STRESS AND RESILIENCE

STRESS AND RESILIENCE
THE SOCIAL CONTEXT OF
REPRODUCTION IN CENTRAL HARLEM

Leith Mullings

Graduate Center, City University of New York
New York, New York

and

Alaka Wali

The Field Museum of Natural History
Chicago, Illinois

KLUWER ACADEMIC / PLENUM PUBLISHERS
NEW YORK, BOSTON, DORDRECHT, LONDON, MOSCOW

An earlier version of Section 6.2 on pages 163–165 was previously published in Mullings, L., 2000, African-American women making themselves: Notes on the role of black feminist research, *Souls: A Critical Journal of Black Politics, Culture and Society* **2**(4):18–29. Copyright 2000 by Leith Mullings.

ISBN 0-306-46638-4

Published 2001 by Kluwer Academic/Plenum Publishers, New York
233 Spring Street, New York, New York 10013

http://www.wkap.nl

10 9 8 7 6 5 4 3 2 1

A C.I.P. record for this book is available from the Library of Congress

FOREWORD

In the opening years of the twenty-first century, we are realizing more than ever the importance of a healthy beginning to life. Reproductive health outcomes not only reflect the immediate medical, social, political, environmental, and economic status of women and children in our society, but also influence health status over the lifetime (Wise, 1993; Hargraves and Thomas, 1993; Hack et al., 1995; Kramer, 2000). Although the United States dramatically led other industrialized nations in per capita expenditures in 1996, twenty-five other countries had lower infant mortality rates, a primary indicator of reproductive health status (National Center for Health Statistics, 2000). Notably, despite the technological advances in health care in the last century, we made very little progress in reducing the twofold excess risk of death that African American infants experience before reaching 1 year of age.

How we perceive and address reproductive health disparities will determine our effectiveness in eliminating them. The disparity in infant mortality should not remain simply a statistic to be reported, with no subsequent action to address it. Nor should we assume that the disparity is genetically determined, and therefore immutable, or only ameliorable by biomedical intervention (Rowley et al., 1993). Disparities should be *prevented* in populations and not *treated* individual by individual. Further, despite their impact on other health outcomes, improved access to care and new medical/technologic advances have not had major impact on reducing reproductive health disparities and are not likely to play a major role in the future. New public health approaches are needed to improve population health and to eliminate disparities in maternal and reproductive health.

Improving reproductive health outcomes and reducing racial and ethnic disparities are key national objectives of both the U.S. Department of Health and Human Services' *Healthy People 2010* initiative and the Department's related initiative to eliminate racial and ethnic disparities in health (U.S. Department of Health and Human Services, 2000; Satcher, 1999). However, because the risk and protective factors for health and disease include both social and biological factors, we need to better understand both, and their interactions, to make improvements in population health. While biologic sciences continue to advance our understanding of the micro-level of disease causation, the complementary macro-level (or social causation) has not received appropriate attention within public health. We must begin to understand the social contributors to health disparities—that is, those real experiences that are lived out daily in individual lives and communities across the country—so that we can improve our society as a whole or, at the very least, improve

our community-based efforts at health promotion and disease prevention. This consideration necessitates developing an information base that allows us to better integrate medical
and sociocultural models of health.

Since 1991, the Preterm Delivery Research Group at the Centers for Disease Control
and Prevention (CDC) has conducted research to understand the social and biological
factors leading to the consistently increased risk for poor pregnancy outcomes among
African Americans so as to inform the development of appropriate prevention programs.[1]
Specifically, qualitative research was conducted using community participatory methods to
describe the influences on maternal health during pregnancy among African Americans—
that is, to answer the question, "What is unique about the experience of being a black woman
in America that places her at higher risk for morbidity and mortality?" Qualitative research
was necessary to identify potential new explanatory factors, to better understand how known
factors interact in women's lives, to provide in-depth description, and to let community
voices be heard. It was also important to understand and describe the diversity within the
African American community, since it is not a homogeneous population, as well as to
understand the similarities of experiences across educational and socioeconomic groupings.

Stress and Resilience: The Social Context of Reproduction in Central Harlem, a product
of this CDC initiative,[2] describes how women's experience of race, ethnicity, and gender
translates into cultural, social, political, economic, and other environmental experiences
that in turn provide the settings and exposures that influence health and disease in Central
Harlem. The methodology provides a model process for how to translate this research into
public health and social action: the community-partnered research process behind this
book resulted in stronger commitments to collaboration, better understanding of risks and
resiliency, greater community empowerment, the design of viable solutions, and a committed local group of people ready to address the roots of racial and ethnic disparities in
their community.

Until now, a proper, comprehensive understanding of the social context of pregnancy
as experienced by urban African Americans has eluded the vast majority of public health
researchers, program planners, and medical providers responsible for designing and imple-
menting prevention and intervention programs. Indeed, this knowledge has also eluded
funders, who have not adequately supported a diversity of community-partnered intervention projects. This book fills a large gap in the literature on the social context of reproduction and will be accessible to medical and public health payors and providers alike. In
public health today, we continue to rely too heavily on interventions defined by those who
live outside the community that is to be "intervened on." What is needed now, on a national level, is support for other communities to make similar efforts to research and understand the social environment through the eyes of the women who live there. But the larger challenge is for public health researchers, program planners, medical providers, policy
makers, and public and private funders to finally move public health into the 21st century.
They must play their diverse roles to ensure that this and similar research is translated into
action to improve our efforts at health promotion, disease prevention, and the final eradi-
cation of the social disease we now call racial disparity.

Cynthia D. Ferré and Vijaya Hogan
Centers for Disease Control and Prevention
Atlanta, Georgia

NOTES

[1] See articles in the *American Journal of Preventive Medicine* supplement to volume 9 (1993), issue 6, titled *Racial Differences in Preterm Delivery: Developing a New Research Paradigm.*

[2] See the *Maternal and Child Health Journal* supplement (in press, 2001) for findings from other studies.

PREFACE

Few things are more important to a community than the assurance of its continuity through generations. What could be more devastating to a mother than the loss of her child? The research results presented here document the daily efforts of the African American community, particularly the women, to protect their children against deeply oppressive conditions. The results suggest that these conditions take a toll on the health and well-being of the women.

Recognizing that medical and epidemiologic studies that narrowly isolate individual risk factors cannot fully account for the difference between the infant death rates of whites and blacks, the Division of Reproductive Health at the Centers for Disease Control and Prevention (CDC) undertook a bold initiative to examine the social context in which reproductive behaviors are practiced. Using qualitative methods, this research initiative incorporates the interrelationships of social, epidemiologic, and physiologic determinants into research protocols and instruments. Such qualitative research documents the processes through which economic circumstances, environmental issues, and social conditions create situations that expose African American women to stress and chronic strain and examines the individual and community assets and strategies used to address these conditions. Funded through this CDC initiative, the research reported in the present publication should be useful for improving epidemiologic research and intervention protocols and for formulating more exact hypotheses about the relationship between risk factors, protective factors, and reproductive health, leading to better understanding of chronic disease patterns and to more effective interventions to reduce rates of infant mortality.

This monograph is a substantially revised version of the final report of the Harlem Birth Right Project, which was submitted to the CDC in September 1997. As originally envisioned, this research project was the first phase of a three-stage initiative by the Division of Reproductive Health of the CDC's National Center for Chronic Disease Prevention and Health Promotion to reduce the disproportionately high rates of infant mortality among black women across social strata. Because this monograph is intended to be helpful to people in public health and related fields, findings are reported in terms of potential sources of stress and chronic strain from social, economic, and political conditions. In a subsequent work, the authors intend to discuss the implications of the research findings from a broader theoretical framework, particularly with respect to recent anthropological and sociological work on race, class, and gender hierarchies.

The ethnographic fieldwork on which this monograph is based was carried out by Alaka Wali, Sabiyha Prince, Deborah Thomas, Denise Oliver, and Leith Mullings. Throughout the project, community participation was solicited in the design and implementation of the research. A draft of the final report was read by the Findings Committee of the Community Advisory Board: Colin Bull, Donna Chandler, and the late Marshall England. Georgia McMurray, a well-known Harlem activist and social worker who died soon after the contract was awarded, originally forged the team of principal investigators and encouraged the New York Urban League to apply to the CDC for a grant. The project's four principal investigators had significant ties to the Harlem community where the work was done. Leith Mullings, an anthropologist who lived in Harlem for 20 years and was involved in a number of research and intervention projects in the community, directed the ethnographic research. Diane McLean, an epidemiologist who was then working at the Harlem Prevention Center, directed, analyzed, and wrote the summary of data from the ethnographic questionnaire. Portions of the summary are incorporated where appropriate in the body of this monograph. Janet Mitchell, then Chief of Perinatology at Harlem Hospital, was in charge of project administration. Dennis Walcott, CEO of the New York Urban League, was the subcontractor for the research grant, provided administrative support, and facilitated access to key informants. Alaka Wali, the senior ethnographer, supervised the student ethnographers and conducted field research at most sites.

The principal concern throughout the project was to provide and disseminate a holistic framework in which to understand infant mortality. To this end, the authors waived royalties derived from the publication of this book so that it can be distributed to a wide public health audience.

Finally, because of the Harlem Birth Right Project's reliance on ethnographic methods and because of the participation of community members in the study's design and implementation, this monograph attempts to incorporate the voices of the community and of the women themselves, both through their own words and through documentation of their actions. Throughout the monograph, we have assigned pseudonyms to all participants in order to protect their anonymity and preserve confidentiality.[1]

It is to these women, with their continued insistence that they be heard, and to the community that supports them that the authors dedicate this book.

NOTE

[1] We assigned given names to the 22 women who participated in the longitudinal part of the study. We use first names, not out of disrespect, but to better allow the reader to follow their experiences, which appear numerous times throughout the monograph. Other men and women interviewed or observed in the fieldwork are designated by an initial to differentiate them from the longitudinal participants.

ACKNOWLEDGMENTS

The authors acknowledge with gratitude the assistance and guidance we received from many people who were instrumental in putting this work together.

First and foremost, we express our deepest gratitude to the participants in this study, all of whom gave generously of their time and selves. All the researchers were immeasurably enriched by the experience. We hope that this book documents the creative ways women continually struggle to improve the lives of their families and their communities.

For preparation of the book we are greatly indebted to research assistants Andrea Queeley and Gretchen Fox, who provided invaluable help in preparing the manuscript and constructing the charts. We also thank Lori Arquilla and Kevin Karpiak, who also worked on the manuscript.

We are particularly grateful to Donna Chandler for her critical reading of the text and her many helpful suggestions. We greatly benefited from her deep knowledge of Harlem and her unwavering commitment to its people.

The book is based on field research funded in part by the Centers for Disease Control and Prevention (CDC) under contract #200-92-0664 to the New York Urban League. After the project was completed and the final report delivered to the CDC, Vijaya Hogan, PhD, epidemiologist in the CDC's Division of Reproductive Health, became the senior project officer and has been instrumental in supporting the dissemination of the research results through various conferences and publications. She has also undertaken several major efforts to find additional support to continue the project through the work of members of the Harlem Birth Right Community Advisory Board. We are grateful to Dr. Hogan for her work on this project, for her counsel, and for her careful reading of the manuscript. We are also grateful to project officer Cynthia Ferré, MPH, and Kendra Hatfield-Timajchy, MPH (who was a project officer during the research), both of whom provided many thoughtful comments along the way. We also acknowledge the many contributions of Diane Rowley, MD, MPH, who was senior project officer during the research. She was instrumental in promoting the use of qualitative research to explore the gap in the rates of infant mortality between blacks and whites.

Harlem Birth Right was a team project and could not have been accomplished without the contributions of all members of the team. We are especially grateful to our colleagues Diane McLean, PhD, MPH, Janet Mitchell, MD, MPH, and Dennis Walcott, MA, who served as co-principal investigators. Diane McLean directed, analyzed, and wrote the summary of data from the ethnographic questionnaire and provided substantive and editorial comments on the initial report to the CDC. We particularly appreciate the tireless work of the Harlem Birth Right Community Advisory Board during the field research process as well as during preparation of the report. Here we would like to mention those members who have continued to participate in the process and who continue to give us critical support and unfailing encouragement: Ms. Donna Chandler, Mr. Colin Bull, Mr. Abukarriem Shabazz, Ms. Yvonne Sawyer, and Ms. Betty Wilson. We note with profound sadness the untimely and sudden death of Mr. Marshall England, also a member of the Community Advisory Board. Marshall, who worked with us until his death, was a leading Harlem activist in the area of public health. The Advisory Board's work on the project—entirely on a voluntary basis—attests to its members' deep commitment to the Harlem community. Listed below are the members of the Community Advisory Board.

COMMUNITY ADVISORY BOARD

Linda Alexander	Betty Hughley	Linda Randolph, MD
Yvonne Barno	Jamal Josephs	Hon. Charles Rangel
Colin Bull, Esq.	Lionel McIntyre	Yvonne Sawyer
Donna Chandler	Vernice Miller	Abukarriem Shabazz
Helen Daniels	Sydney Moshette, Jr.	Nonkululeko Tyehemba
Marshall England	Mark Payne	Linnette Webb
Andrew Gauldin	Muriel Petioni, MD	Betty Wilson

The field research and data analysis conducted for the project benefited greatly from the hard work and dedication of the ethnographers, who at that time were students pursuing doctoral degrees in anthropology. Denise Oliver, Sabiyha Prince, and Deborah Thomas, all women of color, were committed to participatory action research and new approaches to the practice of anthropology. We are also grateful to Patricia Tovar, PhD, who was instrumental in coding the field data, collecting data on the media representation of Harlem, facilitating data analysis, and preparing the original report. We also acknowledge the work of all the research assistants who participated in the project. Darlene de Graffenreidt, Sharon Chekigian, John Friedwald, Suzanne Harris, Yvonne Robinson, Carol Moorer, Mary Floyd, Audrey Grady-Lamkin, Nancy Poor, Marcel Rosin, Lisa Copeland, and Dawn Misra worked on the ethnographic questionnaire. Johanna Fernandez and Sayida Self did important research for the project. Carol De Ortiz, Johanna Goodman, Heather McMillan, Madeleine Tudor, and Mary Futrell helped prepare the CDC report. Editorial staff from the CDC's National Center for Chronic Disease Prevention and Health Promotion and from Palladian Partners, Inc., helped prepare the final typeset manuscript. Significant research support during the analysis and reporting phase of the project was provided to Dr. Alaka Wali by the Field Museum of Natural History. Dr. Leith Mullings also received support from the Graduate Center of the City University of New York and from the National Science Foundation.

Finally, we thank our husbands, Manning Marable and Richard Hubbard, and our children, Alia and Michael Tyner and Shanti and Eric Hubbard, for their support throughout the 8 years of the project.

CONTENTS

STRESS AND RESILIENCE

REPRODUCTIVE HEALTH, HARLEM, AND RESEARCH

SCENES IN HARLEM

Men and women were gathered at the local public hall for a regular meeting sponsored by the community policing unit of the local police precinct. The group was diverse in age and occupation, but it was united in its concerns for the safety and well-being of the neighborhood. They engaged the police representatives in a forceful discussion of their needs and offered many suggestions for improving police procedures. There were two special guests that evening: ethnographers from the Harlem Birth Right Project. The ethnographers described the project and its significance, and lively debate ensued about the causes of infant mortality and the best focus for research. Some argued that research that was narrowly focused on women's bad behaviors (substance abuse and smoking, for example) was not useful because it just reinforced the negative portrait of Harlem that residents had to confront all the time. Others acknowledged that the problem of infant mortality was a grave one (one woman said, "Every week in my shop someone buys a card for a baby's funeral.") but wondered why the project did not examine other pressing issues such as lack of employment.

When asked to participate in the Harlem Birth Right study, Ms. Sandra Bourne lived and worked in Harlem. She was in her early 30s and her family was scattered: in Long Island, Virginia, and other places. She worked at a fast-food restaurant and lived in a building for single mothers sponsored by a nonprofit social service agency. During her pregnancy, she received considerable support from her coworkers and from the owners of the restaurant, themselves African American women. Her coworkers hosted a baby shower for her, and she received many gifts, including a baby carriage, clothes for the baby, and a car seat. From the restaurant owners, she received several pieces of baby furniture, including a crib.

Ms. Gina Jones was a young woman who lived in Harlem and attended college on the Lower East Side of Manhattan. She shared her apartment with two foster children (her relatives' children) and two other young women (also distantly related to her). Both of the young women in Ms. Jones' household were pregnant when she agreed to participate in the study. She provided them with emotional and instrumental support, sometimes accompanying them on their prenatal visits or to parenting support classes as well as providing food and shelter. She and her mother hosted a baby shower for one of the young women, which about 50 people (mostly kin) attended. The young woman gave birth prematurely, so the shower was held after the baby was born. In addition to receiving gifts, both the young woman and the father of the baby received counsel from Ms. Jones' mother and other relatives about their responsibilities as parents.

Mr. John Morris worked as a security guard at a fast-food restaurant in Central Harlem. He was in his mid-20s and had been married 3 years to a young woman who worked for a large hospital. They lived in Brooklyn, and both took the subway every day to work. After his shift ended, he went to his second job as a data entry technician for a private corpora-tion. He and his wife were expecting their first baby when the ethnographers met him. His wife was diabetic and knew that posed a risk for her pregnancy. The stress of her job as an administrative assistant in a surgery unit also was taking a toll on her. Mr. Morris said he intended to quit one of his jobs after the baby was born so he could help at home.

1.1. INTRODUCTION

The purpose of this study was to use ethnographic inquiry to identify the broad social context of gender roles and pregnancy outcomes among a sample of African American women, fully describing the social, economic, and political influences on maternal health during pregnancy. As the foregoing accounts indicate, for women in Harlem, pregnancy and reproduction take place in a social context. Implicit in popular assumptions about pregnancy are presumptions about individual choices and individual lifestyles. How women in Harlem perceive and experience pregnancy reflects complex conditions and relationships, which, at first glance, may appear to be individual histories and behaviors. Although individual risk factors are important, what appear to be personal risk factors and individual lifestyle choices are best understood in the context of a larger structure of con-straints and social choices conditioned by race, class, and gender.

The Harlem Birth Right Project was a response to a Request for Proposals (RFP) cir-culated by the Division of Reproductive Health in the National Center for Chronic Disease Prevention and Health Promotion of the Centers for Disease Control and Prevention (CDC). The RFP grew from an initiative sponsored by the division to address the current state of knowledge about racial disparity in infant mortality rates in the United States. Impelled by studies demonstrating that black women have problematic birth outcomes regardless of their socioeconomic position, that they fare worse than white women at every economic level, and that even college-educated African American women have twice the infant mortality rates of college-educated white women (e.g., Schoendorf et al., 1992), and lacking explanations for these events, CDC called for a research paradigm that would use qualitative ethnographic approaches to assess infant mortality and risk within a social con-text.

1.2. THE SETTING

1.2.1. Harlem and New York City

The study was carried out in Harlem, which is located in northern Manhattan. Despite the area's declining population and ebbing fortunes since the 1970s, Central Harlem has been historically recognized as the mecca of urban African American culture in the United States; the area continues to serve as an entry point to city living for migrants from the southern United States as well as those from foreign countries. Various historians and social scientists have described Central Harlem as a complex, diverse community, populated by residents of all socioeconomic classes (Greenberg, 1991; Huggins, 1995; Johnson [1930] 1991). For the purposes of this study, we defined the Harlem community as people who live and work in Harlem.

Harlem's complexity and heterogeneity stem from a history of settlement and economic change dating from its emergence as an African American community. In the past quarter century Harlem, along with the rest of New York City, has been deeply affected by global economic restructuring reflected in the shift from an industrial economy to an economy based on information and service (Low, 1999; Mollenkopf and Castells, 1991; Sassen, 1991; Smith, 1996).

In New York City, this global economic shift resulted in a financial and economic crisis in the mid-1970s that led to drastic cuts in the city's budget and in the provision of services. Loss of manufacturing jobs has also led to a decline in the unionized sector of the labor force, accompanied by a decline in wages and benefits for workers. In the mid-1970s, there was an expansion of women's participation in the labor force, but they entered largely in the low-wage service sector of the economy. At this time, in contrast to earlier periods (as has been historically the case for black women), women's wages were not largely supplemental to their spouses' wages, but essential to household support. From the early 1980s to the mid-1990s, wages stagnated. In the late 1990s, wages rose slightly as a result of high employment, low inflation, and a small increase in the minimum wage. Still, "the income gap between rich and poor remains wide and the ratio of black to white median family incomes (.56) was as low in 1996 as in 1972" (Conrad and Lindquist, 1998:3). In fact, New York State currently has the largest gap between rich and poor in the nation (CBS, 2000).

During the 1980s, New York began to emerge from the economic recession and experienced a boom driven by the growth of the financial sector. Ironically, compared with previous economic booms, this one did not lead to a narrowing of the gap between rich and poor. In fact, the poverty rate increased from 15 percent in 1975 to 23 percent in 1987 (Mollenkopf and Castells, 1991). By 1998 in New York State, the poorest families earned an average of $10,770, down $1,970 from 1988 (CBS, 2000). This is in part attributable to the types of occupations fostered by the postindustrial economy: a two-tiered structure with high-wage, information-based, highly skilled jobs at one end and low-wage, service-sector, part-time and shift-work jobs at the other end. Downsizing by private industry has further reduced the pool of jobs available for people with little postsecondary education or with moderate skills.

Race and gender have intersected with these socioeconomic transformations in new ways. The civil rights and feminist movements of the 1960s and 1970s increased the opportunities available to African Americans and women. There has been a significant expansion of the black middle class overall (for example, nationally, black-owned businesses experienced a 46 percent growth from 1987 to 1992 [U.S. Census Bureau, 2000]). White women in particular have moved into higher-income professional occupations previously inaccessible to them. However, the distribution of occupations of the black middle class is disproportionately concentrated in the public sector and the social service sector of the economy. The fastest-growing sector of the economy, the financial sector, is still dominated by white men. As white women have moved into higher-income professional occupations, African American and other minority women have moved into clerical jobs (Jones, 1983). Both these trends indicate that racial and gender discrimination continue to influence occupational structures and mobility.

The economic changes wrought by the transition to a postindustrial global economy have been accompanied by social and demographic changes visible in the built environment. The financial crisis of the early 1970s led to a widespread collapse of housing markets and a major decrease in the availability of affordable housing. Most severely affected in New York were portions of the South Bronx, northern Manhattan (including Harlem), and parts of Brooklyn. As the economy recovered, people who were in a position to take advantage of the newly developing occupational structure escalated the demand for upscale housing and renovated old housing, abandoned warehouses, and industrial lofts ("gentrification"). In some areas, this transformed the character of neighborhoods and created enclaves of young professionals living in the renovated buildings in the midst of continued poverty and decay for the neighborhood at large.

In 1989, a narrow majority of voters coalesced across racial lines to elect Democrat David Dinkins, an African American, as mayor of the city. The Dinkins Administration allocated relatively greater resources to improving conditions for poor and low-income New Yorkers. This principally took the form of some extension of social services (particularly health care) and expansion of entrepreneurial opportunities through awarding contracts to businesses owned by women or people of color. In Harlem, these policies encouraged a mini-revitalization: a small growth in retail and commercial outlets and services, construction of new housing and renovation of abandoned buildings, and moderate growth in social services.

Although these changes were promising, they were far from sufficient to address the enormity of problems caused by long-entrenched poverty and discriminatory practices. In 1993, Mayor Dinkins was not reelected, and Republican Rudolph Giuliani became mayor of New York on a platform that pledged to cut the city's budget (because of a projected deficit) and improve the "quality of life." Soon after he took office, Mayor Giuliani decreased the budget for education and schools by $1 billion, initiated efforts to privatize public hospitals and public housing, and increased the budget for the police force, which began a citywide campaign to arrest petty criminals (i.e., subway turnstile violators, unlicensed street vendors, and others engaged in the informal economy) and street-level drug dealers.

Our research was conducted within this political and economic context from 1993 through 1996. Those years marked the beginning of a significant transition in Harlem, characterized simultaneously by increased neglect by the city and state governments, as reflected in the budget cuts and subsequent cutbacks in services on the one hand, and an increase in specific types of investment by the private sector (for example, investments in high-end housing and in new retail establishments) on the other hand. These processes significantly changed the physical landscape of Harlem after the fieldwork phase of the study was completed.

1.2.2. Demographic Characteristics of Central Harlem

These political and economic changes were accompanied by changes in the demographic characteristics, settlement pattern, and overall health profile of Harlem's residents.

From 1970 to 1990, the population decreased substantially, from 159,267 to 99,519 in the area defined as Community Board 10 in Central Harlem (see the appendix), a loss of 37.5 percent.[1] This decline is true for children as well as for people over 18, and the decline is reflected in similar statistics for the Central Harlem Health District, an area with slightly larger demographic boundaries than Community Board 10 and a correspondingly larger 1990 population base of 115,483. Central Harlem is predominantly African American and non-Hispanic, although the Hispanic proportion of the population is growing (from 3.1 percent in 1970 to 10.1 percent in 1990).[2] A recent increase in immigrants to Central Harlem, predominantly from African and Caribbean countries, is reflected in the growing proportion of the population that is foreign born. From 1970 to 1990, that proportion more than doubled.

Currently Harlem is a community[3] with a median age of 33, with substantial proportions of adolescents, young adults, and older adults. According to the 1990 census, 23.7 percent of women are of reproductive age (15–44), and 75.8 percent of the population report themselves as living in families. The statistics on marital status show that a smaller proportion of people are married in Central Harlem than in New York City as a whole; in 1990, more than twice as many families in Central Harlem with children under 18 were headed by women as in New York City overall (69 percent versus 34 percent). In Central Harlem, 30.6 percent of households include children under 18 years of age. The prevalence of adults who live in Central Harlem with at least a high school education has increased by 10 percent since 1980 (42.8 percent versus 55.8 percent), and the percentage of those with only a high school education has remained fairly stable during this period (28.8 percent versus 26.9 percent).

Residents of Central Harlem are employed in a variety of occupations. In 1990, over 50 percent of employed adults were in service or clerical occupations. Almost 20 percent were in executive/managerial or professional jobs; smaller percentages of adults were employed in sales, repair, labor, transport, and other technical positions. While the percentage of the population employed in service jobs has declined since 1970, the proportions of adults in clerical and high-status professional and managerial jobs has increased, with a loss in the percentage of people employed as machine operators and assemblers from 1970 to 1990 (17.8 percent versus 3.3 percent). A substantial proportion of adults work in government positions—over 31 percent of all employed adults over 15 years of age. Interestingly, compared with New York City as a whole, employed Central Harlem adults are more likely to work in professional and related fields and in public administration. This is not surprising because the Harlem Hospital Center is the largest employer in Central Harlem, and the New York State Office Building is also a major work site for Harlem residents.

Most working women in Central Harlem have family responsibilities. Fifty-two percent of women in the labor force in 1990 had children under 18, and 43 percent had young children under 6.

Although residents of Central Harlem are employed in a range of occupations, unemployment is high. In 1990, only 41 percent of persons 16 or older in Central Harlem were employed compared with 56 percent in New York City. The unemployment rate for women in Central Harlem is a little less than 50 percent higher than in New York City (13.7 percent versus 8.7 percent); it is more than twice as high for men (22.3 percent versus 9.3 percent).

The impact of high unemployment can be seen in the distribution of household income. Almost 50 percent of total households had incomes under $10,000, about twice the percentage for all Manhattan and for New York City as a whole. In 1990, 65.6 percent of families were above the federal poverty level, approximately a third less than in New York City as a whole. In 1996, the percentage of households with incomes under $10,000 was 18.9 percent for Manhattan, 20.9 percent for New York City, and 36.9 percent for Central Harlem (Citizens' Committee for Children, 1999). Conditions have worsened since 1970, with a larger proportion of families whose income is above the federal poverty level but not sufficient to buy health insurance or adequate housing. Although more people were on public assistance in Central Harlem overall in 1990 than in 1970, 71 percent were not on public assistance, which belies the stereotype that Central Harlem is largely a welfare community. According to a 1998 report, 39.4 percent of Central Harlem residents, 18.8 percent of Manhattan residents, and 21.7 percent of New York City residents receive some form of public assistance such as Aid to Families with Dependent Children, Home Relief, Supplemental Security Income, and Medicaid. Of people receiving public assistance in 1998, 44.2 percent were children 17 years old or younger (Citizen's Committee for Children, 1999).

One reason the population of Central Harlem has declined steadily is the decline in available housing. The number of available housing units dropped by 27.1 percent from 1970 to 1990. Within the Central Harlem District, the percentage of vacant housing ranges from 5.4 to 17.7 across the health areas, but the percentage of vacant units varies substantially within subareas of Central Harlem. Despite the reduction in available housing and the related population decline, Central Harlem is a more residentially stable community than Manhattan or New York City as a whole.

1.2.3. Morbidity and Mortality

Overall mortality has been declining for the U.S. population since 1950. Age-adjusted mortality rates have declined for all racial and ethnic groups in the United States, although the disparity in mortality rates has remained constant. In Central Harlem, the overall age-adjusted mortality rate has not decreased but has increased steadily since 1950. In 1950, the Harlem population had a lower mortality rate than other minority racial or ethnic groups in the United States. In the last 30 years, however, the Harlem mortality rate has risen to 50 percent higher than that of other minority racial groups and almost 60 percent higher than that of U.S. whites in 1980. Since 1980, there has been some improvement in mortality rates associated with the leading causes of death (cardiovascular disease, neoplasms, cirrhosis, homicide) for men and women under 65. In Harlem, death from cardiovascular disease decreased by 30 percent, from cancer by 24 percent, and from cirrhosis by 67 percent. But since 1990, death from infectious diseases such as tuberculosis and AIDS has increased by 85 percent. Mortality rates in Central Harlem were two to three times higher than in New York City.[4]

1.2.4. Reproductive Health

The Central Harlem health district has had the highest infant mortality rate of all of health districts in New York City, more than twice that of New York City as a whole and substantially more than most other poor African American communities. Since 1980 the infant mortality rate for Central Harlem has been consistently higher than that for New York City. When we began the fieldwork in 1993, the infant mortality rate in Central Harlem was 25.2 per 1,000 births. Between 1994 and 1997, the gap between Central Harlem and most other health districts remained, though the the overall rate in Central Harlem decreased to 6.6. However, the rate increased to 11.4 in 1998 and to 15.8 in 1999. Low birth weight and preterm delivery rates parallel the infant mortality rates. In 1991, 18.8 percent of births in Central Harlem were low weight, nearly twice the rate of New York City. In 1997, this gap between the low birth weight rate in Central Harlem and New York City narrowed to 4.7 percent (13.5 percent in Harlem and 8.8 percent in New York City). A substantial proportion of preterm live births occur at less than 34 weeks gestation. Reported rates of prenatal smoking and illicit drug use are also higher than in other health districts.

Within the Central Harlem health district, the rate of live births is similar across health areas.[5] Abortion rates are also similar across health areas. However, the infant mortality rate differs substantially by health area. At the time of our research in Health Area 13, the infant mortality rate was 69.9 per 1,000—a rate that rivals that of many third-world countries. Yet in Health Area 8, the infant mortality rate was 8.3 per 1,000. The rates of low birth weight and maternal smoking also vary substantially; Health Area 13 stands out with 34 percent of live neonates being of low birth weight and maternal smoking reported at 34.7 percent. Health Area 13, which includes the Harlem Hospital Center, also includes the highest percentage of vacant housing units. These comparisons speak to the great variability within the Central Harlem community of social situations and pregnancy outcomes that deserve further elaboration. We concentrated primarily on identifying health areas with high or low infant mortality rates, yet with different sociodemographic characteristics. Health Area 10, where historically the elite of Harlem reside, has one of the lowest infant mortality rates in Central Harlem and is relatively well-off in terms of household income; yet it has a smaller percentage of women employed outside the home. Health Area 15 has one of the highest infant mortality rates, a high percentage of households with low incomes, and a large percentage of women employed outside the home. Health Area 12 is intermediate, in terms of infant mortality and its sociodemographic profile, and contains a public housing development. These three health areas were chosen as primary neighborhood sites for the ethnographic fieldwork.

Harlem's heterogeneity is expressed in the physical environment as well as in social and demographic characteristics. The following descriptions of three blocks in Health Area 15 are drawn from field notes.

> The first block is a tree-lined street with relatively clean sidewalks, although there are pockets of decay. On this block, about 20 percent of the buildings are renovated and occupied by urban professionals. Another 20 percent of the buildings on this block are churches. One is a large church that frequently offers space for block association meetings. Two others are smaller churches, and one is a "storefront" church in a brownstone. The remainder of the block is a mix of buildings privately owned by landlords who do not live in the neighborhood and who often do not invest adequate funds in the upkeep and maintenance of the building, and city-owned and managed residences. The latter are managed by the city's Department of Housing and Preservation Development (HPD), which takes over buildings when landlords default on tax payments. HPD has converted a few buildings on this block into single room occupancy (SRO) residences for previously homeless people. Another HPD brownstone on this block houses residents who have lived in the building for over a decade. Residents of HPD-managed buildings, as well as those in the privately

owned buildings, are engaged in a wide variety of occupations. Some are professionals, some are clerical workers, and some are in the service sector. Still others are low-wage workers who have access to Section 8 Federal Housing Subsidies. In addition, there are women who use a combination of federal, state, and city public assistance programs.

The second block fronts Marcus Garvey Park (previously known as Mount Morris Park). It contains a row of well-maintained and recently renovated brownstones. It is frequently a stop on annual spring tours of historic Harlem homes hosted by various community associations. Owners of renovated homes welcome tourists and proudly describe the work they have done to restore luxury interiors replete with mahogany and oak trim and Victorian fixtures. However, this block is not fully residential. One of the brownstones contains a day care center, partly subsidized by city and state funds. On one end of the block is a three-story minimal security women's prison, which houses inmates who are in work release programs and are in transition to parole. Adjacent to the prison are three abandoned buildings with broken windows and crumbling brick exteriors, currently owned by the state of New York. They are littered with trash, and are a potential site for rats and other pests.[6] Although a local community improvement association has continually complained about the decay and blight associated with these buildings in the past 5 or 6 years, New York State has not taken any action to improve the property. State inaction on this property is perceived by neighborhood residents and members of the community association as an indication of the state's racism and consequent neglect of Central Harlem.

The third block consists primarily of deteriorated buildings and HPD-managed buildings. One end of the block is dominated by a large vacant lot, rarely cleaned by the sanitation department. Residents of the block warned ethnographers to be careful walking near the lot because of rodent infestations. The public telephone in front of a small corner grocery-deli adjacent to the lot frequently does not work. Across from the vacant lot, the wall of a building is painted with a mural memorializing young people on the block who died from street violence. Flowers and wreaths are frequently placed in front of the wall. Another building on the block is a shelter for homeless men currently engaged in an economic development project. The block also includes several storefront churches as well as a well-maintained 10-story, privately owned apartment building.

In summary, Central Harlem is a geographic, economic, cultural, and historic community with a diverse population of various socioeconomic classes, marital statuses, household composition, age groups, occupational statuses, and religious affiliation within a context of complex environmental conditions. However, the definition of the study population as "women who live and work in Harlem" provided us the flexibility to examine the heterogeneity of women's experiences and to follow social processes as they crossed geographic boundaries.

1.3. METHODOLOGY

1.3.1. Research Objectives

The Harlem Birth Right project had three objectives: 1) to use ethnographic inquiry to identify the broad social context of gender roles and pregnancy outcomes in Harlem; 2) to involve the community in the research; and 3) to evaluate the community participation process with respect to its utility and impact on data collection.

To address the gaps in our understanding of how the changing social, economic, and political conditions affect the health of African American women and their reproductive experiences by documenting the institutional and social barriers to improving health and well-being and the ways people act to overcome these barriers, we used qualitative and quantitative data. Although quantitative data analysis is extremely useful in forming predictive models, it can be limited in its explanatory capacity in that it may put forward inadequate, single-factor explanations for complex phenomena.[7] Paul Wise observes that there is "[a] remarkable proliferation of studies reporting associations between infant mortality and a vast array of singular variables ... with little regard for their respective prevalence or how these risks interact to actually determine infant mortality patterns in the real world" (1993:8–9). Furthermore, Wise suggests,

> The uncritical interpretation of singular risk associations has led to a kind of tyranny of the P value by which statistically significant risk associations push the public debate to the margins and frame the public understanding of infant mortality as the product of deviant maternal behavior. Not only has this "marginalization" played into destructive stereotypes of maternal responsibility for infant death, but it has also helped generate in many communities a host of specialized programs designed to provide services to a relatively small group of "high-risk" women. Although these programs are greatly needed, they distract attention and resources from the basic infrastructure of comprehensive health care and social service provision in these same communities. (1993:4)

The research design had four components: 1) ethnographic field research, 2) an ethnographic questionnaire, 3) focus groups, and 4) structured community participation. A thorough literature review and pilot fieldwork were conducted for 6 months before the beginning of the field research. Analysis of media reports, archival information, public documents, and academic literature was undertaken throughout the research in order to contextualize the ethnographic work.

1.3.2. Ethnographic Field Research

1.3.2.1. Field Sites

There were two components to the ethnographic field research: participant observation in 10 neighborhood and workplace sites, and intensive longitudinal case studies. In selecting the neighborhood sites, we considered the following factors: the Health Area statistical profiles (particularly socioeconomic status, income, low birth weight, and infant mortality data) as well as ease of entry to the neighborhood. Three neighborhood sites within three different Health Areas (10, 12, and 15—as previously discussed) were selected. While the statistical data suggested some uniformity within each of these neighborhoods, the neighborhoods themselves were, in fact, extremely heterogeneous with respect to housing, income and occupation of residents, physical appearance, and social organization.

It was important to emphasize the experience of work because 1) there is relatively little attention in the scientific literature to the conditions, types of stressors, and coping measures of African American working women and 2) it is important to examine a variety of occupational experiences in order to understand why infant mortality statistics remain higher in the African American community even among college-educated women. Hence a fast-food restaurant (low-wage service workers), an office site (clerical and professional workers), street vending sites (informal workers), and two social service sites located in two neighborhoods in Health Areas 15 and 12 (service and professional workers) were selected as loci to capture the variety and concentration of African American women workers in particular sectors. After consultation with the Community Advisory Board (discussed later in this chapter), we added two additional sites—a large public hospital and a housing court (a special section of the city judiciary devoted to housing disputes) as sites for participant observation.

Participant observation was carried out for 3 to 4 months at each site by teams of two ethnographers. The ethnographers attended meetings and events in the community, engaged people in informal conversation, interviewed key informants, and participated in neighborhood events and activities, where they encountered women who were willing to participate in the longitudinal studies. Participant observation in the neighborhood sites facilitated the ethnographers' understanding of patterns of family structure and social support systems and allowed the researchers to meet women not currently employed, on public assistance, or in the informal sector.[8] Participant observation at the work sites allowed researchers to directly observe conditions and the types of stressors and coping mechanisms of African American women in different occupational sectors. Work at both types of sites allowed observation of interactions across work, family, and community settings.

1.3.2.2. Longitudinal Participants

Twenty-six women were recruited in the neighborhood and work sites for the longitudinal study (see Table 1.1). Four dropped out of the study because of problems such as moving, illness, and difficulty of maintaining contact. The remaining sample consisted of 22 women (11 of whom were pregnant when they were recruited) who reflected varied demographic and socioeconomic characteristics. These extended case studies were based on maintaining contact with participants for approximately 1 year. The number of contacts ranged from as few as 6 to as many as 20; the contacts included home visits, attendance at health care appointments, visits to prisons, attendance at various rituals, meetings at work, and informal discussions.

During the entire fieldwork, careful attention was paid to ensuring sampling from diverse social strata. Social strata were used to include variation by level of education, occupation, and income. It became evident in the research that these criteria could not be conflated, because they may have had varying degrees of salience with respect to other social factors. In our study, "middle stratum" is generally used to refer to people in professional and managerial occupations or with some degree of income security, or with a postsecondary education that could lead to professional careers. Given that the preponderance of ethnographic research focuses on low-income populations, a unique feature of this research was that we also explored the lives of middle-income women in order to gain some insight into possible risk factors as they affect women across socioeconomic strata as well as variation within socioeconomic strata.

Fieldwork methods included traditional ethnographic approaches, such as participant observation (structured observation and unobtrusive methods), unstructured and semistructured interviews, questionnaires, network analyses, extended case studies, life histories, and genealogies. One of the principal investigators, the senior ethnographer, and three graduate student ethnographers conducted the ethnographic fieldwork primarily from summer 1993 to fall 1995. The team approach, in which two ethnographers were stationed

Table 1.1. Longitudinal Participants in Harlem Birth Right Project

Pseudonym*	Age	Ethnicity	Education	Parity	Housing Type	Marital Status	Employment Type
Anita	early 40s	AA	College	2	Rental	Div	Professional
Celine	early 30s	AA	College	1	Rental	S	Self-employed
Ruth	mid-30s	AA	College	2/P	Ten/Rental	Sep	Public assistance
Madeline	mid-30s	AA	College	0	Rental	S	Managerial
Fatima	early 30s	AA	College	3/P	Rental	Div	Professional
Noma	early 30s	AA	College	1/P	Rental	Liv	Self-employed
Gina	late 20s	AA	>HS	0	Ten/Rental	S	Public assistance/ informal
Robin	late 30s	AA	>HS	0	Owner	Mar	Professional
Latoya	early 20s	AA	>HS	2	Rental	Liv	Low wage
Aurora	mid-30s	AA	HS	8/P	Rental	Sep	Vendor/ self-employed
Elizabeth	early 60s	WI	HS	1	PH	Rem	Low wage/ informal
Billie	late 30s	AA	HS	1	Rental	Div	Self-employed
Sharon	early 30s	AA	HS	2/P	Ten/Rental	Sep	Public assistance
Norma	mid-20s	AA	HS	0	Rental	S	Clerical
Diana	early 40s	AA	HS	1/P	Ten/Rental	Liv	Low wage
Reina	late teens	AA	HS	0/P	PH	S	Low wage

Table 1.1. Continued

Pseudonym*	Age	Ethnicity	Education	Parity	Housing Type	Marital Status	Employment Type
Sandra	early 30s	AA	HS	0	Rental	S	Low wage
Rose	early teens	Mixed (Latina/AA)	<HS	0/P	Ten/Squatter	Liv	Vendor/ self- employed
Susan	late 20s	AA	<HS	5	PH	S	Low wage/ informal
Ama	late 30s	AF	<HS	4/P	Ten/Rental	Mar	Vendor/ self-employed
Claire	mid- 20s	AA	<HS	2/P	Ten/Rental	S	Public assistance
Ivory	early teens	AA	<HS	0/P	Ten/Rental	S	None

* Characteristics noted in the table are those at time of recruitment; some women changed, for example, residence or marital status during the study, and these changes are described in the discussion of the ethnographic data. Some information is deliberately vague to protect participant confidentiality.
Abbreviations:
  Ethnicity: AA: African American; AF: African; WI: West Indian
  Education: HS: Graduated from high school
  Parity: P: Pregnant at time of recruitment
  Housing: Ten: Tenement; PH: Public housing development
  Marital Status: Mar: Married; Rem: Remarried; Sep: Separated; Div: Divorced; Liv: Live-in partner; S: Single

at each site, facilitated coverage of a broad spectrum of the heterogeneity of Harlem life without sacrificing the depth of participant observation. Further, it allowed for the interaction of multiple perspectives of "insider/outsiderness." For example, among the ethnographers, one is a complete outsider to Harlem; another lived in Harlem 10 years previously; a third lived there more recently but did not live there at the time of the research; the fourth never lived in Harlem but had done research there for the previous 4 years; and the fifth had lived, worked, and done research in Harlem for the previous 20 years. Perhaps most important, the team approach and multiple perspectives allowed for cross-checking of data, comparison of observations, enhanced validity, and increased reliability. The ethnographers met regularly to exchange information and to plan strategies.

1.3.2.3. Participant Observation

Participant observation—"the study of people in their own time and space, in their own everyday lives" (Burawoy et al., 1991:2)—is a research technique that, despite its vague characterization in most descriptions of methods, stands at the heart of ethnography. It is one of the two most significant techniques associated with qualitative methods of data collection (the other being intensive, open-ended interviews).

Participant observation is not synonymous with unstructured interviewing; it involves working with people, listening and talking to them, and observing them. Ethnographers worked behind the counter at the fast-food restaurant, did photocopying at the clerical site, and talked with participants they met at each site, thus observing both what study participants said and what they did. It is this somewhat insidious aspect of participant observation that has generated the necessity for such a strong code of ethics among anthropologists, emphasizing the confidentiality, privacy, and protection of informants.

Participant observation is time-consuming and labor-intensive; it binds the anthropologist to a particular site.[9] Its limitations in many ways arise from its virtues. As Burawoy suggests, "intensive research limits the possibilities of generalizations" (1991:2). However, proponents argue that "[its] advantages ... are assumed to lie not just in direct observation of how people act but also how they understand and experience those acts.... [This] enables us to juxtapose what people say they are up to against what they actually do" (Burawoy et al., 1991:2). Proponents also argue that it is an effective way to understand the configuration of social, economic, political, and ideological forces from the perspectives of the people who experience and shape those forces.

Though mindful of the many problems of participant observation (see Mullings, 2000), ethnography, and representation, we suggest that when linked to well-structured community participation in research, participant observation—at its best—has the potential to be a vehicle for alternative expressions and interpretations of reality and, at the same time, allow for an analysis of the context in which these interpretations arise. Thus, the approach allowed the research team to retain the local perspective provided by participant observation yet to expand the scope of the analysis beyond the confines of a localized community.

1.3.2.4. Focus Groups

A series of 11 focus groups were convened to discuss specific issues related to the context of infant mortality in Harlem. Topics for the focus groups covered a range of social experience and included budget cuts, bereavement and loss, birth experiences,[10] culture, housing, men, research in the African American community, women heads of households, and young people. The focus groups generally had 5 to 10 participants. Participants were people encountered by the ethnographers during the course of fieldwork or people recruited through word of mouth, sign-up forms at street fairs,[11] or flyers posted in public areas.

Focus groups—"Focus group interviews use group interaction to generate data and gather insights into a research topic that would be less available without the interaction found in the group" (Morgan, 1993:144)—began after the initial field research in order to confirm suspected connections among data and to provide additional insights. In addition, focus groups became important instruments for comparing and measuring the validity of statements made by individuals outside the focus groups.[12]

1.3.2.5. The Ethnographic Questionnaire: The Harlem Women's Survey

Based on the participant observation and focus groups, the researchers developed an open-ended questionnaire to be administered to 100 randomly selected women in Central Harlem (Mullings, Wali, McLean, et al., 2001). Because the questionnaire was based in part on data gathered by participant observation, the survey captures a broad spectrum of the experiences of women. The questionnaire was administered to 83 women, 57 of whom were randomly selected. Of the remaining 26, 22 were interviewed specifically at the work sites where ethnographic research was conducted, and four were interviewed at a shelter for the homeless. The interview covered a range of topics, including work, family, stress, health, and political participation. It also covered women's personal, social, economic, and environmental conditions as well as their pregnancy experiences.

The questionnaire instrument was developed through collaboration by members of the investigative team and members of the Community Advisory Board. The process began with a discussion among the ethnographers and principal investigators of relevant areas to be researched. A theoretical matrix framework was developed that broadened the topic areas and concepts of the life stress paradigm previously considered in stress research (McLean et al., 1993; Dohrenwend et al., 1978; Brown and Harris, 1978). The new framework included new topics such as community life, an expansion of the concept of personal dispositions and coping in order to focus more strongly on women's resources and obstructions. We expanded the concept of social networks to include an assessment of the broader ways women participate in many social arenas. This was followed by an extensive literature review on each topic area. A review of the project's ethnographic data was then conducted, and the topic areas were further expanded on the basis of ethnographic observations, including the addition of a section on environment and neighborhood concerns. The topic outline went through two additional revisions as well. The research team then developed open-ended questions and probes that addressed these topic areas, each time going back to the ethnographic field notes and experiences for insight and additional data. In addition, a community dialogue group discussion was held to review topics suggested for the questionnaire and to develop specific items within each topic. [13]

Two different sampling strategies were used to identify potential participants for the ethnographic questionnaire. First, we selected a random sample of 57 women ages 18–65 who had originally participated in the Harlem Health Survey, a random, population-based survey of households in Central Harlem. Women were selected randomly from subsamples of women with varying levels of educational achievement (less than a high school diploma, a high school diploma or general equivalency diploma [GED], and more than a high school diploma). [14] Women were also randomly selected from Harlem Health Survey participants who lived in neighborhoods that were also part of the ethnographic field sites. Twenty-two of the 26 remaining women were interviewed at the work sites where ethnographic research was conducted, and four were interviewed at a homeless shelter.

In summary, the research design involved maximizing validity by using a range of research operations and methodological strategies—participant observation, case studies, focus groups, unstructured interviewing, and questionnaires—and facilitating the cross-checking of data, observations, and conclusions. We incorporated the traditional ethnographic techniques of 1) establishing the accuracy of statements and their reliability through verification, validation, triangulation, proof and inference, replication, and repetition (Ellen, 1984) and 2) comparing our results with the results of other studies. Data were assessed by using internal triangulation (eliciting the same data in a different way from the same informants), comparing accounts given by different informants, and noting how the results compared with the observations of the ethnographer.

1.4. COMMUNITY PARTICIPATION

The project was premised on community participation in all phases of the research. Participatory Action Research (PAR) was the theoretical approach that guided community involvement in the research process (Fals-Borda, 1984; Freire, 1970; Schensul and Borrero, 1982; Schensul, 1974; Manderson et al., 1998). At the time the project was initiated, community participation in intervention design was gaining popularity, but community participation in research was still a novel concept, although the need for promoting such an approach was generally recognized. PAR projects elicit the participation of community members in both research and intervention strategies. Advocates argue that community involvement in the design and process of research not only improves the research itself but also enables it to be utilized (Chesler, 1991); that this approach not only combines research, education, and action (e.g., Hall and Stevens, 1998) as a powerful tool to empower people to improve their social conditions (Park, 1993), but that it also produces a much more profound understanding of social problems (Stull and Schensul, 1987); and that it helps eliminate errors, informs and develops community leaders, and enables the research to be used for social change.

The community participation approach has important implications for health and medicine. As Gamble suggests, community participation in research has the potential to address the fact that medicine is not a value-free discipline. Rather, it reflects and reinforces the beliefs, values, and power dynamics of the wider society. Accordingly, medicine is influenced by issues of race and racism. History shows numerous examples of medical beliefs being used to support the alleged inferiority of black people. Gamble, for example, asserts that the Tuskegee Syphilis Study "symbolizes for many African-Americans" the racism that pervades American institutions, including the medical profession. A lasting legacy of the study is African American "distrust of medical researchers" (Gamble, 1993:35).

1.4.1. Community Advisory Board

The New York Urban League, the general contractor for the project,[15] and some of the principal investigators already had long-term links with the Harlem community. While utilizing the project's connections to the Urban League, the research team also took care to reach out to a broader cross section of the community. To meet this goal, the team established a 24-member Community Advisory Board (CAB) as a major formal vehicle for community participation in the project. In constituting the CAB, the researchers attempted to make it representative of the socioeconomic, occupational, gender, religion, age, and ethnic heterogeneity of the community. Board members participating as individuals were recruited from community organizations, unions, youth programs, and service organizations. Some members were unaffiliated individuals encountered in the course of doing fieldwork. The participation of the CAB members was critical in 1) designing and facilitating the research; 2) facilitating research contacts and entry into research sites; 3) maintaining continuous dialogue with researchers and providing guidance; 4) representing the project at various public functions; 5) serving as resources in hiring personnel from the community (such as interviewers); and 6) assisting in developing strategies for public dissemination of the project objectives and results. CAB participation was facilitated through quarterly meetings of the CAB as well as through many informal discussions. Once constituted, the CAB actively participated in all phases of research. The opportunity to discuss the project with this diverse group and to listen to their ideas enriched the researchers' thinking about the direction of the research; the research team frequently sought the advice of CAB members on an informal basis, drawing on their various areas of expertise. On many occasions, researchers called board members to discuss some observation or problem that arose in the course of fieldwork. Board members often shared insights based on their experiences of long-term residence or work in Harlem and frequently suggested avenues for further exploration.

On one occasion, discussions with the CAB illuminated the need to develop a community description that presented a balanced picture of the community instead of the traditional deficit-model approach. The resulting community profile was widely distributed and utilized by CAB members and other members of the community. At one CAB meeting, the research team discussed its effort to gather statistics on the ways people in Harlem resist poor delivery of services, which results from the failure of the city or the private sector to meet their responsibilities. The objective was to collect these statistics, because the data from the census and other readily available resources are heavily biased toward reporting negative aspects (i.e., rates of crime and homicide, numbers of vacant buildings, percentages of people below poverty, numbers of pupils in special education) rather than reporting the efforts of people to overcome difficulties (complaints of police brutality, complaints about lack of heat and hot water, complaints about lack of housing code enforcement, resistance to special education placement). When the researchers discussed with the CAB the difficulty of finding these types of statistics, board members were able to suggest five or six different sources for such statistics, ranging from grassroots groups to city agencies.

As noted previously, board members encouraged the researchers to examine an additional site—housing court. This arena provided ethnographers with the opportunity to look at both the tenants who lodged complaints and at their lawyers, giving the researchers a cross-occupational perspective. This allowed the researchers to think about how the contingencies and problems of daily life of one group (poor women who often face homelessness) can affect those of another group (women lawyers who advocate for the poor) and how the resulting areas of "stress" or chronic strain affect both groups. The advice and assistance of CAB members was therefore critical to achieving new insights and to devising ways to prepare material for presentation to the community.

1.4.2. Community Dialogue Groups

Because most CAB members were active in their community and had busy lives, we only could meet every 3 months. Therefore, to supplement the input from the CAB, we created community dialogue groups (CDGs). These were groups of 5 to 10 community residents who met with the researchers regularly to discuss specific aspects of the project. Some CDG members were on the CAB, some were experts in issues related to the topic of discussion, and some were people the researchers met while doing fieldwork. These smaller, more flexible groups relieved CAB members from the time burden of frequent meetings with researchers and, at the same time, pulled more participants into the project. Topics discussed with CDGs included site selection, selection criteria for participants in the longitudinal case studies, topics to be discussed by focus groups, the composition of focus groups, approaches to community participation, and the design and context of the ethnographic questionnaire. The CDGs also gave valuable feedback on research methods and strategies.

In addition, open community meetings were held. The first was at the beginning of the project for the research team to explain the research and discuss community concerns; another meeting was held halfway through the research process for the research team to report on progress to date. In addition to discussing the formal techniques of the research projects, ethnographers elicited community participation throughout the course of the fieldwork through unusually detailed explanations of the project and its design. In informal situations, community residents were able to question the research design and intent. There were moments of revelation when people expressed their anxieties about research and its meaning to them, their conceptualizations of "health" and "infant mortality," and their explanations about the causes of high rates of morbidity and mortality. At several meetings, there were lively debates about the causes of infant mortality.

The participation of community members through these formal vehicles led to important changes in research design and implementation. Sites for participant observation were added, the sample for the long-term study was changed, and topic areas for investigation were amplified. Community participation broadened areas of inquiry and provided the research team with multiple critical perspectives from which to view arenas of health and health care delivery.

1.5. STRESS AND REPRODUCTION

When the study began, clear physiologic evidence of the importance of stress as a factor in pregnancy outcomes was not yet available. During the data analysis phase of the research, physiological evidence that women who experience more prenatal stress and anxiety have significantly higher rates of adverse birth outcomes became available. However, "potential mediators of these relationships remain unexplained and thus are important targets of research efforts" (Rini, Wadhwa, and Sandman, 1999:333–334). For this reason, at the request of the CDC, the research findings are reported in the framework of potential sources of stress and chronic strain from social and political conditions.

As numerous researchers have pointed out, while the study of the role of stress in disease is critical, problems abound in conceptualization and analysis of "stress." The approach to stress in this volume falls within the "environmental tradition" rather than the psychological or biological traditions. We assessed the broad environmental conditions and events that may promote stress (Cohen, Kessler, and Gordon, 1995:3).

One of the problems in stress research "is its failure to grapple with what we might term the 'social organization of stress'" (Dressler, 1991:1). Counterbalancing the difficult conditions in which people find themselves are the institutional and cultural resources that African Americans have historically developed to confront and resist oppressive conditions. These traits, behaviors, and processes have been described as "resiliency" (Aronson, 1999), "resistance resources" (Antonovsky, 1979), protective effects of cultural heritage (Krieger, 1999), or cultural strengths or resources that facilitate stressor resistance (Dressler, 1991). These may be personal coping mechanisms or societal and institutional supports. We agree with Dressler, who notes "what has been clearly lacking in the research on the stress process is a consideration of the social and historical context of stressors, of how these risks are generated out of the historically specific social processes operating within a community" (1991:165).

In the chapters that follow, we explore those historical, economic, political, social, and environmental conditions in Central Harlem, conditions that have the potential to cause stress and chronic strain. At the same time, we describe the mechanisms by which people attempt to address these circumstances. Chapter 2 details the environmental factors that provide the context for reproduction. The chapter contains ethnographic data on community social assets and the ways women's attempts to find and maintain safe and affordable housing and social services shape their day-to-day experiences. Chapter 3 documents the multiplicative impact of economic instability and income insecurity combined with potential work site sources of stress and chronic strain. The experiences of both low-income and middle-income women are described and analyzed. Chapter 4 provides the ethnographic data on the role of social support networks in the decision-making processes around reproduction and pregnancy. It also discusses the findings on the relationships between women and men in different roles. Chapter 5 assesses the data on women's interactions with the health care delivery system. It examines the barriers to early prenatal care, the varieties of facilities women use, and the perceptions of women and the community about infant loss. Chapter 6 summarizes the research findings within the context of an overall framework for understanding the relationship between gender, race, and class.

NOTES

[1] All graphs, tables, and figures illustrative of the sociodemographic characteristics described here are contained in the appendix.

[2] Unless otherwise noted, the source of most data is the 1990 census. The 2000 census data were not available when the manuscript went to press.

[3] In urban anthropology, the community study approach has been modified to account for the increasingly transnational character of cities and their location in global economic and social networks. Compared with the emphasis on geographically bound populations in earlier studies, communities are now considered to be "spatial precipitates of yet larger social relations, termini of worldwide economic, social, political and cultural patterns within which localities are embedded. They simultaneously exhibit patterns which are regionally rooted and also reflect the larger world" (Ross and Rapp, 1980:58–59). Community studies predominate among traditional ethnographic studies. In such approaches, the units of analysis are geographically bound populations—camps, settlements, and villages in rural and remote regions, or neighborhoods, enclaves, or a couple of blocks when the study takes place in an urban community. While traditional ethno-

graphies have been rich in detail and have provided data about localized social relationships and the organization of everyday life, their constraints have been well analyzed by
recent critics of the community studies approaches (see also Williams, 1988; di
Leonardo, 1984). In this study, as mentioned, the community was defined as those who
live and work in Harlem.

[4] In 1997, 21.6 percent of deaths of men and women under age 65 in Central Harlem were
due to infection with the human immunodeficiency virus (HIV), while 17.1 percent were
due to heart disease, 20.2 percent to malignant neoplasms, 0.1 percent to chronic liver
disease and cirrhosis, and 4.7 percent to homicide. For New York City, the figures are
12.9 percent, 19.6 percent, 23.9 percent, 2.5 percent, and 3.8 percent, respectively.
Indeed, 1997 marked the greatest discrepancy between Central Harlem and New York
City in deaths due to HIV infection.

[5] The health areas are composites of census tracts within each health district in New York
City. Because the community profile we created for the purpose of the study is based on
the Central Harlem Health District (a summary of all the health areas), without Health
Area 1600, it is almost identical to the area in Manhattan Community Board 10, the political unit. This facilitates comparison of the sociodemographic data and health data. It
should be noted, however, that the City Department of Health no longer uses health area
designations.

[6] It should be noted that the Giuliani Administration cut funding for pest extermination in
successive years from 1994 to 1997. In August 1997, funding was increased after the
mayor saw a rat run across Gracie Mansion, his residence.

[7] Qualitative data, on the other hand, are not designed to form predictive models, which
are based on and used to determine correlations and casual relationships between variables. Rather, qualitative data and their analysis show which particular groups of interrelated factors should be followed up with quantitative methods of data collection and
analysis. Qualitative research findings can guide quantitative data collection by pointing
to the right emphasis of relationships of variables that need to be explored in a more uniform and standardized fashion. It is from quantitative data that generalizations about
relationships of variables can be drawn. If correlations between variables are to be accu-
rately determined in quantitative analysis, there must be a meaningful link between the
variables being analyzed. Thus, the value of qualitative data is that they may reveal areas
to be explored, rather than allow generalizations to be drawn on the basis of what may be
spurious correlations of variables.

[8] The informal economy is generally defined as activities of production and income generation occurring outside of regulatory institutions and mechanisms of the formal market system and government agencies.

[9] As Bernard (1995) notes, most full-scale anthropological research is not done in less than
1 year, but many applied anthropologists have used rapid assessment procedures (i.e.,
going into a field situation with a list of questions to be answered and data to be collected) without developing the field rapport and trust that is often important in obtaining certain forms of data. Clearly there are forms of data that can be collected in this manner
(for an introduction to rapid assessment in anthropology, see Scrimshaw and Hurtado,
1987), but as several anthropologists have observed, an inability to develop rapport and
trust can lead to serious problems, and anthropologists who stay in the field for less than
a year are less likely to be able to collect data on sensitive issues (Bernard, 1995; Naroll,

1962; Foster et al., 1979). Rapid assessment techniques and certain types of interviewing may be more successful after traditional ethnographic research has been conducted in the study area.

[10]A particularly interesting aspect of this research was the difficulty of forming a focus group composed of women who had experienced infant loss. While the research team encountered few difficulties putting together any of the other focus groups, it was difficult to persuade women to attend a focus group on infant loss.

[11]During the Harlem Health Fair week in August 1994, approximately 80 people read the Harlem Birth Right materials (fact sheets about demographics, housing, family, and mortality in Central Harlem) and signed up to be contacted for participation in focus groups.

[12]The research team was particularly interested in noting how individuals may present information in focus groups compared with other circumstances.

[13]The summary results of the preliminary analysis of the ethnographic questionnaire data cited throughout the report were written by epidemiologist Diane McLean, Ph.D. The summary was included as an appendix of the original final report to the CDC.

[14]We used level of education to stratify the sample to conform with the criteria used in the original CDC study (Schoendorf et al., 1992), which demonstrated that regardless of their level of education, African American women fare worse than white women in birth outcomes.

[15]This was one of the first initiatives between CDC and a community organization to conduct a research project.

2

WHERE PEOPLE LIVE: THE ENVIRONMENTAL CONTEXT OF REPRODUCTION

2.1. INTRODUCTION

This chapter begins exploration of the broad social context that shapes the sources of stress and the "resistance resources" (Antonovsky, 1979) with which women confront stressful conditions. We are concerned here with the ways resource inequality, institutionalized racism, and gender discrimination mold the structure of risk, and we argue that only such a systemic view permits a comprehensive understanding of the potential sources of stressors and chronic strain. We also demonstrate that the women we studied were not passive victims but actively struggled to improve their quality of life. Ironically, both the conditions of the environment and women's attempts to ameliorate those conditions are potential sources of stress. This discussion is divided into three parts: 1) the broader urban environmental conditions that characterize Harlem and affect women's daily lives, 2) specific issues related to securing and maintaining safe and decent housing that appeared to be significant sources of stress and chronic strain, and 3) the impact of the delivery of social services (education and public assistance) on women across strata. In each part, we examine the interaction with and perceptions of social and environmental factors that shape exposure to stressors and sources of chronic strain and then document the types of strategies women develop to protect themselves. In each part, we look at similarities and differences in women's experiences across social strata.

2.2. ENVIRONMENT AS A POTENTIAL SOURCE OF STRESS AND CHRONIC STRAIN

M. T. Fullilove suggests that "place" is an environmental unit that is useful in assessing psychological and social health because it represents the immediate portion of the environment to which people are attached:

> Thus, place can be understood as the sum of resources and human relationships in a given location. As such, place sets the conditions for human consciousness.... It also provides

the physical structures within which human relationships unfurl.... Place is, on the one
hand, the external realities within which people shape their existence and, on the other
hand, the object of human thought and action (1996:1517–1518).

In Harlem, the sense of place is mediated by contradictions that emerge from the struggle to overcome negative conditions and to preserve remembered and created healthy environments. Negative aspects, such as neglect of streets, sidewalks, and buildings because of
historical patterns of discrimination, compete with positive aspects, such as the pleasures
of living in a historically significant and culturally vibrant black community. First, we
explore the condition of public space, the quality of stores and retail space, and the concerns with drug-related violence and police protection as they contribute to the difficult
conditions of existence. We then examine the quality of parks, the value of cultural and
spiritual resources, and the importance of living in a black community for feelings of safety and well-being, highlighting the ways residents draw on social community assets to try
to mitigate stress. The ethnographic case material used here is drawn primarily from field
research conducted in the neighborhood settings in the three health areas that composed the
study site. Additional material is derived from the longitudinal study of 22 women, the
focus groups conducted at the end of the field research phase, the ethnographic questionnaire (EQ), and the analysis of quantitative data from city agencies and published sources.

2.2.1. The Condition of Public Space

The heterogeneous character of public space in Harlem is a major factor influencing
exposure to stressors across social strata and shaping people's perceptions. It lends an
uneven character to the degree of decay, abandonment, cleanliness, and overall environmental strain found in different neighborhoods. Health Area 15, for example, reflects a
pattern of "gentrification" in which renovated residential buildings exist side by side with
deteriorated buildings. Renovated buildings interspersed with poorer housing stock may
expose people in a wide range of economic and educational strata to multiple environmental stressors. In one neighborhood in Health Area 15, the owners of newly renovated
brownstones live adjacent to a row of decayed and abandoned buildings, a source of pest
and rodent infestation. The homeowners frequently complained about the city's neglect of
street lighting, sanitation service, and delay in addressing building abandonment.

A slightly different situation exists in Health Area 10, which contains the famous
Strivers Row section of Harlem. Strivers Row, a four-block enclave formed in the 1920s
as the domain of an elite African American bourgeoisie, has largely maintained its exclusive character. The two blocks of Strivers Row consist of brownstones with a wealth of
architectural details, wrought iron gates, and landscaped frontages. Near Strivers Row is
the renowned Abyssinian Baptist Church, the home pulpit of Adam Clayton Powell Sr. and
Adam Clayton Powell Jr. and currently occupied by the Reverend Calvin O. Butts III. The
church has a largely middle-class African American membership who come from all over
the city to attend Sunday services (approximately 75 percent of church members do not
live in Harlem). It is also a popular tourist destination.

In Health Area 10, however, there has been less broad-based gentrification of the sort
that exists in Health Area 15. New black professionals in this area tend to consolidate along
Strivers Row. Other blocks adjacent to or near Strivers Row contain uniformly poorer
housing stock and abandoned buildings as well as vacant lots. Most buildings on one block

are managed by the New York City agency in charge of city-owned residential properties, the Housing and Preservation Department (HPD), which received them after years of landlord mismanagement and neglect and has been slow to rehabilitate or repair them. While no building was entirely abandoned at the time of fieldwork observation, there were vacancies in many of the buildings, with some units left in states of extreme disrepair (broken windows, rusty fixtures, peeling paint). Residents in occupied units experienced continuous problems with plumbing, heat, and hot water. In 1994, after a community-based organization exposed the conditions on this block, HPD agreed to undertake a major rehabilitation of 13 buildings on the block. A plan was developed to temporarily relocate residents while the buildings were rehabilitated, with the promise that the residents could eventually move back. However, there was a delay in funding approval for this plan and, as a result, rehabilitation proceeded erratically without comprehensive services for the residents during the fieldwork period.

Health Area 12 presents a third type of public space, one dominated by a public housing development. These developments, managed by the New York City Housing Authority, are large complexes of high-rise apartment buildings landscaped with small parks and playgrounds. Within the development in Health Area 12 are two child care centers. The development is located on a main boulevard that contains small shops, deli-grocery stores, and a few restaurants. Liquor stores, most of whose owners live outside Harlem, are located on several corners; they display prominent posters of a heavily promoted malt liquor. On a corner several blocks near the development is a large billboard advertising Camel cigarettes (at the time of fieldwork, this displayed the cartoon figure Joe Camel). Side streets, however, may contain brownstones or a mix of brownstones and small apartment buildings.

In summary, each of the health areas reflects different patterns of physical use of space, but in each the uneven development results in cross-strata environmental effects. In the EQ, respondents discussed their perceptions of the cleanliness of the neighborhood and the conditions of streets, sidewalks, and buildings. Sixty-eight percent of EQ respondents overall reported lack of cleanliness as a negative aspect, and this did not vary significantly by level of education, which reflects the broad-based exposure to adverse environmental conditions discussed above. Fifty-six percent of respondents overall perceived the conditions of streets and sidewalks as negative, again relatively uniformly by education level. Forty-four percent of respondents overall found building conditions to be a negative aspect of the neighborhood, and this differed slightly by education level (less than high school, 33 percent; high school or equivalent, 45 percent; more than high school, 50 percent) (Figure 2.1).

The quality and accessibility of public telephones was also a physical space issue for low-income residents who do not have telephone service in their homes. Among the 22 long-term study participants, 8, all low income, did not have regular telephone service at home. They had to rely on public telephones to conduct their business with social service agencies, employers, and others. The impact of nonworking telephones as a potential source of stress that affects women of all social strata is supported by the following data from the EQ: 25 percent of women with less than a high school diploma reported telephone inaccessibility as a negative aspect of their neighborhoods, 48 percent of high school graduates did so, and 39 percent of women with postsecondary education did so.

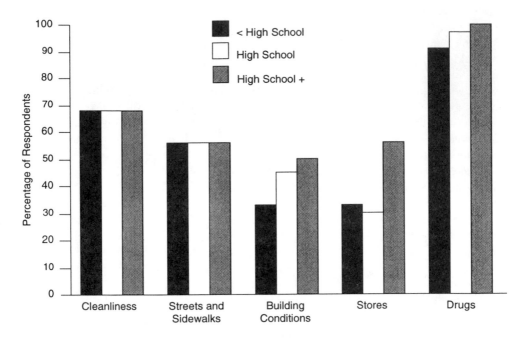

Figure 2.1. Negative Aspects of Public Space Reported on the Ethnographic Questionnaire, by Education Level.

It is important to note that Harlem is subject to a larger load of environmental pollutants than other parts of Manhattan. Data gathered in 1994 for preparation of the Upper Manhattan Empowerment Zone proposal indicated a high incidence of polluting facilities in Central Harlem. Six of the city's 19 bus depots are located in Harlem. There is also a large sewage treatment plant and a sanitation transfer station. Furthermore, there are over 1,800 vacant lots; all are potential sources of rodent infestation (Upper Manhattan Empowerment Zone, 1994). These sources of pollution, coupled with neglect by city agencies of sanitation, pest control, and street and building maintenance, are potential sources of strain that threaten the health and survival of all Harlem residents (see Fullilove, 1996).

Individually and collectively, women were active participants in the efforts to ameliorate the quality of public space in Harlem. Individual actions often took the form of frequent complaints to city agencies (such as the sanitation department) and requesting removal of garbage and cleanup of the vacant lots. Women across social strata also frequently attempted to beautify public space by planting flowers and shrubs in small window boxes or on the front stoops of buildings. Collective action often took the form of turning vacant lots into community gardens, working with neighborhood associations to raise funds for beautification, or more vocal confrontations. For example, members of the Abyssinian Baptist Church and others organized protests against the pervasive cigarette and alcohol advertising in Harlem, which they claimed specifically targeted young African Americans. In addition, several local environmental action groups, organized around issues of "environmental racism," attempted to document the ill effects of the concentration of pollution sources in Harlem and tried to organize people to address these issues.

During the research period, we observed what appeared to be an influx of middle-stratum African Americans into Harlem. Preliminary statistics on rising home ownership and renovation rates gathered after the research ended indicated that this was indeed the case. In May 1998, for example, over 3,000 Harlem residents attended the First Annual Harlem Community Home Buyers Fair, which was sponsored by a variety of organizations, including the Upper Manhattan Empowerment Zone and the Fannie Mae Foundation (*EZ Works,* 1998). The rise in home ownership and building renovation, however, has not been accompanied by significant investment in affordable housing for low-income residents of Harlem. Indeed, the Giuliani administration's policies toward homeless and displaced populations have become more punitive. (For example in 1999, the administration attempted to institute an ordinance to force homeless people without jobs out of shelters, but the initiative was rejected by the court as illegal.) Further research will determine the consequences of these transformations for the physical and social landscape of Harlem.

2.2.2. Access to Food and Other Necessities

A particularly salient issue for pregnant women is the access to healthy food, because attention to diet has long been considered an important aspect of prenatal care. Yet until very recently, women in Harlem have had to expend significant time and effort to obtain quality food and other retail items.

The women who participated in the study acquired information about nutrition and where to obtain good food from various sources. They reported receiving information about proper nutritional practices from their doctors and midwives as well as from family and friends. Most were aware of what they "should" do, but the degrees of compliance were variable, as was their sense of what constituted compliance. Women we encountered in the course of our fieldwork pursued a wide variety of dietary practices. All took prenatal vitamins as prescribed. However, most followed dietary recommendations on a haphazard basis.

One exception was longitudinal study participant Noma, a performance artist, who was very conscious of her health and actively searched for alternative paths to well-being. Along with prenatal vitamins, she added extensive supplements to her diet, including green algae and echinacea as well as many fruits and vegetables. However, she could not get the food she needed in Harlem; she regularly went all the way to Brooklyn to shop at a special food cooperative that sold health foods and organic produce.

Women had various degrees of control over diet. Women with more education appeared to be more conscientious about the types of food they ate and emphasized vegetables and fruits in their diet, although even women with less than a high school diploma generally followed some dietary restrictions. Some women avoided fried foods, and others avoided certain kinds of fruits. However, there did not appear to be any consistent pattern to the dietary changes. The lack of consistent dietary habits may be one reason we had difficulty collecting systematic data in this area during fieldwork. Women had trouble recalling what they ate, and our attempts to get them to write down their dietary intake failed.

The lack of consistency was also supported by the data from the EQ, which demonstrated that although most women (80 percent) considered that they ate special foods for pregnancy, the types of food varied greatly. These included some foods with known health benefits, such as liver, vegetables and juices, meat and fish, shrimp, spinach, and milk. But also included were egg rolls, raw onion, tomato paste with pepper, licorice candy, and baking soda. Almost twice as many respondents with more than a high school diploma reported eating special foods (33 percent) than those with less than a high school diploma (18 percent). Moreover, 17 percent of respondents reported eating Argostarch, clay, or dirt; one woman reported eating ashes.

We observed that what women ate often depended on their daily circumstances. Whether they worked and regardless of how flexible their jobs were, we found that women had little organized time to pay attention to their diet. This did not differ across social strata. If a woman noticed that something was on sale at a supermarket, she might buy it; if, on the other hand, she and friends went to eat at a fast-food restaurant, she was likely to eat fried foods. Although some of the women realized they should pay attention to their diet (making comments about not gaining weight or gaining too much weight or about eating one thing or another), few were able to take consistent measures to "eat right." Nationally, the greatest consumers of fast food are working women with children, and among respondents to the EQ, 70 percent reported that they ate at fast-food restaurants at least once a week; of those, 71 percent reported that they did so up to three times a week.

In general, it appeared that the degree to which women had control over their eating schedules and access to nutritious foods influenced the extent to which they could heed medical advice on nutrition and diet. Access to nutritious food through the Special Supplemental Nutrition Program for Women, Infants and Children (WIC, a federal subsidy designed to facilitate pregnant and lactating women's access to healthy food for themselves and their infants) was especially important in facilitating women's efforts to maintain a good diet. Studies have found WIC participation to be associated with improved pregnancy outcomes, including decreases in low birth weight and neonatal mortality (Devaney, 1992; Devaney and Schirm, 1993; Kotelchuck et al., 1984). In Harlem, the WIC center at a large hospital was able to arrange for a farmers' market during the summer months, when local New Jersey farmers sold fresh fruits and vegetables nearby once a week.

Women we observed as part of the longitudinal study used the WIC foods to supplement their diets. Longitudinal study participant Sandra, a cashier at a fast-food restaurant, said she was always careful to keep her shelves stocked with baby food and powdered milk bought through the WIC program. The food came in handy, she said, when her public assistance budget was cut and she was short of funds. The 1996 welfare reform legislation enacted by the federal government (after the field research ended) had the effect of making the WIC benefits more difficult to obtain despite their demonstrated success. More research is needed to determine how this change has affected women's abilities to maintain healthy diets during pregnancy and in the postpartum period.

However, even with access to WIC resources, women in Harlem had difficulty locating healthy and nutritious foods because of the types of retail food stores nearby. In all three health areas, the quality and quantity of stores were similar. In all three, the predominant type of store was a small deli-grocery that carried a variety of groceries, dry goods, beer, wine, and cigarettes. These stores also sold lottery tickets, newspapers, and magazines. Residents in these areas perceived these stores as a convenience for their small-item shopping. Typical of New York, the store operators come to know their clientele, and the stores can become sites for neighborhood social interactions. A potential negative aspect of these stores, however, is the sale of beer, malt liquor, and cigarettes to minors. During the fieldwork period, these stores typically displayed large poster advertisements for St. Ide's Malt Liquor, a popular beverage for young teens. In a workshop at a social service agency, Harlem parents expressed their anger about the campaign to promote St. Ide's and commented that it was sold in large bottles and made to look like a soft drink, when in fact it has a higher alcoholic content than beer.

The supermarkets are located on the main boulevards. The typical small supermarkets in Harlem contain the usual variety of dry goods but a poor variety of fresh produce and meats. One ethnographer shopped weekly for 3 months at a supermarket in Health Area 15 and discovered that she could rarely get the quality or variety of fresh produce that was available in the adjacent upper west side supermarkets. On several occasions, the produce she bought was rotten. The fresh fruit and produce markets found on virtually every corner of the upper east side and upper west side of Manhattan are more limited in Harlem. Participants in the ethnographic study in all three health areas reported that they tried to avoid shopping at these small supermarkets, which they found to be unsatisfactory for a variety of reasons, including quality of products and price. Participants instead traveled to larger supermarkets outside of Harlem. This was true regardless of income level or level of education, or whether they were pregnant.

- Elizabeth, a high school graduate and family child care provider in her early 60s, lived in Health Area 12. She usually shopped at a large supermarket in the Bronx every 2 weeks, taking advantage of sales and promotions. Sometimes her son drove her, and other times she used a "car service." She used the local supermarkets only for emergency shopping.
- Gina, in her mid-20s, an unemployed woman who lived in Health Area 15 and was enrolled in a community college, also shopped outside of Harlem. She made regular shopping trips to the upper east side or to the Bronx with her cousins, Ms. A, a high school dropout who was unemployed and lived in Health Area 10 as well, and Ms. B, also a high school dropout who lived in Health Area 15.
- Celine, in her early 30s, had a bachelor's degree and worked as an independent consultant; she lived in Health Area 15, shopped for groceries on the upper west side, and sometimes even went to Westchester County.
- In Health Area 10, Ms. C, a resident of Strivers Row who worked in the private sector, shopped in the suburbs just north of New York City. She commented, "Now, that's something I don't do. I don't shop right here. That may be because I have a car. So, I can jump in a car and I'll go all the way up to Yonkers, Mt. Vernon, and New Rochelle because I had the opportunity to do those things. I don't shop in Harlem. I don't like the quality of food. I don't like the people that own those stores. The Mets and the Associated and all that. I don't like their food. I can find a better quality of food and at a better price if I go out of Harlem."
- Also in Health Area 10 was Robin, a longitudinal participant in her late 30s who worked for a downtown firm and lived in a brownstone she owned with her husband. She shopped at a large supermarket outside of Harlem.

Until mid-1996, there were no major large upscale supermarkets located in Harlem. In 1996, the first modern state-of-the-art large Fairway supermarket opened in West

Harlem, at 133rd Street at the West Side Highway. In late 1999, a long-awaited Pathmark supermarket opened on 125th Street and Third Avenue, in East Harlem. These large stores have made a significant difference to Harlem shoppers, affording them the access to quality goods without having to travel a great distance. However, particularly in the case of Pathmark, community residents have raised questions about prices and employment practices.

The ethnographic data on residents' dissatisfaction with the stores in Harlem are supported by the EQ, where one-third of respondents with less than a high school education (33 percent) and about one-third of those with a high school education (30 percent) reported that poor-quality stores were a negative aspect of their neighborhoods. More than half (56 percent) the women with more than a high school education felt this way. While 74 percent of women reported that they shopped for food in Harlem, however, this does not indicate whether they also shopped outside of Harlem; 40 percent reported that food was more expensive in Harlem, and only 39 percent said the quality of food was better in Harlem. Ninety percent said transportation was available. Women reported a desire for more stores in Harlem, including department stores such as Macy's and JC Penney; other large retail chains such as Pathmark, Caldor's, and Duane Reade; and specialty stores including The Gap, Blockbuster, bookstores, and stores that would provide "good vegetables and foods good for our health."

Finally, in a telephone survey of 1,000 Harlem households that was conducted for the Upper Manhattan Empowerment Zone Proposal, only 1 of 10 goods and services listed— laundry and dry cleaning—was regularly purchased by a substantial majority of residents in their neighborhood or in Harlem (67 percent and 66 percent, respectively). Sixty-six percent of the respondents shopped outside their neighborhoods and outside Central Harlem for food, fruits, and vegetables (Upper Manhattan Empowerment Zone, 1994). In summary, the lack of suitable supermarkets and, in general, the dearth of adequate retail stores posed a significant obstruction and source of chronic stress for Harlem residents of all strata during the research period. To acquire basic necessities and to make simple purchases, almost all residents had to travel outside their neighborhood.

As indicated by the advent of the two new large supermarkets, this situation began to change in Harlem after our research concluded. The Upper Manhattan Empowerment Zone (which began operating in the summer of 1996 with funding from the federal government, the state, and the city) together with a coalition of private businesses began to promote the development of new retail enterprises in Harlem, principally on 125th Street. Chain stores such as The Gap, Duane Reade drug store, Old Navy, and Blockbuster video store have opened franchises in Harlem and will be joined by other nationally based establishments. However, promises to incubate small businesses and increase affordable housing have not materialized. More research is required to determine how these changes affect low-income residents, small entrepreneurs, and others. Furthermore, the social implications of the homogenization of public space as a consequence of the expansion of retail chains should be further explored.

2.2.3. Drugs, Violence, and Police Protection

A major problem perceived by people across all social strata as a negative environmental factor in Harlem was the traffic in illegal substances. Drugs received the highest negative rating of all environmental factors in the EQ. Overall, 97 percent of the women interviewed identified drugs as something they disliked in the community, and there was little difference across educational level (less than high school, 91 percent; high school, 97 percent; more than high school, 100 percent).

Between 1965 and 1970, drug use expanded in inner-city communities. By 1985, crack cocaine had become widely available, with far-reaching consequences for Harlem, and was directly related to escalating rates of violence (see Mullings and Susser, 1992). The Centers for Disease Control and Prevention (CDC) cited crack use and related practices of exchanging sexual favors for illegal substances as a factor for the rise in sexually transmitted diseases in 1988 (cited in Goldsmith, 1988). In addition, linkages were found between crack cocaine use and prevalence of infection with the human immunodeficiency virus (HIV) (Watkins and Fullilove, 1999).

Documentation of the extent of illegal drug traffic, or its social patterns, was not an objective of the field research, but ethnographers recorded participants' perceptions and concerns. Drugs were perceived by study participants as a negative environmental factor and stressor in several ways. First, the multiple ways drug abuse rends the social fabric was universally deplored. Across all neighborhood sites, people discussed the consequences of addiction on the families of people they knew. Grandmothers who had to take care of their grandchildren because their daughters had become addicted were frequently cited. Addiction to crack cocaine, in particular, was perceived as significantly destructive because of its ability to severely incapacitate an individual (see Watkins and Fullilove, 1999). Participants in the study were also aware (as has now been documented by other anthropologists; see Hamid, 1992) that crack cocaine addiction had disproportionately affected a stratum of mid-level professionals (such as teachers and civil servants) who lost jobs and careers as a result. Ms. D, in Health Area 15, for example, discussed teachers she knew who had fallen victim to crack addiction. Mr. J, a social worker we encountered, recounted how he had been a teacher, became addicted to crack, was incarcerated, managed to overcome the addiction, and reestablished himself.

Second, people were concerned about the violence associated with drug traffic. They were concerned not only about the violence among people actually engaged in drug traffic but also about violence that resulted from the increased police effort to control street-level drug sales. The Giuliani Administration stepped up police efforts in this area during the period of fieldwork and targeted inner-city areas as the foci for massive drug sweeps and anti-narcotics undercover work. There was a visible increase in police presence in Harlem, whose impact was felt by neighborhood residents. This concern was reflected in discussions in public meetings, such as those held on a monthly basis at the police precincts as part of their community policing efforts. Here, participants in both Harlem police precincts were supportive of the police efforts to control the drug trade, but they were vocal in their criticisms about the tactics used by the police and the haphazard nature of the enforcement of laws.

For example, meeting participants expressed concerns that the police were spending too much time making "quality-of-life" arrests for activities they did not consider criminal while they often ignored dangerous crime. They also believed the police could offer no guarantees that residents would not suffer retribution from drug dealers if they cooperated with police work. This significant source of stress is documented in an ethnographer's observations of a precinct community meeting.

At that meeting, a senior citizen voiced a concern about giving names to the police. Other people concurred. She went on to say that she was afraid that if she informed on them, the drug dealers would retaliate, and the police would not protect her. Another person at the meeting commented that the street narcotic unit officers only drive the dealers off the streets and into the buildings, where they remain. The person was not convinced the drug dealers were actually being removed. A third woman then asked how many of the people arrested were still in jail, to which the police officers responded that it was the fault of the judges and the politicians that criminals were let go and returned to the community. The woman who made the original comment about her reservations about calling in reports on drug dealers finally said, "This is why you have to be careful—you lock people up, they get out and they come to get you."

Skepticism about the ability of police to protect residents who cooperate with them was coupled with skepticism about police sincerity in resolving the problem of drug traffic. At several meetings, people complained that the police were not doing enough and that they were in fact turning a blind eye to drug activity. For example, at one meeting the ethnographers attended, a young woman recounted that she had witnessed two police officers just standing by while several people used crack cocaine in their vicinity. She expressed the opinion that the police attitude was that this type of activity was "normal" in this community and that this was a racist attitude. She was told that she should provide the precinct captain with the names of the offending officers. Thus Harlem residents did not have confidence in the police efforts to protect them against the consequences of increased illegal activities related to the drug trade.

The increased levels of public and random violence in recent years has been related to the influx of drugs and weapons into inner cities (see Mullings and Susser, 1992; Canada, 1995). Public violence and its unpredictability affected community residents across the spectrum of educational and occupational strata. This was most compellingly demonstrated by a report of two incidents of violence experienced by a middle-stratum participant and a low-income participant, respectively.

Longitudinal study participant Celine was a college-educated, self-employed consultant who lived in a recently renovated brownstone in Health Area 15. In an interview with an ethnographer, where she appeared visibly upset, she recounted that the previous night she and her son had witnessed a police confrontation with a criminal suspect in front of their apartment. They had heard and seen the police fire and shoot the suspect. Then they watched as the police let the suspect lie on the street unattended, without calling an ambulance. An ambulance came about 45 minutes later, even though the hospital was less than a mile away. Celine said that her son, who lives in North Carolina with his grandmother, was not used to seeing this type of violence and was very frightened. She made her son stay away from the window, and neither of them slept much after the incident. Celine perceived the police action as insensitive to the community residents, and she wondered why they chased suspects in such a fashion, shot them on the street, and then left them there for so long. She placed some calls to the local police precinct to try to get some answers to her questions and was waiting for a reply. She was seriously considering whether to curtail her son's visit and send him back to North Carolina early.

Another longitudinal study participant, Claire, an unemployed mother of two with less than a high school education who lived in a tenement in Health Area 15, told the ethnographer about a violent incident that occurred on her block. During the night, there was a shootout between several men on the streets. Terrified that stray bullets might enter her apartment, Claire pulled her children from their beds, and they all huddled together in the middle of the room on the floor. Claire and the children were very upset by the incident and talked about it for weeks afterward.

Many of the women in our study remained constantly alert about the possibility of violence and its impact on themselves and their children. An ethnographer was attending a tenants' association meeting in Health Area 10 during the summer. The tenants, all low-income women, had gathered to discuss strategies for getting repairs made to their apartments. Their children were playing on the building stoop. Suddenly, the women ran out of the meeting, collected their children, and shepherded them inside. The ethnographer, surprised at the action, asked what had happened. The women stated that they had heard a police siren, shouts, and loud noises; they recognized these noises as signs of a possible police action and brought their children inside to protect them.

Environmental noise pollution was also associated with violence. At a focus group on housing and environmental concerns, a participant in his mid-30s, who was a father of two young children, spoke about moving from an apartment on a block with a high frequency of drug-related violence because the constant nighttime noise from shouts and gunshots kept him, his wife, and their children awake. He said they were reawakened so often throughout the night that they were chronically exhausted. He stated that he was happy to have moved to a new apartment on a better block and that now his family could sleep through the night.

Related to the concerns about drug traffic and violence and their impact on the neighborhood were study participants' perceptions about the level and type of police protection they received. In the EQ, people responded that overall they perceived police protection as a positive factor in their neighborhood. Only 33 percent of women with less than a high school education perceived it as negative, while 19 percent of women with a high school diploma or equivalent did so, and 34 percent of women with more than a high school diploma did so. However, this overall approval may reflect the fact that they liked the idea of police protection. In a 1994 survey for the Upper Manhattan Empowerment Zone Proposal of 1,000 Harlem households, 68 percent described police protection as only fair or poor.

Harlem residents often appeared to be negotiating between the need for protection against crime and drugs with very real complaints about police behavior. Despite residents' lack of confidence in the police, they continued to attend community meetings and press for action that would increase safety in their neighborhoods. In late 1995, for the first time in the city's history, an African American woman police officer was appointed as precinct captain in Harlem. Community residents expressed satisfaction with this decision and hoped it would lead to an improvement in the quality of police services. It should be noted, however, that overall New York City's police force remains largely white and male (according to the 1995 report of the New York City Civilian Complaint Review Board, 72.5 percent of the police force was white). In the past few years, several nationally publicized cases of reported police brutality and use of excessive force (such as the case of the sodomization of Abner Louima while in police custody and the shooting death of Bronx resident Amadou Diallo) highlight the continued persistence of the problem of police–community relations and contribute to residents' distrust of the police.

In summary, the data indicated that the fact that communities such as Harlem have become marketplaces for the international traffic in illegal drugs and sites for the concomitant escalation in levels of violence has seriously affected residents, and these negative influences were widely perceived as a significant source of chronic strain and acute stress. As coping strategies, women (both low-income and middle-stratum) undertook collective action through participation in community meetings to secure police protection; they also engaged in individual actions through vigilance against often unpredictable episodes of violence.

2.3. COMMUNITY ASSETS

We now turn our attention to perceived assets in the Harlem environment that residents identified as positive factors associated with living in Harlem. The consideration of assets in poverty-stricken regions has received considerable attention in recent social science literature. The debate has centered on the presence or absence of so-called "social capital" and how such capital can be used for economic development or poverty amelioration (Kretzmann and McKnight, 1993; Putnam, 2000; Sowell, 1994; Wilson, 1987). Anthropologists have long examined the ways social organization and use of available resources become the building blocks of community struggles to improve the quality of life (Mullings, 1987). The location of assets in the physical environment is related to the ways people imbue public space with meaning and value (Low, 1999). During the Harlem Birth Right study, we identified three major community social assets in the physical environment: parks, faith institutions, and the desirability of living in a black community.

2.3.1. Parks and Cultural Resources

All three health areas had one or more neighborhood parks, generally with a playground. An important improvement in the parks during the period of fieldwork observation resulted from the Harlem Injury Prevention Program of Harlem Hospital. The Injury Prevention Program has collaborated since 1988 with a community advisory board, Harlem parents, and the city park district, among others, to resurface all Harlem playgrounds with safe rubberized material. In addition they started alternative recreation programs such as a baseball league, an arts and dance program, and a bicycle repair shop. These initiatives have significantly lessened pediatric injuries in Harlem, and this program success has been reported in the *American Journal of Public Health* and other health publications. Generally, the ethnographers observed the parks to be in constant use during the daytime by a wide variety of people, including children with parents, young people, and senior citizens, as is evident in the following descriptions from fieldnotes:

- Late one afternoon in early summer, an ethnographer visited a park near Health Area 10. In one corner, the Harlem Grace Choir was practicing. A small crowd gathered to listen to what turned into an impromptu concert. Nearby, men seated on park benches were playing checkers. In another corner, young boys were playing basketball.
- Mount Morris Park in Health Area 15 is the site of the annual neighborhood spring festival. In 1995, the local Community Improvement Association joined

with a social service agency that works in the park's recreation center to broaden the fair and include youth and children's activities, such as storytelling and face painting. The festival was a vehicle to bring together several different community organizations and to stimulate initiatives to provide recreation alternatives for youth. Throughout the park, there were booths with plants and garden products (sold by the association as part of its home improvement effort), activities, and food. A special program at the outdoor theater behind the recreation center featured speeches by community leaders, poetry readings, and youth group dance and song performances.

- In the summer, almost every morning, around seven o'clock, Ms. E practiced tennis against the backboard at the recreation center in Mount Morris Park. She liked the convenience of having the facility across the street from where she lived.

- Ms. F regularly took her young day care charges out to play in the little playground on the grounds of the public housing development in Health Area 12. Nearby, young adolescents played basketball in the fenced-off court that was also on the housing development's grounds. Elderly residents sat on the park benches and chatted with each other.

- Riverbank State Park opened in summer 1993. Part of the New York State Park System, it was built in part to mitigate the negative impact of a huge new sewage treatment plant completed in 1985 in West Harlem. The plant was originally planned for the upper west side, south of Harlem. However, powerful members of the upper west side community board successfully resisted having it located in their neighborhood. Consequently, the $1.1 billion plant was built in Harlem despite the objections of community activists, who cited the existing environmental burden of a marine garbage transfer facility adjacent to the new plant. The combined odors from the two facilities and the bus depots were perceived as a real hazard by community residents, although plant officials claimed that odor and toxic emissions were under control. The Riverbank State Park, however, with spacious grounds, several playing fields, a track, huge indoor and outdoor pools, and a recreation center, was immediately popular with community residents.

The positive advantages of parks, as recorded in the fieldwork, was also supported by perceptions expressed in the EQ. Overall, 71 percent of respondents viewed parks as a positive aspect of the neighborhood, while 61 percent viewed recreation centers as a positive asset. There was little difference by level of education.

The beneficial uses of parks, however, are tempered by the fact that they may also become dangerous zones if they become a site for illegal drug transactions. Informants (particularly elderly people) generally said they avoided going to parks after dark. Random inspections revealed that certain areas in parks were littered with used crack cocaine vials. After Rudolph Giuliani was elected mayor of New York City, the police stepped up their campaign against street level narcotics dealers, and the parks became prime targets for drug sweeps, which created situations of unpredictable tension and danger for community residents (as discussed above).

In addition to the parks, Harlem residents frequently use other cultural resources, such as the Schomburg Center for Black Culture; other branches of the New York Public

Library; theaters, such as the Apollo and the National Black Theater; and museums, such as the Studio Museum of Harlem. During our study, schoolchildren regularly visited the branch libraries to use the books and do their homework, and block associations held meetings in these spaces. The Schomburg Center was frequently the site of film screenings, book signings, lectures, and discussion groups.

2.3.2. Faith Institutions and Spiritual Resources

Institutions of faith abound in Harlem. They range from well-known large establishments to small storefront churches to even smaller ministries run from the minister's home. There are also a wide variety of centers, practitioners, and street vendors who offer African, African-centered, Eastern, New Age, or eclectic spiritual resources, including books, therapies, and advice. Christian institutions predominate, but there are several mosques (the two best known are the Malcolm Shabazz Mosque at 116th Street and Lenox Avenue and Mosque 7 of the Nation of Islam near the corner of Fifth Avenue and 125th Street), a large black Hebrew temple near Mount Morris Park, and various smaller institutions of other faiths. These institutions were important in the everyday lives of women in our study, and many study participants belonged to some institution, although not necessarily in the neighborhoods where they lived. Ethnographers could discern no particular pattern indicating the reasons women chose one or another faith institution. Many commented on the quality of a particular minister or the tenor of the service. In the EQ, virtually all the respondents (94 percent) described faith institutions as a positive aspect of their neighborhoods. Descriptions of four different institutions in the three health areas illuminate their role in the social life of women and the potential ways they may act to mitigate stressors.

2.3.2.1. Abyssinian Baptist Church in Health Area 10

This church is perhaps the best known of all Harlem churches. As previously noted, it was the pulpit of Adam Clayton Powell Jr., a ranking Black Congressman whose sermons attracted nationwide attention. Currently, the Reverend Calvin O. Butts III presides. He is a controversial figure who is active on the state political scene and is a leader of the church's efforts to acquire and develop significant real estate holdings in Harlem. He is also a leader of community efforts to reduce alcohol and cigarette advertising in inner cities. The membership of the church is largely middle-class African American, and members from all over the city come to Sunday service. The church is also a major tourist attraction, and large numbers of tourists from Europe and Asia arrive in buses to view a portion of Sunday services during the year. The tourists, often dressed in casual clothes, may seem jarring in the context of the regular church members, who are dressed in more traditional church attire. However, members appear to tolerate tourists with no particular discomfort.

An ethnographer observed a Sunday service and recorded the proceedings:

> There was a mix of older and younger people as well as some obvious tourists. The serious churchgoers were predictably well dressed, with the older ladies in hats and the men in suits despite the heat. The tourists (many Europeans and some white Americans) were more casually dressed in shorts and tee-shirts. Inside the church, the ushers, dressed in white with white gloves, showed people to seats. Two special events occurred in the serv-

ice: blessing of babies and acknowledgment of graduates. All the parents of the babies were married couples (as indicated by husband and wife with same name), and the two baby girls were dressed in fancy white "baptismal" type dresses.

Dr. Butts, presiding at the service, talked of the importance of children and how the blessing of the babies is a way of showing the babies to the congregation and providing the parents with additional integration into the church. Dr. Butts also acknowledged the graduates, to reinforce the importance of "intellect" in the service of God. The graduates (from any institution of higher learning, high school and up) lined up in the aisle. They came forward one by one to receive congratulations and a book (*Sermons from the Black Pulpit*) from Dr. Butts. Dr. Butts asked each one to say their name, the institution from which they had graduated, and the level of their degree. He knew quite a few of them and took the time to joke with them, praised them, and asked family members to stand. Twenty graduates were so acknowledged.

2.3.2.2. A Storefront Ministry in Health Area 15

This is a storefront church located in a brownstone on a quiet block. Regular services are held at the church, but it also serves as a gathering place and meeting hall for other activities. One of the members, Ms. G, a woman we encountered as she was vending (she sold spiritual literature and accessories on 125th Street), organized a support group/workshop that had three or four sessions at the church. They met on the ground floor of the brownstone in a large room with a long rectangular table (the room was set up like a conference room). About seven people attended the workshop (not including the ethnographers); all were women, except for one man who came with his partner. Two of the women lived in the Bronx and two lived in Brooklyn. Three of the women actually worshipped at this little church.

The discussion ranged from personal to professional issues and ways to better cope with stress. Ms. G, for example, was worried about how long it was taking her to find a job. She had a college degree, but could not find appropriate work. Ms. H talked of her travails when she discovered her son was a crack addict. She relied on support from her mother and held on to feelings of love to overcome her fears. Ms. G offered a variety of strategies, including spiritual nourishment from the Bible as well as physical remedies. For example, she suggested taking a bath with kosher salt added to the water. She maintained that this practice purified the water and was especially good for the feet. After the workshop, the ethnographers were given a tour of the church. The ground floor also had a sizable kitchen. Upstairs was the main chapel, with an altar and about 10 rows of pews. The church was decorated with religious pictures and a photograph of the founder.

2.3.2.3. Salem Baptist Church in Health Area 12

This large church is also one of the leading churches in Harlem. It is located adjacent to a large public housing development. The church is the site of a number of social service programs, including a day care center, a subsidized program for infants and toddlers, and a senior center. Church members and governing officers sit on the boards of the social service agencies, and there is a close connection between the two. The services are housed in a four-story "office" building annexed to the main church. On any given weekday, the building is lively and in constant use. In addition to housing the child care facilities, it is a meeting place for youth groups, senior groups, and other community organizations.

2.3.2.4. A Mosque in Harlem

The mosque at 116th Street and Lenox Avenue is known as the Malcolm Shabazz Mosque. The mosque offers regular prayer services, runs a parochial school, and has a bookstore and a small restaurant. In October 1994, when vendors were evicted from 125th Street (discussed in the next section), the mosque, working with city government, created a small outdoor market for them in the vacant lot across the street.

The variety of ways faith institutions serve the neighborhoods indicates their significant role as community assets and resources. Spiritual guidance and support, while important, is by no means the only service offered. Faith institutions are increasing their social roles in the community as the public sector shrinks. One innovative program, for example, facilitated by a faith institution, was a discussion by a panel of prominent male artists, social theorists, and political activists on the ways men can help reduce the levels of domestic violence against women. The invited audience included women (some of whom were pregnant) from a battered women's shelter.

2.3.3. Living in a Black Community

It is interesting to note that respondents to the EQ reported a fairly uniform feeling of comfort with the level of safety in the Harlem community. Only 33 percent in each level of education described safety as a negative factor in their neighborhoods. Study participants encountered in the ethnographic fieldwork did not seem to experience their neighborhoods as inordinately unsafe (that is, more unsafe than New York City in general). Women discussed the violence and criminality associated with drug traffic but in general did not appear to be overly concerned about other types of crime. This distinction may indicate that stressors resulting from drug-related crime and violence should be treated separately from overall perceptions of safety. For example, two ethnographers accompanied a longitudinal study participant, Rose, a vendor, to a Jazzmobile concert at Grant's Tomb in Riverside Park. Jazzmobile is a Harlem-based not-for-profit arts initiative that provides free jazz concerts during the summer and offers educational programs for children in poor neighborhood schools. After leaving the concert at 9:30 p.m., the ethnographers and Rose walked back to 125th Street because Rose was going to sell tee-shirts outside the Apollo Theater (it was amateur night at the Apollo, a weekly event that draws a large crowd during the summer months); 125th Street was lively and full of people, and many of the restaurants and a few retail stores were still open. As the group approached the Apollo Theater, they saw many street vendors with their tables set up to sell to the large crowd of mostly young people, who were waiting in an orderly fashion.

Another woman interviewed by the ethnographers was Ms. I, who lived in Strivers Row. She characterized her neighborhood as city living that is "wonderful." Typically, on weekends, people are out barbecuing and chatting in a neighborly fashion, and, while the lack of clean air and open space bothers her, she believes that family activities and camaraderie thrive in the relaxed environment. She told the ethnographer that even if she "won the lottery" and had as much money as she wanted, she would keep her house in Harlem as a legacy for her son.

Ms. C, also a Strivers Row resident, said the following:

> First of all, let's say ... the warm sense of your neighbors. Harlem is like ... it's like a little town. You know people in a block. I know people up there. They used to see me every day and I used to go work and come home and feel more comfortable. The transportation is good. You can get to Long Island. To the Bronx. To Staten Island. Transportation is wonderful....

As shown by the cases above, people's sense of safety in Harlem partly resulted from the positive feelings they had about living in a predominantly African American community. In the EQ, 99 percent of the respondents identified living in a black community as a positive aspect of their neighborhoods. Across the broad spectrum of income and educational levels, the degree of comfort people felt in living in Harlem was uniform. Overall, 67 percent of the women reported that they thought it was important to live in a black community, and 32 percent thought it was not important. Women with a high school education or general equivalency diploma (GED) were the most likely to believe it was important to live in a black community. Among women with less than a high school education, 58 percent reported that it was important to live in a black community; 8 percent were not asked. Among women with a high school education or GED, 74 percent reported that it was important to live in a black community. Among women with more than a high school education, 61 percent reported that it was important to live in a black community.

In the EQ overall, 11 percent reported that neighbors were a negative aspect of the neighborhood, and 84 percent reported that neighbors were a positive aspect. Among women with less than a high school education, 0 percent reported neighbors as a negative aspect of the neighborhood, and 91 percent reported neighbors as a positive aspect; 8 percent reported both positive and negative feelings about neighbors. Among women with a high school education or GED, 14 percent reported neighbors as a negative aspect of the neighborhood, and 82 percent reported neighbors as a positive aspect. Among women with more than a high school education, 11 percent reported neighbors as a negative aspect of the neighborhood, and 83 percent reported neighbors as a positive aspect.

In the EQ overall, 25 percent of the women sampled had lived in Harlem their entire lives. The number of years ranged from 1 to 55. Approximately 50 percent of the women had lived in Harlem for 28 years or less. Among women with less than a high school education, the range was 4 to 54 years. Among women with a high school education or GED, the range was 8 to 55 years. Among women with more than a high school education, the range was 1 to 54 years. The proportion of women who had lived in Harlem their entire lives did not appear to differ according to educational status. Among women with less than a high school education, 25 percent had lived in Harlem their entire lives. Among women with a high school education or GED, 22 percent had lived in Harlem their entire lives. Among women with more than a high school education, 28 percent had lived in Harlem their entire lives. Overall, 96 percent of the sample reported living in Harlem year-round. Among women with less than a high school education, 100 percent lived in Harlem year-round. Among women with a high school education or GED, 96 percent lived in Harlem year-round, and 4 percent lived somewhere else part of the year. Among women with more than a high school education, 94 percent lived in Harlem year-round, and 6 percent lived somewhere else part of the year.

Overall, among EQ respondents, 86 percent of the women considered Harlem to be home; of women with less than a high school education, 83 percent called Harlem home; of women with a high school education or GED, 78 percent called Harlem home; and of women with more than a high school education, 100 percent called Harlem home.

Residents interviewed during field research expressed frustration that the representation of Harlem in the national and local media, in popular perceptions, and in the political arena focused on the single negative dimension of crime and inner-city poverty. A compelling example of people's frustration with the representation of Harlem was evident in the reaction of residents in several of the study sites to a three-part front-page series that appeared in the *New York Times* in September 1994 about a block in Harlem (Lee, 1994a, b, c). The series, entitled "Another America," described the lives of block residents as being caught up in the hopelessness of the "underclass." People on the block were characterized as generally dependent on public assistance, involved with illegal drug activities, destitute, and hopeless as well as apathetic about their own condition. The very title "Another America" and references in the article that these people lived "a world apart" from mainstream America seemed to imply that their lives were not related to or affected by events, policies, or structural conditions in national life, but that theirs was a deviant and abnormal lifestyle.

Coincidentally, the block reported in the article was part of the Harlem Birth Right research site in Health Area 15, and the ethnographers were familiar with the residents who were portrayed in the article as well as with others on the block. The ethnographers met the reporter who wrote the article, although the reporter did not formally interview them as part of her series. When the article appeared, the ethnographers received a call from a block resident who was outraged by the article, its portrayal of people, and its tenor and tone. Upon reading the article, the ethnographers immediately recognized that it contained several substantive errors of fact and interpretation. Over the next few days, the ethnographers observed and recorded people's reactions to the article.

First, on the block itself, the day the article came out, the ethnographers observed people on their stoops reading the article and discussing it among themselves. One woman commented, "[The reporter] got everything distorted." Another woman, in her late 20s or early 30s, shook her head in disgust and said, "I'm not part of the underclass ... I hate this underclass business. This is totally irresponsible journalism." Another woman pointed to a photograph of an arrest that accompanied the article and said, "I remember when that happened" and continued, "Why don't they write about any of the good things on this block? They've doomed us. They didn't mention the picnic at the park and 50 pounds of chicken that ... [we] cooked. We had lots of food for the kids and had a great time. And the bake sale." (Here she referred to a picnic organized by block residents to raise money for children to buy school supplies.) Several other people on the stoop agreed. They strongly expressed anger about the depiction of the block and what they perceived to be serious inaccuracies.

Over the next 2 days, when the second and third installments appeared, residents appeared to be even more angry. Most upset were some of the people who had cooperated with the reporter and were featured in the article. They expressed feelings of betrayal. The reporter had portrayed them as cooperative with the drug trade. She had also described the life of a former drug dealer who had been paralyzed as a result of a shooting. Those featured in the article claimed that the reporter had excerpted partial pieces of information from their accounts and created a false picture of the events. Furthermore, she revealed information they had given her off the record and believed that she had placed their lives at risk because rivals of the former drug dealer might seek revenge. A woman commented, "All they want to do is make black people look bad. And I had to stop some guys from beating up that woman ... because when they read the article it looked like she said they were drug dealers.... [Reporters] can get a lot of people in trouble."

A few of the women who were featured wrote letters to the *New York Times* to respond to the egregious inaccuracies. The Harlem Birth Right team felt very strongly that the article warranted a strong response to the factual inaccuracies and the biased nature of the reporting and also wrote to the *New York Times*. The letter was signed by the entire research team. None of the letters was printed by the paper.

Reaction to the article was not limited to residents of the block itself but reverberated throughout Harlem. On the second day of the series, Celine, a middle-stratum longitudinal study participant, received a phone call from a friend in Brooklyn who had read the article and was angered by it. Celine, who was familiar with the block through work she had done, said it was an inaccurate and unwarranted portrayal of the people. She pointed out that the block was the site of the Hark Homes residence for homeless men, which had pioneered efforts at job training and entrepreneurship and had a franchise agreement with the Ben and Jerry's Corporation to operate a retail ice cream store on Fifth Avenue and 125th Street. The failure of the reporter to cite this positive example on the block angered Celine.

Furthermore, at a police precinct community meeting for the 32nd precinct, about a week after the series came out, there was a lively discussion of the article. People were very critical of the press and the representation of Harlem. One person commented that "every article is negative, but there is good here, that doesn't get reported." Another person said, "Harlem is a quiet place." Another person commented that people in Harlem who were caught committing crimes didn't live there—they came from outside.

This powerful case demonstrates residents' frustration and resentment created by negative stereotypes and perceptions of Harlem as portrayed in the media and in popular culture. Our analysis of newspaper articles on Harlem—from summer 1993 to summer 1994—revealed that the bulk of articles concerned negative issues such as the illegal drug traffic, crime, physical decay of the environment, and poverty. More positive articles generally appeared in February, during black history month, or around the winter holiday season, during the celebration of Kwanzaa in Harlem. Positive articles also sometimes appeared in the real estate section, featuring the renovated brownstones. Thus, Harlem residents' perceptions of negative representation were based on substantive facts about media treatment of their community.

The possible health consequences of representation were also evident in the experience of Ruth, one of our long-term participants. Ruth's clash with outsiders' negative perception of life in Harlem brings to the foreground the complex interplay of behavior, social conditions, and negative representation. It is described here in detail because it is the only case of infant loss directly witnessed by an ethnographer.

Ruth was a bright, friendly, and talkative woman who was 5 months pregnant when we met her. At the time, she lived on the sixth floor of a tenement building with no elevator. Although the outside of the building was run down and the hallways were ill-kept, her own apartment was immaculately clean. The block where the building was situated had a number of vacant, abandoned lots as well as brownstones and apartment buildings. Although Ruth had a difficult history with episodes of dysfunction (including substance abuse), she remained strong and active in the care of her children and her community. The man responsible for the most recent pregnancy she had thought was too old to impregnate her. "He must be hitting 60," she said. She had not realized she was pregnant until 19 weeks into the pregnancy. Once she had made the decision to continue with the pregnancy, however, she assiduously went for prenatal care, returned to a drug recovery program, and scheduled herself for a cesarean section.

One day, shortly before she was scheduled to give birth, an ethnographer went to visit her and found her sitting on the steps, no longer pregnant. She said that the week before, she was walking down the street when the person walking next to her was shot in what appeared to be a drive-by shooting. She fell to the ground screaming, and a passerby pulled her into his car for safety. The next day, her water broke while she was sitting on the stoop. She climbed all the way back up the six flights of stairs to her apartment and lay on her bed to rest. Soon she noticed she was bleeding. Lacking a phone of her own, she used her neighbor's to call an ambulance.

With her bag packed, Ruth went downstairs to wait for the ambulance. Her neighbor sat with her on the stoop and held her as she grew progressively weaker. After an hour the ambulance had not arrived. Neighbors called again and they also called the police. Finally, the police and the ambulance arrived together.

According to Ruth, the paramedics in the ambulance refused to take her to the east side hospital, where she had received prenatal care, and finally took her to the nearest hospital on the west side. Once admitted, Ruth said she begged the doctors to get her files from the east side hospital, but she was unable to get anyone to do so. She also said she requested a cesarean section, but no one responded. She was in labor for 14 hours before the babies were finally born. One of the twins died of asphyxiation during childbirth. The other, she was told the next night, "had a hole in his heart" and was rushed to Mt. Sinai Hospital across town. Immediately after the operation on the baby's heart, the surgeon informed Ruth that the baby was HIV positive. Ruth, realizing at that moment that she, too, was HIV positive, was very upset. Unfortunately, Ruth received no counseling from the hospital on self-care.

The above account is the one Ruth herself provided, and its specifics cannot be confirmed. What is important here, however, is the way Ruth remembered and explained the loss of her pregnancy. She attributed the death of the first twin to the delay in getting her to the hospital and because the doctors did not respond appropriately to her. Ruth believed some of these problems were due to the perceptions the officials had about the block where she lived. She vocalized her feelings in the focus group on grief and loss: "And I'm angry. I'm still angry, you know. And I want somebody to pay for it because I know what goes on the block, but the block ain't got nothing to do with a person that is sick.... they were supposed to come no matter what rumors that [they] have of our block."

During a focus group on the birth experience, one of our cofacilitators, a psychiatrist, asked: "What would anyone say to help Ruth?" A participant responded, "Missing someone who died is like I'm missing her and I just feel so sad about the loss and it is also ... it just makes you so angry when you just think about, you know, the state of the way things are and the way that we are treated within our communities and the way we are neglected to the point that ... you know, to the loss of life and our family. And it just ... you know ... it's no excuse. You know, there's no rational excuse for it."

While Ruth's loss may be dismissed by some because of her complex behavior history, it is nevertheless clear that infant loss affects a wide stratum of women, many of whom do not have histories of high-risk behavior.

Despite such experiences, attachment to Harlem was expressed across a broad spectrum of education level and occupation, but it was more strongly expressed by people of middle income or by people with more than a high school education, who were more vocal in their criticisms of popular representation and the negative stereotypes generated about Harlem.

The following interview with one of our long-term participants, Robin, who owned a brownstone and worked as a professional in a publishing company, reveals the conflicting feelings generated by the positive and negative aspects of living in Harlem. The transcript has been modified to protect the identities of people and specific institutions and to provide anonymity.

> Ethnographer (E): Well, I'm going to ask first of all about the services that you were using in the community. I want to know how you [became] interested in this stuff. I would like to know, for example ... if you could tell me about a group that you're a member of.
>
> Robin: We're members of the Adopt-a-Block program, which is in conjunction with the 30th Precinct. [The block] got like a bad reputation. And the church, which is run by Reverend _____ and people who live on _____ Place meet every second Wednesday of the month to discuss their concerns about the neighborhood. And we've been involved with that organization since we've moved here. Like we moved in April and we were at the first meeting in May.... we [also] belong to _____ Homeowner's Association. We've been to a few of their meetings and it's different. The difference between these two organizations is so interesting. The Homeowner's Association are the people who own the homes up here who have nothing to do and don't even associate with the people who live in a lot of the apartment buildings for the most part. I know a lot of people in the time that we've moved here and I know people all up and down this block more so than my neighbors who are the homeowners on this side who only necessarily associate with a lot of the ... Homeowner's Association people.
>
> E: That's interesting.
>
> Robin: The elderly women who sit in their windows and watch outside the building. They tell me who comes to my house: "Guess who I saw knocking on your door the other day." And then there's ... this woman who lives up the street who has a garden in front [of her] place. She brings me collard greens from this garden and we have tomatoes.... I met those people when I became a part of the Adopt-a-Block. And they're all elderly.... So, they've seen the neighborhood change from bad to worse and some of them say it's getting better and some of them say it's getting worse and it's just depending on your perspective the day that you ask them a question about how are things.
>
> E: Sure, which is understandable because that's how we are, too. Optimism varies from day to day.
>
> Robin: That's true. So, those are the two organizations that we are involved with, but I would say we're more involved with Adopt-a-Block. We have been instrumental in getting them to get their [act together]. I [had] one of these buildings over here boarded up because it was a crack building 'cause I got on the city's back about it. I said, you know, people have children who play out here and it does not make sense for them to have to trip over all these crack vials coming out of this building and the city owns this building and you need to board it up 'cause there's no one living in there. So, we fought and fought and fought with them and then we finally got that closed.... So, we fought and we got that one closed up.

Robin: [continuing the discussion of Harlem] I lived on 71st Street before I moved to Harlem and I wanted to move to Harlem and then I come up here and it's like things just don't seem to happen up here like they do downtown. Below 96th Street, those people get services like that. Quickly. People respond immediately. Up here it's like they figure, "low income, not paying any taxes, they're all on welfare, they're all black" and it's all this negative stigma that's attached to us up here. Which is frustrating.

E: And not accurate.

Robin: Oh, definitely not accurate ... but they don't see it that way, even the policemen.... So, it's frustrating in that sanitation is not conscientious even when they pick up the sanitation up here. Compared to the way it was when I was living on 71st Street. Street cleaning, you're lucky if you see them sometimes.... I rarely see them and when I do, I'm like oh, wow, they're finally here. But, they will give us fines constantly about garbage staying in front of our building.

E: Because of the dumpster [Robin and her husband were renovating the brownstone].

Robin: Well, not even because of the dumpster, but because of the fact that they don't clean the streets like they're supposed to, which makes it harder for us, so now it's like, they say ... by law we're responsible for cleaning 18 inches into the street. So, we do that. And wind blows up here all of the time. So, they're like, well, you're supposed to have somebody up there cleaning your house periodically so that the dirt is just not there. So, I'm supposed to hire to clean in front of my house on a continual basis?

E: And what about what you were saying about the sidewalk, it was cracked or something?

Robin: The city owns this building and the other building and they recently sold the one next to me that's having work done on it now. And prior to that, the sidewalk was literally sinking out there and all these elderly people come by with their carts and everything, because there are quite a few elderly people who live up there.... None of the young people ... when I first came here, there were a few that went and they said, they just got frustrated with trying to work with the police department and turning this block around and nothing was happening and they just did not get involved anymore, they just said, I don't want to be a part of it, I don't want to have to deal with that. And they dropped out....

Robin: [continuing the discussion of Harlem] And the thing is ... there are things about Harlem that I love, and there are things about Harlem that bother me. Things that bother me are the things that I just mentioned. Because the things that I love ... like the elderly who speak to me and sit in their windows watching out for things. It's the little old geezers that are on the corner that are harmless.... you know they don't mean anything, but ... they're there. They're part of the landscape in a sense.

E: They give character to the community.

Robin: And a lot of the cultural things that are available. We went to see black filmmakers and black music in Aaron Davis Hall. You know, things that would not be available to us elsewhere in the city unless it's black history month are available up here all the time. A lot of cultural things that we have access to which I enjoy. That aspect of it. And there's no place else in New York City that I could afford the space that I have except for Harlem.

It is evident that the mix of emotions middle-stratum people felt about Harlem derived from their relative assessment of their frustrations with the negative qualities (which they linked to institutionalized discrimination) versus the many advantages they perceived to living in a black community. Middle-stratum African Americans in Harlem thus may have exchanged one set of stressors for another. They were willing to live under conditions of systematic neglect of community and higher levels of violence in exchange for the protective features offered by living in a black community, including the feelings of community, access to cultural resources, and a more limited exposure to everyday acts of racism in their neighborhoods.

In sum, the environmental conditions that structured study participants' daily lives and their exposure to stressors reveal the complexity of relationships between negative and positive environmental factors. Some negative aspects, such as the poor physical conditions of buildings, the interweave of decay and renovation, the poor access to public telephones, and the lack of quality retail and grocery stores, affected poor women directly and immediately but also affected women in professional occupations who considered these factors to be part of their general environment. Everyone who lives in Harlem has been affected by the violence of the international drug wars fought on Harlem turf. Acting as a buffer against some of these negative factors are the community's considerable assets, including the easy access to public transportation, the parks, and the cultural resources such as the faith institutions. Many people we encountered in the course of participant observation linked the negative representations of Harlem and the narrow focus on crime and poverty to the difficulties they encountered in getting access to resources (such as bank loans for small-scale businesses) and services (such as rehabilitation of housing stock and provision of police services). These responses are indicative of the mixed emotions people have with respect to living in Harlem. The positive aspects of the comfortable social environment and the close relations between neighbors compete with the negative impact of drug-related violence and crime and the pervasive discrimination. It is clear from our research that the positive and negative characteristics of environments, and the diverse ways in which environment acts as both a source of acute stressors and chronic strain and a source of protective resources, interact in complex ways.

2.4. HOUSING CONDITIONS

The research strongly suggests that women's lives and well-being are significantly affected by their effort to gain access to or maintain good housing. The level of significance varies with the type of housing, which itself correlates to some extent with occupation but not necessarily with educational level. It is important to investigate the extent to which pregnancy becomes a point at which problems about housing may produce multiplicative, rather than additive, stresses. This section describes not only the types of housing problems women face in Harlem and the implications for their health, well-being, and reproductive health, but also the ways women act to resolve their problems. While it is well known that New York City is characterized by severe housing problems for low- and middle-income people, housing has also been documented as a problem for single women with children nationally. Thus, we anticipate that some of our findings will be broadly generalizable in other communities. In this section, we discuss the types of housing women live in and the problems of maintaining safe and clean shelter, both of which are indicative of the ways structural conditions contribute to the difficulties of daily life.

2.4.1. Types of Housing

The range of housing in Harlem reflects the city profile and includes a variety of housing types, such as large, privately owned brownstones and condominiums and cooperative apartment buildings, privately owned and often poorly maintained rental apartment buildings, city-managed rental buildings, single-room occupancy shelters, and city-run public housing developments. Although Harlem had some of the highest vacancy and abandoned building ratios in the city, there was a modest improvement in the availability of affordable housing between 1989 and 1993 (see Upper Manhattan Empowerment Zone, 1994).

Among our 22 longitudinal study participants, 4 of the 5 who had less than a high school education lived in privately owned or city-managed tenements.[1] One woman in this group lived in a public housing development. Among the 7 women who had graduated from high school, 2 lived in public housing developments, 2 lived in tenements, 1 lived in a building for single women operated by a nonprofit organization, 1 lived in a rented apartment in a privately owned building, and 1 rented three floors of a brownstone. Among the 10 women who had more than a high school education (6 of them had finished college), 2 lived in tenements, 1 owned a brownstone, and the others lived in rental apartments in either brownstones or privately owned buildings.

A range of housing types was also found among respondents to the EQ; of those women with less than a high school education, 67 percent lived in apartments (the EQ does not distinguish between poorly and better maintained apartments), and 33 percent lived in public housing developments. Among women with a high school diploma or GED, 67 percent lived in apartments, 7 percent lived in brownstones, 22 percent lived in public housing developments, 7 percent lived in city-managed buildings, and 4 percent lived in single-room occupancy residences. Among women with more than a high school diploma, 62 percent lived in apartments, 11 percent lived in brownstones, 33 percent lived in public housing developments, and 6 percent lived in city-managed buildings.

While there are nuances of difference within each housing type, we can broadly characterize the general situation of each. The months of participant observation in each health area are reflected in the summary discussions and examples reported below. Landlord neglect of property is a primary cause of housing problems. Rent in tenement buildings varies tremendously depending on length of occupancy, building condition, and size of the apartment. Much of the subsidized housing provided by the federal government in the form of Section 8 (named after the section of the federal legislation that created the subsidy program) rent vouchers is used to rent tenement-type apartments. When landlords default on tax payments to the city for these buildings, the city takes them over and manages them.[2] Residents in these buildings then must deal directly with the city's HPD to have repairs done. They may also go to HPD if they have complaints about their private landlords. Harlem has one of the highest concentrations of city-managed buildings in the city.

Three of the longitudinal study participants lived in a six-story walk-up tenement building in Health Area 15. When the ethnographers first met them, the lock on the front door of the building was broken, and so was the intercom. The paint in the halls was peeling, and there was a leak from one of the pipes in the foyer. The tenants were in the process of organizing themselves to begin a rent strike. After a year and a half of tenant activity, the landlord had made some of the most badly needed repairs, including installing a new intercom.

In the focus group on housing and environment, participants who currently lived in tenements, or had done so in the past, described their perceptions of this type of housing:

> ... and I'm pretty sure a lot of people know about HPD apartments and how they're tore down. You know, you get in and you [feel], 'Oh, wow, this is really sweet,' and you stay in there a couple of months, the heat doesn't come on. You know, the water's not working or it's brown or your ceiling is falling out. I mean, you see all of this after being in there for a couple of months.

> ... and I remember moving into this apartment [a privately owned tenement] and there were no lights, there was no stove, there was no refrigerator. And by the time the child was born, about a month later, it was time to do something.

Single-room occupancy residences are generally managed by the HPD and are designed as transitional housing for people who were housed in homeless shelters. Single-room occupancy residences generally contain two or three rooms per floor, with a shared bathroom on each floor. A small kitchenette may be part of the room, but usually residents rely on hot plates or similar portable cooking devices. This spartan arrangement has obvious implications for the prenatal nutrition of pregnant women, because even though these housing units are intended as temporary transitional residences for single people, staff members at HPD interviewed by ethnographers reported that a growing number of single-room occupancy residents were women with young children. Because occupancy by more than one person was technically not permitted, there were no official figures on how many single-room occupancy resident units were occupied by more than one person. In one single-room occupancy residence we visited, we found a young woman with an infant in the unit. She had requested a transfer because the man she shared bathroom facilities with was harassing her.

In contrast, rental units in better-maintained apartment buildings constitute another type of available housing, but these are often difficult to procure. These units include the large complexes such as the Riverton, located behind Harlem Hospital, and Lenox Terrace on Lenox Avenue. Both provide well-maintained buildings and grounds. Apartments vary in size and rent.

The brownstones are one of the hallmarks of Harlem. The recent revitalization of housing stock in Harlem (mentioned previously) has centered on brownstone renovation, and many blocks are now dotted with newly renovated brownstones with restored ironwork, Victorian-era brass fixtures, and other distinctive features. In the spring, several homeowner associations in Harlem sponsor tours of historic and renovated brownstones. Typically, people buy a brownstone, renovate it, and rent out one or more units while they live on one or two floors. Such was the case with Ms. J and her husband. They bought a brownstone in 1984 and renovated it, taking advantage of a low-interest loan available from the city for this purpose. Ms. J taught at a nearby college and her husband worked as an administrator for a major transportation corporation. They had two young children. The family occupied the first two floors of the building. Ms. J installed her mother in one apartment in the building, which allowed her to care for her mother more easily. The other four apartments were rented out.

Public housing developments are managed by the New York City Housing Authority (NYCHA). Generally, these are large complexes of multistory apartment buildings. The grounds of the complexes often contain small parks or playgrounds. A variety of services may be located in the complex, including child care centers and health clinics. Perceptions and experiences of people in our study who lived in public housing developments (colloquially referred to as "the projects") varied tremendously and depended on the specific situation of each development.

Longitudinal study participant Susan, who lived in a public housing development at the time of the study, initiated a discussion of the projects during the focus group on housing and environment. Susan commented first on her experiences with getting repairs or other services in the projects:

> ... with housing [i.e., the NYCHA] they don't get to it right away either, but they get to it, you know, after ... you have a lot more to fight with housing than with HPD apartments ... you know somewhere down the line, somebody's going to get to it. You keep calling the right people, and that's another thing, knowing the right people. Like you have people [who are in] the tenants' association, PTA, presidents, you know. If you know you can get to them, they fight for you. That's what they're there for. If you know these people, you can get to them and, you know, really get information on how you can go about it. You know, if something isn't fixed right, keep on calling. Sometimes it takes a $60 phone bill, but you can call it and you can get some kind of help.

Another participant in the focus group reminisced about one housing development and how it had deteriorated over time:

> You know, what is sad, you're talking about [a public housing development]. I remember when it was built and I thought they were the most beautiful apartments I have ever seen. In '61–'62. As a matter of fact, I had some family that had bought into there and I was wondering whether I should be struggling with a house because that place was so big and it had terraces and everything and all this stuff and what saddens me, because I used to go in that courtyard, it was gorgeous. And [I] still thought it was gorgeous up until a few years ago.... And it's such a beautiful construction, but what comes to my mind is what happened.... It makes you wonder.... and a few other buildings are some magnificent pieces of property and it makes you wonder why is it that one day [it can be] a gorgeous place, [and suddenly] it hits rock bottom....

People in the various focus groups agreed that public housing developments engendered a sense of identification and community, but Susan, one of our longitudinal participants, also commented on the positive and negative consequences for young girls. She suggested that, on the one hand, everyone knew each other, and there was a sense that people watched out for each other's children. However, she noted that, in the closed community, young people (teenagers) may acquire reputations. For example, if a young boy was deemed "popular" or "cute," the young girls tried to attract his attention. Susan said that when she was growing up, this kind of attraction was limited to mild flirtation, but in today's climate, girls were more likely to engage in the full range of sexual activity, often leading to early pregnancy. It was appealing to girls to be popular with the popular boys, but once a girl got a reputation in the projects as willing to engage in sexual intercourse, the boys took advantage of her, according to Susan. Susan thought that the adults in the projects were not educating their children adequately about the dangers of these types of activities and that the adults were, to their detriment, overlooking the behavior of young people. While these may be issues relevant to any setting, it is interesting that Susan linked this to the positive aspects of community associated with the projects. It is also interesting to note here that some studies have linked lower infant mortality rates to residence in public housing. In public housing developments, the infant mortality rate was 19.2 per thousand, while among people who were not living in those housing developments, the infant mortality rate was 28.6 per thousand (McCord and Freeman, 1990).

In sum, each type of housing in Harlem has specific characteristics that influence the presence, types, and degree of stress that people may experience. Because level of education does not correlate easily with type of housing, it is important to look specifically at the type of housing to explore the level of exposure of housing-related stress across educational and income levels.

2.4.2. Housing Problems

Maintaining safe and clean housing is a well-known problem for most low-and middle-income New Yorkers. This is particularly true where discrimination and isolation may magnify the stressors. Of the respondents to the Empowerment Zone telephone survey, 55 percent reported that affordable housing was a serious problem facing the neighborhood, and another 22 percent reported that it was a somewhat serious problem. Similarly, half the respondents described poor housing and homelessness as very serious problems in Harlem, and about one-quarter of the respondents reported that these were somewhat serious problems.

The housing problems faced by women affected many of the other aspects of their lives, and struggles to resolve housing problems exposed them to long-term stressors. Fully 50 percent of the longitudinal study participants were engaged in some efforts to resolve housing problems. Most relevant for understanding the impact of housing-related stressors on reproductive health were the types of problems faced by the women in our sample who were pregnant. In the following case material, we seek to capture the ways in which the larger social constraints of racism in the area of housing affected the daily lives of these women during pregnancy.

All four women who were pregnant and had less than a high school education experienced significant problems with their housing during pregnancy. Claire lived in a tenement that needed major repairs. While she was pregnant, the tenants organized a rent strike to attempt to compel the landlord to undertake repairs. The major problem in Claire's apartment was that there were sizable holes in the kitchen and bathroom walls through which rodents entered from the alleys. Several months after Claire reported an incident of a rat entering the apartment, the landlord finally patched up a hole in the bathroom. Soon after, however, a rat entered through a hole in the kitchen. Claire was so startled that she ran screaming from the apartment with her children into the hallway and, in her fright, locked herself out of the apartment. After that incident, she went to stay with her mother temporarily. Finally, the landlord patched the hole in the kitchen. After Claire delivered the baby, she obtained a cat from her neighbor to protect the baby against rodents. Unfortunately, she concluded that she was allergic to cats because she soon developed a rash on her face but nonetheless preferred allergy problems to the possibility of rats. Thus she was willing to trade exposure to one type of stressor for relief from another type of stressor. Claire's household tasks were made more difficult by a broken pipe in her kitchen. As a result, she was forced to wash all her dishes in the bathroom. Her apartment was also infested by cockroaches, but her landlord did not provide regular extermination services. Claire complained that the problems with rats, cockroaches, and broken pipes as well as the general disrepair of the building placed physical stress on her during her pregnancy.

Ivory, a high school student who initially lived with her mother, also faced serious housing problems during her pregnancy. Her mother's apartment, on a very poor block in Health Area 10, was located on the fifth floor of a dilapidated tenement building. At one point in Ivory's pregnancy, the heat and hot water were turned off for several days in her building. A broken window allowed cold air to enter. The lack of hot water and, consequently, Ivory's inability to wash, prevented her from attending prenatal visits. In addition to these difficulties, after a dispute with her mother, who began drinking heavily after Ivory's brother died from a hit-and-run accident, Ivory was forced to move from the apartment when she was close to delivery. Ivory took up residence with her sister, who lived in the Bronx.

Ama, who was a 37-year-old Senegalese vendor of African cloth and mother of four children (two of whom remained in Senegal), faced two types of problems with housing while she was pregnant. First, like Claire and Ivory, she had problems getting the landlord to do proper repairs on her tenement building. For example, during the course of her pregnancy, there was a leak through the ceiling into her bathroom, which resulted from bathtub overflow on the floor above. When she and her husband requested repairs from the building superintendent, they were informed about the source of the leak, but the damage was not repaired. Ama's husband called the fire department, who investigated and promised to make a report. With the help of the ethnographer, Ama wrote a letter of complaint to the housing court. In another instance, the superintendent had turned the hot water off in the building, and the tenants' requests to have it turned on were unsuccessful. This time, Ama and her husband called the police, who forced the superintendent to turn on the hot water. In addition to these problems, there were also minor problems, such as broken windows. Ama and her husband also filed complaints with the HPD to try to compel the landlord to make repairs, and they withheld rent. Finally, soon after the baby was born, Ama and her husband decided to look for a new place to live. In addition to the poor condition of the apartment, the one bedroom with a small living room and kitchen was too small for their needs. Furthermore, the rent was $600 a month, and, because this was high for Ama and her husband, her brother lived with them and paid half the rent. When the new baby was about 3 months old, they found another, slightly larger apartment at $700 a month. They were hoping to rent out a room there as well. Ama and her husband also applied for the federal Section 8 housing subsidy and hoped to move to better quarters if they received the subsidy.[3]

Rose, an adolescent street vendor, was a minor who had run away from home. She and her partner lived on the streets for several months before they moved into the apartment of the mother of one of Rose's friends, whom she considered to be like an aunt. Although she rented out rooms in her apartment, she allowed Rose to live there free of charge. However, when we met Rose, her "aunt" had not been able to pay her rent and utility bills, and Con Edison had turned off the electricity in the apartment. About a month before Rose's new baby was due, her aunt asked Rose's partner to leave because he was unable to pay rent. Rose decided to leave with him and, after a desperate search for new quarters, they finally moved in with a friend of her partner. This housing situation was unsatisfactory and Rose moved in with another friend shortly before she gave birth. We cannot know to what extent these housing problems contributed to the general stress that Rose experienced as a result of her situation, but we do know that she had a difficult labor and was delivered by cesarean section. The baby, although not premature or low birth weight, was in distress at birth and was placed temporarily in intensive care.

Of the four pregnant women who had completed high school, two experienced difficulties with housing during the course of their pregnancies. Diana, a fast-food restaurant worker in her early 40s, spent much of the time she was not working searching for a place to live. When the ethnographers recruited her to participate in the study, she was about 4 months pregnant and lived in a small, two-bedroom tenement apartment rented by her partner's grandmother. Her partner was living in a separate apartment with a roommate. Diana was uncomfortable with the roommate and did not want to move in with her partner for that reason. His grandmother's apartment was too small for her and the baby, but her search for a new apartment proved to be futile and, at the time of the baby's birth, she was still living in the same place. Her partner moved in with her so he could be with the baby, but everyone complained that the apartment was too crowded.

Sharon, a mother of two who was unemployed when she was recruited to participate in the study, also spent considerable time during her pregnancy looking for a place to live. She had separated from an abusive husband on whom she had placed a restraining order. She felt obliged to move because she lived in the same building as her ex-husband's family, and this placed her at risk of harassment from him. Under these circumstances, the HPD was obligated to help her find an apartment and provided her with several possibilities. Sharon searched for several months before she found a suitable apartment in the Bronx. However, she was unable to move until after the baby was born.

Of the four pregnant women with more than a high school education, only one experienced difficulties with housing. Ruth, a mother of two, had a college degree but was unemployed and recovering from drug addiction when she was recruited into the study. She lived in the same tenement as Claire and therefore experienced the same difficulties with the landlord, who was severely negligent about maintenance. Ruth was active in the tenants' association and worked to organize the rent strike. Because the intercom and front door buzzer were broken during much of her pregnancy, she had to walk up and down the six flights of stairs every time she had a visitor. While she kept her own apartment very clean, she constantly complained about the condition of the hallways and the stairs. For several months during her pregnancy, Ruth complained of a rash that she attributed to contact with piles of garbage in the hallways, stairs, and alleys.

Among our longitudinal participants, Susan, Latoya, Ruth, and Claire were homeless at some point in their lives, although we did not directly observe these situations. In addition to these seven women, five others in the longitudinal study also experienced difficulties with housing similar to those described above (thus 12 of the 22, more than 50 percent, had problems with housing during the course of the study). Either the conditions of the buildings were poor and they needed repairs (this was the case for women who lived in the tenements and to a lesser degree for women who lived in public housing developments), or women were in unsatisfactory living arrangements and spent a considerable amount of time trying to find another place to live (of course, as in the case of Ama, some women faced both crises). Longitudinal study participant Gina's description of her housing situation demonstrates her perception of these issues and is representative of the comments of others:

> [The landlord] doesn't want to fix anything. He wants his rent, and he wants it on time. All he wants is money, money, money, money. The intercom is not fixed, it's always broken. There's been no buzzer for almost a year. There are roaches and rats. There are floods

> in the walls and water dripping from the ceiling. He harasses us so bad for the rent money. If we don't have it he'll have a fit.... The problem is, he's cheap. He buys the cheapest materials for everything and employs cheap labor, so nothing is ever done right, and falls apart as soon as it's done.... You should see the big hole in my bathroom behind the sink, where the rats come in. I had to buy a cat and feed it to get rid of the rats but he isn't gonna pay for the cat food. He costs me money!

Other women we encountered in the course of the fieldwork, but who were not in the longitudinal study, described similar housing problems. Finally, the focus group on housing and environment also allowed community residents to voice their concerns and problems with housing issues. The focus group participants discussed directly their perceptions of the relationship between housing conditions and their own health and well-being. At one point the ethnographer asked if they thought housing issues affected their health, and the group responded unanimously that it did. One participant described his problems in the following way:

> I got a situation. I got a hole in the wall right over my tub, mildew that God only knows, I can't take it anymore. That's stress city, you know, involving my health.... the bathroom and kitchen are adjacent.... all that water has been building over a period of 2 years, and I put in an order 2 years ago, and this is a health hazard and it has come to where I'm going to have to do something about it because I'm watching something on my medical chart.... something's not right here and I'm not sure what it is.... My health is so bad that I had to take last month and hardly ever stay there in the apartment.

Another focus group participant described how she began to experience health problems when a sewage line broke and spilled into her apartment after the landlord had initiated repairs in another part of the building. A third participant described a cough she had developed, which she attributed to fumes from the oven or the stove. Other participants suggested that it might be carbon monoxide and counseled her to keep her windows open a crack and to place water on the stove to humidify the room. Another man counseled her in this way: "Also [here's] what you do. Each part of each room, put a glass of water in the corner facing east. Because that's where the sun comes up."

After analyzing these accounts of women's housing problems, the research team developed questions for the EQ about exposure to specific housing-related stressors. In the EQ, the following problems with housing were reported: peeling paint, running faucets, broken elevators, broken stairs, rats, mice, roaches, poor lighting, inadequate size, inadequate heat, lack of hot water, unremoved garbage, broken mailboxes, and lack of repairs.

In general, among the EQ respondents, peeling paint, broken elevators, pests (mice, roaches, rats), and difficulties getting repairs done were the major problems reported, which is consistent with the fieldwork findings (Figure 2.2). It is interesting to note that, except for the category of running faucets and mice, a smaller percentage of women with less than a high school education reported problems than women in the other two categories of education. This was not entirely consistent with the fieldwork findings, as reported above, but it was consistent with the findings that women of all levels of education lived in both good and poor housing. Another possible interpretation of the fact that women with less than a high school diploma reported fewer problems overall might be their general reluctance to report problems because of the humiliation they might feel about their living conditions. Women with more education might have been more willing

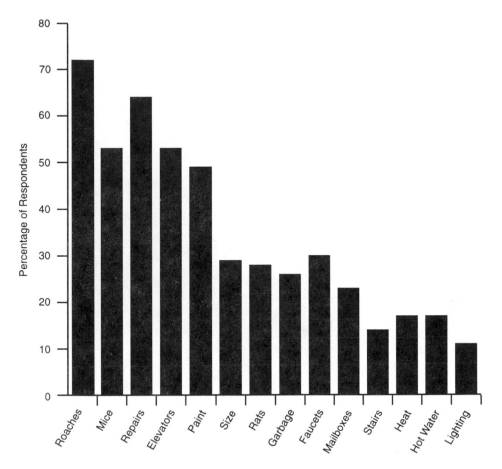

Figure 2.2. Housing Problems Reported on the Ethnographic Questionnaire

to openly discuss their problems, which they attributed to the necessity of having to live in a neighborhood that was discriminated against, despite their education.

In general, women across educational levels shared expectations and disappointments about housing conditions. This was revealed in a poignant statement made during a focus group by a low-income participant:

> For myself ... you can settle for what you have, but I want more. [I] want to get something better.... I live at housing [i.e., a public housing development] and that is where I have to live right now. This is what I can afford, this what I have to deal with until I can make my situation better for me and my children. But, this is something that I have to deal with. That doesn't necessarily mean that I'm comfortable with it. That I want to be there. So, that's saying, you know, whatever I have to do to get where I want to be at, it takes time. It takes someone helping you or you learning how can you go about, you know, getting somewhere. So, it's really on you, what you're willing to do, what you're willing to sacrifice or give up to get where you are going, where you want to be.

It is also significant that overall, a high percentage of women (64 percent) reported that getting repairs done was a problem, and that it was relatively consistent at all levels of education (57 percent, 66 percent, 67 percent) is also significant. Women depended on their landlords for repairs, and they perceived that landlord neglect of proper maintenance of their buildings was related to living in an inner-city neighborhood stereotyped as unimportant or not worthy of attention. This perception of landlord discrimination appeared to have contributed to a sense of frustration and stress that women felt when it came to coping with housing problems.

One of the participants in the focus group on housing and environment encouraged others to confront feelings of anger or frustration toward the landlord:

> The first thing is ... you don't have to be afraid of the landlord. I've noticed a lot of people, a lot of tenants are afraid of the landlord. But this man usually does not ... live in the community with you. So, a lot of your problems, they have no inkling that these things actually exist. Then, our environment, the neighborhood, they don't live there, so they don't see them and they don't know....

Another commented:

> The only problem that I ever had is that whenever they wanted to come out and do repairs, they didn't ever want to let me know. They just [show up and say], 'we're here,' you know. And it's like they expect you to be here because you're on public assistance, [but] I'm not trying to just sit on my butt and do nothing.

The focus group participants also discussed their perception that major repairs were made only when the city or private agencies were interested in taking over the property and renovating it for a higher-income clientele. One woman commented:

> What a lot of times happens is that when certain people in power decide that they want them to be a condo or a co-op [both of these are forms of private ownership of apartments] it miraculously changes into another beautiful place to live. And what comes to my mind is, what happens. All somebody political, or whoever, decided is that this is where he wants to move people off 125th Street, no problem. If they want to change a neighborhood, it happens.

Another woman commented:

> You won't get any help, they won't fix that apartment until you move out and somebody else is ready to move in. That's how it goes.

In summary, the bulk of people's problems with housing were related to the ongoing neglect and lack of maintenance by private landlords and city agencies alike. Residents often directly linked these problems with ill health and also with exposure to acutely stressful situations and ongoing chronic stress. They also perceived the poor condition of housing in Harlem to result from discriminatory practices and the negative stereotyping of the community. Furthermore, because of the poor conditions of the housing, women found themselves engaged in long-term struggles to improve their living conditions. The research suggests that housing problems clearly conditions the lives and well-being of women in Harlem, and poor housing has been linked with a variety of health issues

(Health and Hospitals Corporation, 1991; Wallace and Wallace, 1990; Fullilove, 1996). In our study, however, housing scarcity may have become a particular stressor during pregnancy when the need for extra space arose. This was particularly true for low-income women, whereas middle-strata women had more resources to ameliorate these conditions. However, the resources of middle-strata women were often insufficient to completely offset the stressors produced by lack of affordable quality housing in the community. Furthermore, the large-scale destruction and scarcity of housing contributed to weakening support networks that were so important to women, as we discuss in a later section. Finally, Fullilove has discussed what she refers to as the "loss of 'place' as a source of mental distress" (1996:1517). For Harlem, in particular, she notes the loss of more than one-third of the area's housing in over 30 years, and the ways it has "undermined community structure and altered individual lives" (p. 1517).

2.5. FIGHTING BACK: COPING WITH HOUSING-INDUCED STRESS

Women in Harlem were not willing to be passive in the face of the considerable difficulties generated by the lack of safe and affordable housing. The activism women engaged in around housing concerns included using the housing court to lodge complaints against landlords and participating in neighborhood tenant and homeowner organizations.

2.5.1. Housing Activism

Women's activism around housing issues ranged from daily actions to maintain a clean and safe space for themselves, their children, and their extended networks, to more organized collective struggles for long-term solutions, to problems such as affordability of housing and the quality of residences.

Although often unlabeled and seemingly an innocuous and routine task in which most women everywhere engage, housecleaning is by no means a trivial aspect of women's lives, especially when women are forced to confront a daily struggle against a deteriorating environment. When buildings are poorly maintained; peeling paint is prevalent; repairs are left undone; pest control is nonexistent; streets, sidewalks, and alleys are left uncleaned; or garbage removal is delayed or irregular, removing the dirt and pollution inside the home can consume a significant proportion of women's time. The ethnographers were often impressed with the time and effort women spent to keep their homes clean. There was a stark contrast between external decay, disrepair, and dinginess and well-kept, clean, often bordering on immaculate apartments in even the worst of the tenements or public housing developments. This cleanliness was true in all instances except some of the more chaotic homes, where there may have been alcoholism or substance abuse, or perhaps a disorganization stemming from youth (there is only one documented case of a persistently untidy home in our ethnographic record). Even women who lived in renovated brownstones, but not in the middle-income enclaves, faced some of these problems and had to expend extra effort to maintain clean homes. Women spoke of their efforts to keep the house clean, the cupboards stocked with food, the children dressed well, and the furniture well-maintained. For example, longitudinal study participant Sandra, who worked at a fast-food restaurant and lived in a privately owned building, showed off with pride a cupboard fully stocked with baby food for her daughter. She used the WIC allotments to buy the food and kept the cupboard stocked in case she was cut off from her payments (as discussed below). Her studio apartment, although small, was well-organized and orderly, with a place for everything. Every day she vigorously searched for cockroaches in an effort to minimize their number.

In another instance, Reina, who lived with her aunt in a public housing development, paid rent by doing household chores and caring for her young nephew. The hallways of the building were dingy, the elevators were musty, and the stairways were littered in places with used crack vials, but inside Reina's aunt's apartment, the atmosphere was cozy and bright. Trophies the children won in sporting events and class and graduation photos decorated the living room.

One of the women who was featured in the *New York Times* article discussed above was most angry about the description of her apartment as dirty, bare of furniture, and having no food. The reporter described the apartment as "gloomy," and then stated "... a single overhead bulb illuminates the narrow living room.... The linoleum floor is dirty and missing some tiles" (Lee, 1994b:B4). Furthermore, the reporter claimed that when a friend came to visit, the only food in the house was a box of cookies. The featured woman, extremely angry about the distortions, called one of the ethnographers the same day the article appeared. She was particularly angry about the description of the lack of food, which she claims was entirely untrue. The ethnographer, who had visited the home on a number of occasions, always found it clean. On one visit, the ethnographer had found the woman's young cousin (described in the article as listless and hopeless) busy polishing the woodwork. The article did not mention the woman's attempts to obtain repairs to her apartment by taking the landlord to housing court.

In summary, in addition to the exposures to specific stressors and chronic strain brought on by poor housing conditions, women in tenements and public housing developments also had to expend extensive time and effort to keep their homes safe and clean. The continual representations in the media (much of it inaccurate) of poor people's homes as dirty and unkempt added to their frustration and sense of discrimination.

The daily efforts to keep homes clean could not, however, compensate for the structural problems women experienced as a result of systemic neglect and failure to maintain the buildings. Women took a number of actions to get repairs done, including doing repairs themselves and filing complaints with HPD or other city authorities. For example, a woman in the focus group described how she was frustrated when she could not get the NYCHA to repair the leaks in her bathroom wall, so she eventually purchased the plaster and made the repairs herself. In another instance, an elderly woman who lived on a block in the field site in Health Area 15 discussed her numerous efforts to get HPD to repair leaks in her apartment. She wrote letters to the head of the regional office, telephoned numerous times, and finally called the television and print news media, hoping that negative publicity might force some action.

In addition, Noma, one of the longitudinal study participants, experienced problems in a previous apartment, which included the ceiling caving in. She recounted that she had refused to pay rent until the landlord fixed the building. Later, she and her partner moved to another apartment. Finally, a woman who worked in construction participated in the focus group on housing and the environment and described how she helped renovate a building. The building she referred to was on the block that was written up in the *New York*

Times article. She discussed the significance of the project as a statement against discrimination and the difference the renovated building made in the lives of the tenants (previously homeless people) and the block:

> ... I've always been the only female out of the group to participate in the construction field. And it always seems that I always start with the paperwork first, and then things wind down and the money runs short, I always end up helping in the field ... the building was set on fire accidentally ... we took it from a burnt out hull. There were no floors, except the fifth floor and the first. The basement was ... full of debris. We removed it. We cleaned it out from scratch and we renovated it ourselves. Through the help of the men from the neighborhood, all community-hired men, and ... we took it upon ourselves to give the building back to the people who don't have places to stay. For instance, the homeless minority, that's what we really wanted ... that's the large majority of those who don't have homes. Everybody can find a home if you're blond and white and have a college education. But if you're black and it doesn't matter how much education you have, they really ... they take one look at you and they don't want you in their ... in the good environment like you don't deserve it. So when we focus on the minority ... the homeless minority and I inspected the building for HPD. I looked at the overall picture of 'twenty-four/seven' good-looking, well-put together apartments. Nice clean homes. Square corners, not tons of plaster stuck on the wall. Not [infested] with roaches and mice. No holes in the floors. [She meant here that she took the time to guarantee a nice building for these homeless people, while other contractors may have cut corners.] We proceeded to screen, lightly screening [selecting tenants for the building], and we got people in. And these people are now working together ... to protect this building. They have become very possessive and I thank God that they are possessive because this is their territory now. I mean, they patrol the steps all hours of the night. They fuss with each other ... "don't leave a bag in the hallway. Pick up the paper".... They love having their own. They love having this piece of ground. They cherish it. Their houses ... 90 percent of the people, you can walk into [the apartments] and eat off the floors. They are so clean. They take great pride in their children, they have a home. Now they can focus on their kids. Their kids are going to school. I mean, their whole attitude. We had a block party and each building donated to the block party ... and I'm telling you, you have never seen such a sense of community in your life. Never have you seen such sense. Like the oldest woman in the building ... she works so hard.... I look at her as my elder and we would not open our table until she came home from work, which is about three o'clock in the afternoon ... and they actually waited respectfully. I mean these are human beings and everybody ... they get along, they take pride, they love their children....

As this case material demonstrates, women spent considerable effort to address structural problems with their housing situations. The frustrations they experienced when the approved channels for redress did not work seemed to add to a sense of anger and contributed to a general skepticism about the fairness of the system, as was demonstrated by respondents to the EQ; this skepticism was an important source of chronic stress.

Finally, as illustrated by the last case, women made a direct link between racism and discriminatory practices and their lack of access to decent and adequate housing. This perception of discrimination was also reported in the EQ, where 83 percent of the respondents believed that discrimination affected housing (with no significant variation by level of education) and 26 percent reported housing as a stressor. Only 41 percent of the EQ respondents were hopeful that discrimination in housing would lessen any time soon. About 20–30 percent of the respondents reported that discrimination in housing had affected their daily lives.

2.5.2. Housing Court

While women sometimes appeared to be overwhelmed by their housing problems, they persisted in seeking solutions. One recourse that women used was to take landlords to housing court for neglecting repairs. The ethnographic team followed the cases of two of the long-term participants who used the housing court, interviewed legal assistance lawyers who worked with tenants, and conducted several days of observation at the housing court. Questions about housing court were also included in the EQ. The director of the Harlem office of a legal services provider that offered services for the indigent discussed at length his experiences with housing issues. He stated that most of the clients in the housing practice were women, many of whom had already been involved in the legal process, as indicated by the fact that they had already been served with petitions or orders to show cause by the time they came for legal assistance. Because many women first tried to represent themselves, the legal services office got cases in various stages of development. Almost all the landlords, on the other hand, were represented by lawyers.

The director of the legal services agency pointed out that this state of affairs, where women represented themselves in court actions while landlords had legal counsel, obviously put these women at a significant disadvantage. He stated:

> People do not have a lot of options about housing and often wait until the last minute to come in [to the legal services office] because they first try other means—negotiating with the landlord, [or] with the janitor who claims to be in touch with the landlord.... You can't find more common sense per capita anywhere else in the world. They have managed to keep the wolf at bay and then things get out of hand.

He admired the women for going to court alone:

> They have the courage to walk into court past demeaning court officers, into a courtroom where the court is not sympathetic to poor people and is pressed with an enormous calendar.

However, as another lawyer later pointed out, taking actions to use housing court without legal assistance or proper information had its costs for the women. She reported that she had observed a pattern of depression among people who were trying to deal with housing problems. When clients were suicidal and depressed, there were few resources to which they could be referred.

The housing court is located at 111 Center Street, which is in lower Manhattan. All clients and visitors must pass through metal detectors and have their bags searched by court officers. Only attorneys and court employees are exempt. Inside, in the middle of a large lobby, there is a guard's booth where three court officers sit. The officers are uniformed and carry nightsticks, guns, and handcuffs. The building is divided into a public part and a section that is not open to the public and that houses the offices of the judges, clerks, and court officers. Here, according to attorneys, the facilities are better maintained. For example, at the time of this research, in the part of the building open to the public, only the 5th-floor women's bathrooms had stalls that closed and included toilet paper.

On the ground floor, there is a child care center run by the Tenants Assistance Association. Nearby is a table staffed by the City-Wide Task Force on Housing Court, Inc., that is stacked with literature to assist tenants. The pamphlets include titles such as "How to sue your landlord for repairs," "Holdover proceedings," "A non-payment dispossess," and "What to do if you receive a 72-hour notice of eviction." Across from that is a table titled "Owners' Assistance" with appropriate material to aid landlords.

Also on the ground floor is an enormous courtroom, where cases are "calendared" for the first time and where tenants can request inspection of their property. A large sign at the front of the room reads, "No questions will be answered during calendar call."

At the time of the ethnographer's visit, the room was filled with about 200 people who were overwhelmingly African American and Latino. Several court officers patrolled the room, aggressively informing people not to talk or to read newspapers or magazines. All newspapers and other reading matter had to be put away. A judge in a black robe presided at the front of the courtroom while a court officer called out names, such as, "Martin Smith against Jim Jones." When called, the tenant and landlord (or more likely the land-lord's lawyer or paralegal) answered to say whether they were ready.

To someone unfamiliar with the procedures, the situation could be confusing and stressful. It was difficult to hear and to figure out when a particular case would be called. The confusion seemed to be shared. A person sitting next to the ethnographer asked if she knew what number was being called. As the ethnographer could not help her, she asked the person on the other side, who also did not know. The ethnographer was later told by the legal services lawyer that those in the know (usually lawyers) can consult a chart in the lobby for the order in which cases will be called.

On the 8th floor, where the housing courtrooms are located, there is a long hall where the landlords' lawyers may intercept the tenants and suggest channels of negotiation. The hall spans the length of the floor and is lined with benches where people sit and wait or talk. Lawyers in business suits usually can be easily distinguished from clients, who are often working class and casually dressed and whose faces often appear marked by anxiety and concern. Everyone must leave between one and two o'clock, when the facilities are closed for a lunch break. Thus, if a tenant returns for the afternoon session, she must go through the metal detectors and search process twice.

The experience of Ama—one of four long-term participants—in housing court has been described above. With the assistance of the ethnographer, Ama wrote a letter inform-ing the court that she had sufficient funds to pay rent but was withholding rent because repairs had not been made to her apartment. The case remained unresolved, however, and Ama and her family moved to another apartment.

Gina, another long-term participant, went to housing court to attempt to force the landlord to do repairs. In her case, the landlord initially served her an eviction order based on nonpayment of rent. Gina obtained a legal aid attorney. The first time she went to court, accompanied by two of her friends, the landlord's attorney did not appear, so the case was rescheduled. The second time she went to court, Gina arrived armed with photographs of the damages to her apartment. She was also able to present the judge with a housing inspector's eyewitness account of her leaking ceiling. The judge awarded her a 2-month rent abatement and scheduled a date for final resolution of the case.

At Gina's third court appearance, it took a half hour merely to pass through the metal detectors and to be searched because the line to get into court was so long. The delay resulted in part from the number of women with infants and small children, since all the bags with the children's paraphernalia had to be searched. Once in the courtroom, Gina pointed out the landlord's lawyer, a white male.

Gina's lawyer was a young Latino who worked for the legal services agency. He discussed the landlord's demands with Gina: $1,300 in back rent. Gina informed her lawyer that the landlord had been receiving $312.00 a month from her public assistance subsidy, which he continued to receive even after she began participating in the rent strike. The lawyer appeared to be surprised by this revelation because the landlord had not told the judge he was receiving most of the rent. The lawyer and Gina confronted the landlord, and the lawyers finally worked out an agreement: Gina paid $400.00 of back rent and the landlord agreed to repair the apartment. Gina also requested the inclusion of a clause that stipulated a date when the repairs should be completed and that they should be done "during regular working hours—9 to 5," because she thought the landlord might send repairmen at all hours of the day and night, interrupting her sleep.

Everything was finally settled to Gina's satisfaction, and the lawyers presented the case to the judge. Repairs were to be completed within 6 weeks; however, the ethnographer observed that the repairs were not actually completed until 4 months later.

As these cases demonstrate, "homelessness prevention" and the attempt to maintain adequate housing could be an arduous and difficult process. Tenants had difficulty negotiating housing court by themselves, and lawyers from legal services agencies improved the tenants' chances to get redress from the court. However, this was an uncertain situation. The procedures were not rigidly defined, and the outcome was often influenced by the judge the case was brought before, the negotiating abilities of the lawyers, and the level of documentation that might be produced by the plaintiff or defendant. The process of attending court was time-consuming, confusing, and sometimes frustrating for tenants. Even if the tenant was somewhat sophisticated in her knowledge of the system (as in Gina's case) there was no guarantee the remedy would be satisfactory. One of our middle-stratum informants described her experience in housing court as "mortifying theater."

Finally, in the EQ, respondents were asked about their experiences with housing court. Overall, 39 percent of the women had been to housing court. Among women with less than a high school education, 25 percent had been to housing court. Among women with a high school education or GED, 52 percent had been to housing court. Among women with more than a high school education, 28 percent had been to housing court.

Interestingly, among women who had experience with housing court, most reported positive experiences. Overall, 91 percent of the women reported having dealt with competent people. Among women with less than a high school education, 100 percent reported having dealt with competent people compared with 86 percent of women with a high school education or GED and 100 percent of women with more than a high school education. Overall, 45 percent of the women reported having waited a long time. Among women with less than a high school education, 33 percent reported having waited a long time compared with 50 percent of women with a high school education or GED and 40 percent of women with more than a high school education. Overall, 45 percent of the women reported having been given respect. Among women with less than a high school education, 100 percent reported having been given respect compared with 86 percent of women with a high school education or GED and 100 percent of women with more than a high school education.

Overall, 76 percent of the women reported having had a good experience. Among women with less than a high school education, 100 percent reported having had a good experience compared with 57 percent of women with a high school education or GED and

100 percent of women with more than a high school education. In addition, overall, 27 percent of the women reported having other experiences.

Overall, 55 percent of women represented themselves in housing court, 36 percent were represented by a lawyer, and 14 percent had other representation. Among women with less than a high school education, 67 percent represented themselves in housing court, 33 percent were represented by a lawyer, and 0 percent had other representation. Among women with a high school education or GED, 50 percent represented themselves in housing court, 43 percent were represented by a lawyer, and 14 percent had other representation. Among women with more than a high school education, 60 percent represented themselves in housing court, 20 percent were represented by a lawyer, and 20 percent had other representation. Overall, 27 percent of women dealt with the landlord directly in housing court, 72 percent dealt with the landlord's lawyer, and 14 percent dealt with other representation of the landlord. Among women with less than a high school education, 33 percent of women dealt with the landlord in housing court, 100 percent dealt with the landlord's lawyer, and 0 percent dealt with other representation of the landlord. Among women with a high school education or GED, 29 percent dealt with the landlord in housing court, 71 percent dealt with the landlord's lawyer, and 14 percent dealt with other representation of the landlord. Among women with more than a high school education, 20 percent dealt with the landlord in housing court, 80 percent dealt with the landlord's lawyer, and 20 percent dealt with other representation of the landlord.

That most respondents described their experience in housing court as a good experience may suggest, as some researchers have, that the ability to take some action to address one's circumstances has positive consequence. Nonetheless, the constant struggle to retain and maintain shelter must also affect women's reproductive health.

2.5.3. Tenant and Block Associations

The daily effort to maintain clean and safe homes and the recourse to housing court to force landlords to make structural repairs were strategies to cope with and ameliorate housing-related stresses pursued by individual women. In addition to these individual measures, however, women pursued collective strategies toward improving housing conditions. Most prevalent among these were participation in tenant and block associations and directly confronting city officials about specific policies. Also present in Harlem were community improvement or homeowner associations, whose memberships were dominated by brownstone owners either in historically middle-class enclaves or in newly gentrified neighborhoods.

Tenant associations typically involve tenants of the same building banding together to provide collective representation in dealing with the landlord. There are a range of such associations functioning in buildings as varied as high-rent luxury apartment buildings to city-managed buildings for low-income residents. Ethnography at the field sites did not provide us an opportunity to observe the workings of tenant associations in buildings populated by relatively high-income tenants, but there was some opportunity to observe tenant associations in low-income buildings and to a lesser degree in NYCHA public housing developments.

In tenements, there are two types of associations: informal, loosely structured organizations and formal, highly managed associations. In both instances, most participants are women. The men who are involved tend to be elderly. This membership might suggest that women are most heavily exposed to stressful situations that result from having to confront a nonresponsive system.

2.5.3.1. Informal Tenant Organizations

The ethnographers observed the functioning of an informal tenants association in Health Area 15. This building housed some of the longitudinal study participants, including Gina, Ruth, and Claire (Ruth and Claire were pregnant during the study). Most of the occupants of this building were single women who were the most active in the association. Some of the tenants had moved to the building from a homeless shelter. At the time of the ethnographic fieldwork, the city, which managed the building, was in the process of selling it to a private landlord. Hence tenants had to deal with both the city and the private landlord. The tenants decided informally (by talking to one another) to withhold rent until repairs were made to the building. Instead of holding formal meetings or electing officers, they worked through informal consensus. It appeared that a few women took leadership roles and bore the brunt of the effort. Gina, for example, was quite active in this association, in addition to her own individual efforts to get the landlord to repair her apartment. Although Gina was diabetic and had other related health problems, she managed to remain active. Ruth, another of the participants described above, also was active in the tenants association and encouraged other women in the building to participate.

One of the ethnographers interviewed three women who lived in the same building on a block in Health Area 10. Most buildings on this block were managed by HPD. In the building occupied by the three women, there was no formal tenants organization, but the women, who were related, worked together to try to bring the problem of the building to the attention of HPD officials. According to an HPD official who was familiar with the block, many of the buildings on this block have these types of informal associations arising from close kinship ties among the residents. According to the same official, city agencies do not perceive these kin-based associations as valid organizations because they lack formal structure and rules. The block may be perceived by city agencies and the popular media as a dysfunctional one because of the extremely poor condition of the buildings and the high proportion of vacant units. The central office of HPD decided to relocate the tenants of 13 of the worst buildings on the block so those buildings could be rehabilitated. According to the Harlem-based HPD official, however, this could result in fragmentation of the kin-based networks because relocation would separate them.

2.5.3.2. Formal Tenant Organizations

The more formal tenant organizations develop as a result of the city's Tenant Interim Lease (TIL) program. This program was designed to help tenants buy buildings from the city. Ideally, it functions to help tenants learn to manage the building, allowing them to keep a portion of the rent income and to determine how the money should be used to maintain the building. If tenants successfully manage the building for a stipulated period of time and meet certain other criteria, they are permitted to own the building. The TIL program requires enormous and unpaid efforts on the part of the tenants. They must elect a tenant committee with officers to manage the building, collect the rent, and interact with city agencies, repair contractors, and others.

The ethnographers interviewed a woman who was active in the tenants association of a building in the TIL program in Health Area 10. She worked full-time in a bank downtown. Because of her accounting skills, she was elected treasurer of the tenants association. She discussed the difficulties involved in managing the building. First, because she worked full-time, she had to do all the association-related work in the evenings. As treasurer, she was responsible for rent collection, a difficult task, which involved repeated visits to delinquent tenants. The woman also represented her building at the Precinct Community Meetings (at the time of the interview, she was also secretary of the Precinct Community Council).

Although the TIL program had some positive benefits for residents of city-managed buildings, it also presented difficulties. In separate interviews, different housing activists commented that it was often difficult for poor tenants of city-managed buildings to sustain the level of organization and effort needed to participate in the TIL program. Women who were either in the formal labor force or involved in other activities to make ends meet were often compelled to assume the responsibility of a full-time real estate manager and building superintendent and received no financial compensation for this activity. These women were asked to perform tasks that in buildings inhabited by high-income residents would have been outsourced to paid personnel. Unless the tenants association was fortunate enough to have guidance or assistance from committed agency personnel, it could find itself facing insurmountable obstacles.

The Public Housing Developments managed by NYCHA also have formal tenant associations. None of our long-term participants who lived in these developments was active in these tenant associations, but all were familiar with them and had recourse to them. As a participant in the focus group on housing and environment pointed out, these tenant associations were often an effective broker between tenants and the NYCHA in helping to get repairs done. In the building where Reina, one of our longitudinal study participants, lived, the tenants association had an active patrol watch that helped monitor violence in the housing project. The tenants association also held social functions for the young residents to provide them with alternative forms of recreation.

Block associations are also a popular form of organization for Harlem residents (indeed they are prevalent throughout New York City). Block associations bring together residents of the block in efforts to improve the physical condition of the neighborhood. Typically, there are elected officers. Again, most participants are women.

The ethnographers interviewed Ms. K, who was vice president of a precinct council, president of her block association, and an active leader of the Consolidated Block Associations for Harlem. Ms. K, who appeared to be in her 60s, was retired from her job but always active in these various organizations. She was on 10 different boards of community-based organizations. She lived in Health Area 15. Her block association was involved in improving the regularity of the sanitation department's garbage pickup and in the upkeep of the streets and sidewalks. Ms. K reported that she sometimes felt overwhelmed by the amount of work she had to do in the various organizations, but she was committed to continued participation.

An active block association also existed on the block that was featured in the *New York Times* article. The association held one of its meetings in the chapel of a small church located in a brownstone about a month after the article appeared. Of the five officers of the association, only one was a man (he held the position of sergeant-at-arms). The president of the block association was a young woman, who appeared to be in her late 20s and who was accompanied by her small children. She worked full-time and lived in an HPD-managed building on the block. She had completed high school. The co-president was a woman in her late 50s who had been active in housing issues for a long time. The vice president was a 60-year-old woman; the treasurer was in her mid-40s; and the secretary was in her 30s, had two children, and was pregnant at the time of the meeting.

All the officers lived in tenement buildings. About 17 people (5 men) attended the meeting. The attendees included several social workers who lived on the block. The main topic of the meeting was a discussion of how to raise funds for a community center that the block association wanted to build for the neighborhood children. The association members also wanted the center to serve as a job training site and as a GED facility.

The association president did some preliminary research and discovered there were city-sponsored "beautification grants" they could take advantage of to improve the physical appearance of the neighborhood. She had also heard of the Foundation Center, located in downtown Manhattan, which provides listings of foundations and the types of grants they award. She offered to go there and do more research about possible sources of support. She also volunteered to undertake a survey of the block to collect basic demographic information. Ways to draw more people on the block into the block association were also discussed. Vehicles such as a block party or a celebration of a holiday event were suggested. There was a consensus that the event, or events, should be child-centered and should involve different activities for children.

This block association, while small, attempted to be active on a number of fronts that members thought were critically important to their community. The women who participated represented diverse occupations and a range of ages, and there were significant differences in their perspectives and approaches. However, there was a consensus about the need to focus attention on young people.

Finally, there are a few community improvement and homeowner associations in Harlem. The ethnographers interviewed members of one such association in Health Area 15 and attended several of its meetings. Although most of the members were homeowners, there were also a few tenants at the meetings. The main concerns of the association were to improve the quality of neighborhood. Here, as in the other associations, most participants were women. The association members included long-time residents who had owned brownstones in Harlem for over a decade as well as newcomers who had recently moved to Harlem to buy and renovate brownstones or to rent an apartment in a renovated brownstone. The association had elected officers and developed a fairly aggressive fund-raising effort. Their primary vehicle for fund-raising was an annual tour they sponsored of historic homes in the neighborhood. Tourists were charged a fee for visiting participants' homes. The association also received several grants from historic preservation organizations. One grant received by the association enabled it to hire a part-time executive director.

Thus, tenant, block, and homeowner associations were active sites where the women in our study engaged in efforts to improve their housing conditions and their neighborhoods. Among the EQ respondents, 39 percent participated in tenant organizations and 33 percent participated in block associations. Tenant and block associations were deemed effective by 58 percent of the respondents. Tenant associations were viewed as effective by

64 percent of women with less than a high school diploma, 56 percent of those with a high school diploma, and 67 percent of those with more than a high school diploma.

Generally, as can be observed from some of the case material above, women who were active in housing issues were also engaged in a number of other community efforts, ranging from the PTA to service on boards of local organizations and public institutions. Women who responded to the EQ reported participation in a broad range of community activities. Participation in community organizations varied by type of organization: 21 percent in school boards, 19 percent in community boards, 47 percent in churches or religious institutions, 32 percent in the PTA, 19 percent in self-help groups, 23 percent in social groups, 12 percent in political organizations, 11 percent in environmental organizations, and 25 percent in community activities fighting drugs. Women reported that good things came out of participating in community organizations: "they provide a network for you in many instances," "I got to know a lot of people and help people," "you get to do good for others," "keeps you abreast of what's going on in the community and keeps you aware of what's going on," "get to see an important change that we want to see in our neighborhoods, learn to work with each other," and "you feel like you are not alone."

Participants in the EQ survey described many organizations as effective in community improvement, including school boards (21 percent), community boards (47 percent), churches and other religious institutions (70 percent), PTA (44 percent), and the precinct councils (37 percent).

However, as reflected in the case material above, the participation of women in these organizations took considerable time and effort and therefore was a coping strategy that was also a significant stressor in their lives. What distinguishes these associations from those outside of Harlem in more affluent areas of New York, or even in suburban areas, is the level of frustration residents reported about the lack of cooperation they perceived on the part of city and state agencies. Participants across income and educational levels felt that the neglect of their communities was based on discriminatory practices. This type of neglect means that Harlem women are consistently fighting difficult battles in these associations and not merely cultivating friendly relationships with neighbors.

The cost to women's health of their persistent activism was perhaps vividly illustrated by the sudden death from a heart attack of a well-known housing activist, who had been involved in efforts to increase the number of affordable and mixed-income housing. Other activists spoke of their health problems and levels of stress.

- A middle-stratum independent consultant who had been active in efforts to provide affordable housing for more than 5 years commented that, because of her schedule, she did not eat properly (one day her breakfast consisted of a doughnut and lunch was half a can of tuna fish) and did not get enough sleep because she was up late working most nights. She was a single mother of an adolescent son.
- Two women who were active in the Strivers Row block association reported that they were also on the boards of several different community-based organizations as well as working full-time. Both agreed that this schedule was stressful at times but thought that they must continue. Both women were middle-aged with grown children, and one of the women reported that she often felt tired.
- Ms. L, a clerical worker who was active in her building's TIL program efforts, described her weariness after spending long hours at work and then attending an evening meeting or an evening spent knocking on tenants' doors attempting to

collect rents. Eventually, dissatisfied with the quality of life, Ms. L returned to her home in the West Indies. Ms. L was in her mid-30s and a single mother.

- At a meeting of community health activists, during a break, two professional women commented to the ethnographer about their feelings of stress. Although this was done in a joking manner, they clearly thought that the many different activities they engaged in contributed to this feeling of stress.

- At the Community Advisory Board Meetings of the Harlem Birth Right project, there was always informal conversation about the multiple activities of the board members and how a typical day might consist of work during the day and one or two meetings in the evening. This was true of both the men and the women on the Community Advisory Board.

2.6. ACCESS TO SOCIAL SERVICES

The involvement of women in obtaining social services, such as public schools and public assistance (welfare, food stamps, housing subsidies, and Medicaid), represented another arena where potential exposure to stressors was high because of systematic patterns of discrimination. Here, as in the efforts to maintain clean and safe neighborhoods and homes, women experienced the consequences of the struggle they had to wage to gain access to resources, which in theory should have been provided to them in a smooth and efficient manner as legislated and in fulfillment of the obligations of the state. While the procurement of social services is complex and extensively documented from many different perspectives, the ethnographic data in our study illustrated the ways women experienced these interactions, illuminating social service issues that had the potential to give rise to stress.

2.6.1. Schools

The quality of schools and their impact on the lives of women with school-age children is a multifaceted issue that requires more extensive reporting than can be offered here. Discussed below are the data from the research about women's efforts to obtain quality education for their children and the ways such efforts may be potential sources of stress.

In the EQ, 33 percent of women with less than a high school diploma reported they were dissatisfied with the schools, 23 percent of women with a high school diploma did so, and 39 percent of women with more than a high school diploma did so. As with other quality-of-life factors, women with a higher education more often expressed their dissatisfaction. However, only 56 percent of respondents were currently responsible for children, and this responsibility was more common among the women with the highest level of educational achievement (33 percent of women with less than a high school diploma, 59 percent of women with a high school diploma, 67 percent of women with more than a high school diploma). Of those women with children in school, 46 percent had children in different schools. Eighty-two percent of all women with children in school thought that their children were learning in school; 82 percent visited their children's school(s) and said their children did homework. Family members and partners, including godmothers, sisters, and friends, often helped with homework.

Women in the EQ reported a variety of feelings about after-school safety that cut across levels of education. Positive feelings included "I feel good about it—they have crossing guards," "mine is ok because my daughter goes to her godmother," "good school," "I feel safe about after-school safety because the counselors will keep us informed if kids do not show up or there is a problem," and "I feel safe, it's ok, I trust it." Other women raised concerns: "it's not so safe but I pray," "schools are not safe anymore," "I'm worried about that for my two oldest. The trains, the gangs, the police officers," and "not good. My children have been robbed."

The EQ responses indicated that women in this sample, because of the high degree of involvement in the schools and educational processes, in general appeared to be satisfied with the quality of the schools, although they were worried about aspects of their surrounding environment. However, at all of the field sites, ethnographers recorded complaints from mothers about the school system and the quality of their children's education.

The ethnographic data also revealed, however, that a major source of chronic strain may have been parents' struggles with school officials. In the following two cases, mothers, although of different income and educational levels, experienced similar treatment from school officials. In both instances, school officials seemed hostile to the parents because the parents questioned official decisions.

Ms. M, who depended on public assistance and did not have a high school diploma, was mandated by the New York City Child Welfare Agency (CWA) to attend a parenting class through a Harlem-based social service agency after she argued with school officials about her son's placement in special education classes. According to Ms. M, the boy played hooky several times and also acted up in class, so school officials wanted to place him on the special education track. Ms. M thought this was completely wrong, and she resisted the designation. She opposed it because she thought that once he was put in special education, "that would be the end of him" and he would never learn. She said, "he is a smart kid who doesn't need to be in special ed, but needs some guidance because of his lack of discipline." Her perception was that the school officials were lazy and just wanted to track him into special education as an easy solution. She thought that when she did not acquiesce, school officials became vindictive and called in the CWA, claiming that she was neglecting her children (they claimed, for example, that her son had come to school wearing dirty clothes and looking tired). She explained that she always sent him to school in clean clothes but could not control what he did on the way to school. She said that because of the school officials, the CWA mandated her to take the parenting workshop. She was willing to do this, even though it meant making arrangements for the care of her preschool children. However, she still intended to fight the special education designation for her son. Ms. M was clearly angry at the school system and at CWA for putting her in this position. She seemed determined to persist until she succeeded.

Ms. N was a young single mother with an associate's degree who worked as an administrative assistant for a national television news show. She told ethnographers that the principal at her 5-year-old daughter's school called to arrange a meeting. When Ms. N arrived, three other school representatives were in attendance. They told her they were concerned about her daughter's repeated lateness and they wanted her to work harder at getting her to school on time. Ms. N said she responded that her work schedule was very taxing and was the cause of her daughter's repeated lateness. She reported being surprised at how vindictive school officials were. She said the school officials didn't like her response or her attitude (not remorseful enough, according to Ms. N). They told her she would have to deal with child welfare and indeed she did. The CWA came to interview her and inspect her premises, and she had to take a day off from work. She described the process as extremely demanding and anxiety provoking. Her daughter was enrolled in a school on the upper west side, and Ms. N was especially concerned during the proceedings because, in order to allow her daughter to attend a good school, she had used the address of a friend. However, the agency found nothing wrong and said they would remove her name from the list of people to be followed.

The first case is especially interesting in light of recently published findings about the disproportionately high rates of minorities tracked into special education in New York City (*New York Times,* 1998). The experience of Ms. M indicates that consequences of this practice affect the parents as well as the children. There has been no statistical report, to our knowledge, of how many parents resist the placement of their children into special education and face bureaucratic procedures or punitive measures for undertaking such actions. However, the director of the legal services provider we interviewed informed us that women frequently request legal aid in opposing this designation for their children. Among the respondents to the EQ, there was also a significant correlation between having low income and being required to attend parenting workshops or to obtain other forms of counseling. These same women reported a higher frequency of encounters with forms of discrimination, including being treated with less courtesy, receiving poorer service, and being looked down on.

Two other sources of stress reported by study participants were children's performance and their social relationships at schools. Celine, a longitudinal participant who was self-employed, worried about her 12-year-old son, who lived with her mother in the South. Apparently, the boy had been having trouble in school, acting up, and getting poor grades. Celine made plans to go for a short visit so she could talk to his teachers. Her mother worried that perhaps her son needed Celine to be there.

Another longitudinal participant, Anita, a single mother who worked as a nurse, said that she sent her children to school where they were in contact with children who had access to greater material resources. She recounted that sometimes when she took them to school, she compared herself with the other mothers and wished she had more time to do things like bake pumpkin cookies. She said that sometimes she felt torn but that she always told her children, "there are always going to be people who have more than you and people who have less than you." She hoped someday they would understand. She believed that even though there might not be many children of their socioeconomic status in that school, they were getting the benefit of a better education, which in the long run would be an investment they could bank on.

Another longitudinal participant, Noma, relied on her daughter's teacher to help her out when Noma could not avoid being late to pick up her daughter. But the teacher was not always reliable, and, in one incident observed by the ethnographer, the teacher insisted that Noma pay a late fee. It was the last money Noma had with her, and she reported being angry that she had to spend it this way when she had counted on the teacher to be supportive.

Susan, a longitudinal participant, had sent her two younger children to live in the South with their father's relatives (in a suburb of Atlanta). Because of the violence around the schools in Harlem, she worried about the three older children who lived with her. She commented on the difference in the quality of schools:

I visit their schools [those of the children who live in Atlanta] and it's a big difference from the city. They have computers and everything in the classrooms for the kindergartens. And I look at this and how the teachers really take the time out to spend with each child, I mean, I stood in a classroom and heard a teacher actually call each child by name whereas here, they're like "what is this child's name?" You know I've seen that. It's a big difference and it's what you want, you want the best for your child.

In summary, public schools were a site of women's struggles on a number of fronts, from ensuring the quality of their children's education, which might involve harassment and discrimination from school officials, to a sense of frustration with the daily routine of monitoring bureaucratic procedures. The more general stressors that women experienced around these issues were compounded by race-related discrimination experienced by the women. As such, these stressors appeared to affect both low-income women and those in the middle stratum. While low-income women might have had to expend more efforts daily because they sent their children to inadequate public schools where problems of quality, bureaucracy, and discrimination were compounded by a dearth of resources, middle-stratum women, who often sent their children to private or parochial schools outside of Harlem, had to also confront the discrimination they and their children faced both in the social circle of their peers and from educators and administrators.

2.6.2. Public Assistance

The nexus of social services described under the rubric of public assistance includes a variety of programs from federal, state, and city agencies. Typically these include cash benefits (in the Aid to Families with Dependent Children [AFDC] program), food stamps, rent subsidies, and, depending on the woman's situation, child care subsidies, Medicaid, or other benefits. In the Upper Manhattan Empowerment Zone survey of 1,000 households, cited above, 33 percent had received Medicaid, 29 percent had received social security, 22 percent had received food stamps, 14 percent had received general welfare assistance, and 8 percent had received AFDC. Sixty-four percent of these respondents rated welfare offices as only fair or poor. Among the respondents to the EQ, 33 percent reported that they used public assistance; a higher percentage of women with more than a high school education relied on public assistance than women with less than a high school diploma (45 percent versus 25 percent).

In the EQ, women were asked about problems with procuring needed services such as quality child care, healthy foods, and quality health care. While most did not report problems in these areas, the types of problems with obtaining services included cost (39 percent), time (35 percent), waiting (39 percent), arrangements with other people (23 percent), and location (26 percent). Women were also asked about four specific types of services: personal services, social services (agencies), food shopping (reported in the discussion of stores), and health care. Eighty-four percent of women reported that they used personal services in Harlem, 21 percent reported that these services cost more in Harlem than elsewhere in the city, 62 percent reported that the quality was better in Harlem, and 86 percent said that transportation was available. Sixty-one percent of women reported that they used social services in Harlem, 7 percent reported that these services cost more in Harlem, 42 percent reported that the quality was better in Harlem, and 63 percent said that transportation was available. Sixty-five percent of women reported that they used health care services in Harlem, 16 percent reported that these services cost more in Harlem, fewer than half (47 percent) reported that the quality was better in Harlem, and 90 percent said that transportation was available.

It is well known that women who receive some form of public assistance must manage a variety of paperwork and bureaucratic procedures. If fortunate, they may be able to work with one case manager who links them to the various services. If not so fortunate, they must negotiate the different programs on their own. Women who work at low-wage jobs still may qualify for some benefits from public assistance as part of either state- or city-sponsored "incentive" programs to keep women working while supplementing wages too low to provide adequate resources. Many of the problems of the "welfare" system have been extensively documented by anthropologists (see particularly the work of Susser and Kreniske, 1987; Dehavenon, 1987; and Sharff, 1987) and sociologists (the classic *Regulating the Poor* by Piven and Cloward, 1971, for example, still provides an accurate portrayal of the system; for a more recent discussion, see Edin and Lein, 1997). Currently, a number of studies that examine the impact of the most recent legislation on public assistance (the 1996 reform, for example) are under way. In the course of fieldwork, ethnographers observed the day-to-day experiences of women negotiating this system and the pressure this may exert. Six of the longitudinal participants relied primarily on public assistance, while 12 either had used some form of public assistance in the past or were currently relying on one or more programs to supplement low wages or informal sector work.

The ethnographers observed a typical day at an income maintenance center in Central Harlem. The center occupied two floors in a building. The main waiting area was on the second floor, where there were about 30 plastic molded chairs in the center of a large room. Around the periphery of the room were cubicles where case managers had their desks. On the ground floor were more offices, presumably of supervisors and other personnel. People seeking assistance had to sign in. Often it seemed they had to wait several hours before their name was called and they could see a staff member. Most of the people seeking assistance at the office were women. The ethnographers met one woman who was there with her 18-year-old daughter and her small baby. They had been waiting several hours but had not yet been helped. Agency staff, when ready to see a client, would come to the waiting area and loudly announce the first name of the person next on their list, thus foregoing any privacy the women might have had. Women interviewed at the site were patient about the long waits but unhappy about the extent of paperwork and bureaucratic procedures.

In contrast, observation at a WIC center located near a large public hospital was more pleasant. Here, there was also a waiting room, but clients were called in individually to see staff in a private office. However, the center was small and could become crowded quickly. Again, women had to wait, sometimes for several hours, before they saw a staff member. The WIC director was an older black woman. According to her, there were nine WIC centers in Harlem, which saw a total of 14,500 people per month (this site saw 4,500 per month). The WIC program provided standard nutritional benefits for pregnant and lactating women and for infants up to 1 year old. The WIC director expressed a desire to tailor the nutritional supplements offered under the WIC program to make them more appropriate to the mostly black clientele served by the center (for example, substituting nondairy sources of calcium). While this goal had not been achieved, she had been able to collaborate with a farmers' market and arrange for it to operate near the center one day a week. Through this arrangement, WIC program members had access to fresh produce.

Use of some public assistance programs gave some of the longitudinal participants the opportunity to improve job skills through either finishing their high school equivalency or enrolling in college or technical courses. Longitudinal participants Gina, Latoya, and Susan followed this strategy. Several study participants had difficulty getting access to benefits even when they appeared to be eligible for them. For example, Reina, a longitudinal participant, had difficulty getting public assistance (AFDC) and Medicaid insurance for her newborn infant. She was fortunate that the health clinic she attended agreed to treat her and the baby without forms. Her aunt counseled her to make sure she had proper documentation before she went to the income maintenance center because otherwise they would "give you the runaround." It took Reina at least three visits just to get the paperwork completed to obtain the Medicaid for the baby.

However, access to public assistance did not guarantee that women would be able to make ends meet. Most women combined public assistance with informal work such as selling Tupperware, food, and other items; providing services such as babysitting and hairbraiding; and seeking out charities for food and clothing. Longitudinal participants Sharon, Ruth, Claire (all recruited while pregnant), and Susan found themselves in this situation during the course of our fieldwork.

Perhaps the greatest stressor for women occurred when they were suddenly cut off from access to benefits for what appeared to them to be arbitrary reasons. This happened to Sandra, a longitudinal participant who worked at a fast-food restaurant. Sandra was given a small raise, and this was reported to the social service agency through which she received food stamps, WIC benefits, and a small amount of cash assistance for her baby daughter. Sandra always planned her budget carefully so that she could make purchases without undue stress on her income. She had just made some purchases when she was cut off from public assistance entirely. She was notified that she would lose not only her cash benefits but also her food stamps. This was a major crisis because Sandra would have to spend more money on food and would have no extra money to buy supplies for the baby not covered by the WIC program. She demanded a fair hearing (a chance to appeal decisions about cuts in assistance), and a date was set for a month later. In the meantime, she fell behind in her rent payment. She was able to borrow some money from a friend, and an ethnographer also gave her a cash gift for the baby from her personal funds. Finally, at the fair hearing, all Sandra's benefits were restored because she still was not earning enough income to put her over the limit; and because the system supervisor acknowledged that a mistake had been made in her case, she was compensated for the missed payments.

However, Ms. O, another fast-food worker whose benefits were similarly cut off after her income allegedly increased, was not able to get them restored. She said that it was very hard without the cash payment because even though she could still get certain food items with the food stamps, she had no money to purchase other supplies the children needed (such as school notebooks). Another fast-food worker, Ms. P, suffered the same fate. Ethnographers recorded numerous instances of women being arbitrarily cut off from benefits.

Toward the end of 1994, policy discussions were taking place in Congress to eliminate welfare or to severely restrict it. In 1996, these discussions took fruit and "welfare reform" legislation was passed and signed into law. Policy makers proposed strict time limits on benefits for women, work requirements, and other measures. Women who had gathered for a prenatal care class at a social service agency discussed with an ethnographer the likely impact of such changes on their lives. These women doubted the reforms would lead to work. They expressed doubts about the availability of jobs. Instead, the perception was that cutting people off public assistance would lead to crime and drug abuse. The women also discussed the power of the public assistance system. Once enrolled in it, they felt it was hard to get out, because if one went in for one of the services (such as the rent subsidy), the case worker encouraged the recipient to enroll in a number of different programs. Thus, the women perceived that they became entangled in the web of fragmented services.

As noted above and in the case material, women also had difficulties with enrolling in, maintaining, and using Medicaid. This difficulty had obvious implications for these women's health, and their use of the health care system is discussed in a later chapter. It is important to note here that although access to health care during pregnancy is facilitated through some programs such as P-CAP (Prenatal Care Assistance Program) and WIC, termination of these programs (P-CAP at 6 weeks postpartum and WIC at 1 year postpartum) assumes that women will be able to find alternative sources of support or alternative ways to access health care. However, this may not be the case. Further research is needed on the disjuncture between the termination dates of these special programs (determined in part by medical assumptions about physiological needs) and the actual resources and needs of women.

None of the longitudinal participants in the study relied on institutional child care services. Data on the use of friends or kin for child care are reported in a later chapter. Data on the potential sources of stress for child care providers in institutional settings are reported in the next chapter.

While eligibility criteria were in theory defined by law, the women in our study were not always well informed about which programs they were eligible for, how they might access them, and how they might use them. Both the fragmented ways these programs were delivered and the seemingly arbitrary ways they were administered frequently prevented women from complying with regulations or from fully taking advantage of the programs. While this phenomenon is well documented in anthropological and sociological research, the ethnographic research reported here underscores the time and work involved in piecing together public assistance aid.

In summary, just as with the struggle to find solutions to housing problems, the time and effort women had to expend to attain public assistance may have constituted a significant source of stress. Low-income women found themselves continually having to struggle for access to resources that by law should have been provided to them more efficiently. Instead, whole days could be spent filling out paperwork or waiting to see service providers. The arbitrary and sudden termination of services also disrupted women's lives and upset precarious balancing acts that they constantly maintained in order to survive. These difficulties in obtaining public assistance or benefits legally accorded them by law were compounded by the overall economic instability and insecurity by which women were constrained, as is discussed in detail in the next chapter.

This chapter has demonstrated that the ethnographic research reveals there are significant potential sources of stress and chronic strain associated with environment, housing, and social service delivery. The likely mechanism by which these factors directly affect women's health and well-being is through the day-to-day interactions with these conditions. In our study, these interactions included women's daily attempts to cope with these stressors and strains and to modify their quality of life. Women perceived that these sources of stress and strain could be changed and participated in both individual and collective strategies to address their circumstances. In addition, the ethnographic data revealed that study participants considered the negative representation of Harlem in the media, popular culture, and the political arena attributable to racism and a direct cause of the negative environmental, housing, and social service stressors. As such, the negative representation of Harlem in itself was a significant source of chronic strain for study participants across social strata. It became an additional burden that made the day-to-day efforts to cope more difficult.

Protective strategies and perceived community assets, however, served to buffer the women in their daily lives. It was notable that the middle-stratum participants appeared to be willing to exchange one set of stressors for another in that they were willing to live under conditions of systematic neglect and higher levels of violence in exchange for the protective features offered by living in a black community, including a more limited exposure to racism in their neighborhoods.

An important finding of the research was that, in the context of these chronic strains, the occurrence of pregnancy may serve as a catalyst to increase the magnitude and actual and perceived severity of stress. At the time of pregnancy, the multiple stressors associated with housing, environmental factors, and obtaining of social services interrelate in forceful ways so that the effect is multiplicative rather than additive.

NOTES

[1] The word tenement is used here as a colloquial term to refer to rental units (owned either by the city or by private landlords) that were poorly maintained.

[2] According to the Empowerment Zone proposal, there were approximately 13,000 city-owned occupied housing units and several thousand units within vacant buildings in 1994.

[3] Because Ama was in possession of documentation (a green card), she was more easily able to pursue the legal avenues available to obtain and maintain adequate shelter. As recent newspaper accounts have demonstrated, large numbers of undocumented West African immigrants in Harlem live in extremely dilapidated rooms and apartments and do not have avenue to legal recourse. Furthermore, new and proposed legislation is likely to exacerbate these conditions.

3

WHERE PEOPLE WORK: THE ECONOMIC CONTEXT
OF REPRODUCTION

3.1. INTRODUCTION

As various studies have noted, African American women historically have worked outside the home; thus, occupationally related stressors and strains, as well as those arising from household work and community work, may influence their health status (Mullings, 1984; Krieger et al., 1994). African American women now constitute a slightly greater proportion of the African American workforce than men. Currently, on the national level, while approximately one-fifth of African American women in the labor force are in managerial and specialty professions, most are concentrated in service, technical, clerical, and laborer occupations. Twenty-eight percent are service workers; 12 percent hold jobs as operatives, fabricators, and laborers; and 39 percent hold jobs in technical, sales, and administrative support (Bennett, 1995). While only about 4 percent of African American women report themselves as self-employed (Devine, 1994), their increased participation in the informal sector has been widely discussed by social scientists (Sassen, 1991). Class stratification over the past 10 years has produced a concentration of African American women in low-wage, dead-end jobs and a growing middle stratum of managerial and professional workers.[1] The community description figures in the appendix describe employment and income characteristics of Central Harlem residents, according to the U.S. Census Bureau and other administrative sources of data.

An important issue here is the concentration of African American women in public sector work; in 1990, slightly more than 26 percent of African American women in the labor market worked in the public sector (Burbridge, 1994). The current cuts in federal and state spending, downsizing, and privatization affect women across class. For example, the public sector consistently has accounted for twice as many African American women as white women working as clerical workers (King, 1993). But these processes are also important for understanding the vulnerability of the middle class, since 85 percent of professional African American women work in the three major industries dominated by government and nonprofit employment: health, social services, and education (Burbridge, 1994).

As Krieger and colleagues (1994) note, in assessing the impact of race and class on the status of black women, numerous studies have established that the economic return for the same level of education is lower for blacks than it is for whites (and it is lower for women than for men within each racial group); that within the same occupation, blacks are likely to find themselves in lower-paying and lower-status positions; that black poor are much poorer than white poor; that many black women are segregated in menial, low-paying, dead-end, insecure jobs; and that there are pressures on high-achieving black career women.

According to 1990 census data, the proportion of all households in Central Harlem that had a household income under $10,000 was 43 percent, which was double the rate for New York City. In 1996, according to data compiled by the Citizens' Committee for Children, 36.9 percent of households in Central Harlem had an income under $10,000. This percentage was significantly higher than in New York City as a whole (20.9 percent) and nearly double that of Manhattan (18.9 percent). Households in Harlem also had significantly less income than black households nationwide. In 1990, 65.6 percent of families in Harlem were above the federal poverty level, approximately one-third less than in New York City as a whole. Conditions had worsened since 1970, with a larger proportion of families whose income was above the federal poverty level but was not sufficient to afford health insurance or adequate housing.

Among respondents to the ethnographic questionnaire (EQ), the mean annual income of the women interviewed was slightly less than $17,050 per year (range, $5,400–$70,000 per year). The median annual income was even lower, with 50 percent of the women having an income under $12,125 per year. On average, the women worked 24 weeks (slightly less than 6 months) of the year. Overall, just less than 50 percent of the women reported that work was a current source of their income. Other sources of income were family (35 percent), public assistance (33 percent), boyfriends (29 percent), other friends (14 percent), and babysitting (11 percent). Fewer than 10 percent of the women reported pensions, unemployment insurance, odd jobs, renting out rooms, playing the lottery, collecting bottles and cans, and other activities as a source of income. It should be noted that a larger percentage of women with more than a high school diploma reported being on public assistance (45 percent) than did women with only a high school (24 percent) or no high school (25 percent) diploma.

William Julius Wilson has noted that "for the first time in the twentieth century most adults in many inner-city ghetto neighborhoods are not working in a typical week" (Wilson, 1996:xiii). Although this has been changing slowly since about 1998, it held true during the study period. In Central Harlem, only 41 percent of persons over 16 years old were employed in 1990. The unemployment rate for women in Harlem was 50 percent higher than in New York City (14 percent versus 9 percent) and it was more than twice as high for men in Harlem (22 percent versus 9 percent). In 1990, more than half (55 percent) the Harlem women who were eligible to work were not in the labor force (New York City Department of City Planning, 1990). Nearly one in four (24 percent) respondents to the empowerment zone survey were unemployed (16 percent) or were working part time but looking for full-time work (8 percent).

Among respondents to the EQ, approximately half the women interviewed (49 percent) were currently working. Whether a woman was currently employed did not differ across educational level. Of women who were currently unemployed, 45 percent had not been able to look for work, and 21 percent were retired and not actively job hunting. Interestingly, only 21 percent of unemployed women indicated that having children was the reason they were not working. Finding a job appeared to be more difficult for women who had a high school education or more. None of the women with less than a high school education was unemployed because she could not find a job, whereas 22 percent of women with at least a high school education said they had been unable to find work.

Overall, among EQ respondents, 75 percent of the women who were currently unemployed had previously worked in Harlem (though 47 percent of the total sample had not worked in Harlem). The mean number of years since they had last worked or held a regular job was 6 years. Eighty-five percent of women had worked for more than 1 year in the past. The reasons women left their jobs were diverse. Many were forced to leave because they were laid off, their company was downsized, or a store went bankrupt and closed. In other instances, women retired or left their jobs for health reasons such as "I had arthritis and thought I had to have surgery" or "I had kidney surgery." Women of all educational levels reported both financial and emotional difficulties associated with unemployment, including "hard to function financially, buy the kids clothes, and have money for emergencies" and "the effect was stressful." Lack of income was most frequently reported as what women liked least about being unemployed. However, other negative effects of unemployment included "the boredom after being home all the time" and "not having somewhere to go every day."

In this chapter, the principal and potential sources of stress and chronic strains uncovered during fieldwork at the work sites are discussed in order to explore the relationship between type of work and type of stressors. Comparisons across income and type of occupation are discussed in terms of exposure to work stress. The stressors discussed here fall into two categories: 1) specific stressors related to the nature of work, and 2) general stressors that relate to the overall economic conditions in which women find themselves. The important point to remember, however, is that these two types of stressors interact with each other to create a magnitude of overall stress. The ethnographic fieldwork and responses to the EQ reveal that many women in Harlem are subject to a continuum from employment to unemployment that severely affects their income security and their access to work-related benefits. This continuum is perhaps a chronic stressor of a greater magnitude than those that are specifically work related. As such, stressors associated with employment and income insecurity may underlie and reinforce work-related stressors in such a way as to multiply the effect of all these conditions. In this chapter, findings are reported from the field research on current sources of income and employment insecurity and how such insecurity was experienced across social strata. We also discuss how women coped with the stressors at work sites. Additionally, in this chapter, the perceptions of middle-stratum women about their vulnerability to downward mobility and the role of protective strategies afforded by working in a black community are considered.

3.2. WORK SITE DESCRIPTIONS

The following specific work sites were examined: a fast-food restaurant, an office site, a hospital site, self-employed women (vendors and several middle-stratum entrepreneurs), and three sites of social service delivery (a social service agency, child care work-

ers, and a legal services agency). As discussed in the first chapter, these sites were selected to reflect the concentration of black women in particular occupational categories.

3.2.1. Fast-Food Restaurant

This site was composed of two restaurants, both in Harlem, and both owned by two
African American women (the first time a fast-food franchise was granted to African
American women in Harlem). The restaurant's wage and shift policy was regulated by
franchise contract terms. The women owners, however, had some control over work policy, decor, and other aspects of management. The owners were very attuned to the Harlem
location and to their own position within the business community. The restaurant was decorated with African-centered motifs, and the uniforms were made of distinctive African
prints, reflecting the community's heritage. The owners believed this helped the workers
and customers have a sense of pride about the venue. Each restaurant had a small rest area
for the workers in the kitchen area, as well as lockers for their personal effects. The owners also had offices at each restaurant. The workers and the dining area were monitored by
security cameras. The owners emphasized cleanliness and efficiency in customer service.
They stated that they thought that, beyond being a business, the restaurant was a part of
the community. They frequently participated in Harlem's Chamber of Commerce programs and facilitated charity events.

3.2.2. Office Site

This office was a public state agency, which occupied space on two floors of a prominent Harlem building. There was a large open reception area on the main floor of the
agency. Private offices of higher-echelon staff had access to windows. Lower-level administrative and secretarial staff were located in interior space, generally in cubicles with
modular furniture. A large area of cubicles in the back of the office suite was dubbed "the
plantation" by one worker because she said it lacked ventilation and proper heating or
cooling. The worker's lunch lounge was in the copy and supply room. A small round table
and a small refrigerator were provided for the staff. A group of six or seven women regularly had lunch there and watched a favorite soap opera on a small television owned by
one of the workers.

3.2.3. Hospital Site

This was a large public facility, one of two large hospitals in Harlem. The facility
included newer renovated sections as well as older, more worn-looking areas. The large
public reception area in the main building was staffed by information booth and security
personnel. Security personnel were also located on various floors. Hospital wards were
similar in design to those in other large hospitals, with a mix of patient rooms, central
nurses' stations, and small offices for hospital staff. The emergency room had molded
plastic seats in the waiting room, where there was also a pharmacy station. Outpatient clinics were scattered in various buildings. In early 1993 funds were allocated for a new ambulatory patient care center, and ground was broken for the facility in the summer of that
year. However, after the administration of Rudolph Giuliani took over city governance, the

project was halted, as Giuliani initiated a review of all the city-managed hospitals with a view to developing a strategy for privatization. The ambulatory care facility was finally completed in 1998.

3.2.4. Self-Employed Women

Among the self-employed women studied were street vendors who had stations along 125th Street. These vendors had a variety of arrangements—everything from small card tables and folding chairs to more elaborate carts. The vendors typically started setting up their tables in midmorning and often sold their goods well into the evening. On Wednesday nights, when the Apollo Theater has amateur night, vendors stayed open late into the night to catch the attending crowds. A great range of goods were displayed— homemade arts and crafts, African cloths and art works, oils and scents, herbal health products, books, and tee-shirts, to name a few. Vendors sometimes made arrangements with small businesses on the street to rent storage space for their equipment and wares.

3.2.5. Social Service Providers

The three social service agencies demonstrated the range of work venues and arrangements characteristic of this sector. The nonprofit agency we examined had a local branch in a Harlem park and recreation center. Each department had offices. There were also several meeting rooms where classes and programs were offered. One large room had a stage for community performances and also functioned as a dining room. Local senior citizens regularly were served lunch there. The child care workers, on the other hand, worked from their homes. Each home had to meet state standards for child safety. The workers were coordinated through an agency located in a church building, where they regularly picked up their checks as well as information about changes in regulations. They also periodically attended classes at the agency. Finally, the legal services agency had an office in a prominent Harlem building. However, most of the lawyers spent much of their time in court buildings, especially housing court, as was described in the previous chapter.

3.3. WORK SITE–RELATED STRESSORS

The following strains and stressors related to the nature of work emerged in the course of fieldwork as most salient: the pace of work, the schedule flexibility of work, the physical and environmental strains associated with work, the chronic strain of role hierarchies, the chronic strain of interactions between providers and clients in the service sector, and the perceived level of occupational stress. Examination of these aspects of work includes assessment of their potential role as stressors, whether this differs across strata, and the coping strategies developed by women to counteract the impact of the stressors. While some of these potential stressors may appear to be common to all work, it should be underscored that race and gender constrain employment opportunities, and the work sites studied reflect these constraints.

3.3.1. Pace of Work

The pace of work refers to the day-to-day workload and the way it is scheduled. Each work site had a fluctuating work pace, and at each site it seemed that the unpredictable nature of this pace could be a source of stress, regardless of the type or quantity of work. The fluctuation of the pace of work was most vivid at the fast-food restaurant, the office site, and the hospital site. In the social service delivery sites and in the informal economy site, pace of work was not as salient as a potential stressor because there was more regularity to the rhythm of work. The ethnographic documentation of the effect of the unpredictable character of the pace of work is detailed below.

3.3.1.1. Fast-Food Restaurant

The pace of work at the fast-food restaurant depended completely on the flow of customers in and out of the restaurant. The restaurant was located on a busy boulevard in Harlem and was open from early morning until late at night. While workers could roughly predict peak meal times (breakfast, lunch, and dinner), they could not predict the number of customers at any given time. The following vignettes from two different days over the 3- to 4-month period when the ethnographers worked in the restaurant indicate the ways fluctuations in the pace of work acted as a stressor.

On one day, the ethnographer was working behind the counter at a cooking station. At about 11:25 in the morning, close to 100 schoolchildren (estimated ages 9–11) and their chaperones entered the restaurant. The restaurant managers had no prior warning that the children would be arriving, and the restaurant became extremely crowded in a matter of minutes. Because it was also lunchtime, the restaurant had the usual load of lunch customers as well. The managers requested all workers to accelerate the pace of work immediately. Some were shifted from their stations to others that required more attention. The ethnographer was assigned to the soda dispenser to ensure that there was a continuous supply of filled soft drink orders. At various times, the manager barked orders to the workers to work faster or to work better. When the host (who busses tables) requested help in the front area, he was told no help was available. The ethnographer was ordered to keep the soda area clean and was quickly reprimanded if she filled the soft drink orders incorrectly. For 1 hour, the ethnographer was not able to look up from the soda dispenser machine, felt her heart beat accelerate, and felt a high degree of anxiety about meeting the demand while keeping the area clean. The normally light conversation that generally occurred between workers was curtailed and people spoke only when they needed something or when they observed an error. Once a fellow worker gave a word of encouragement to the ethnographer and told her to keep going. At the end of the hour, all the customers had been served and the pace slowed. The cashiers collectively cheered for having met the demand, and the manager applauded the workers and commented to the ethnographer, "See how it is—now you've really got a taste of it."

On another day, the ethnographers were working the late-afternoon shift. According to the workers, the lunch hour had been very busy, although the restaurant was then virtually empty. The ethnographers had been told that the "bosses" like the workers to always be occupied and to keep busy, even when the restaurant was empty. Hence, the ethnographer working the front area cleaned the tables twice, and the ethnographer working behind the counter swept the floor again. The general manager arrived and decided the flow was slow and sent some of the workers home early from their regular shift. This meant they would not receive their full shift pay that day (workers clock in on time cards and are paid according to the number of hours they work). For the workers who were forced to leave early, the unpredictability of not being able to earn the full amount of shift pay was a constant source of anxiety. One worker, a young woman in her 20s, commented on this to the manager, who nonetheless insisted on his decision.

In general, the ethnographers noted that the pace of work was never the same on any of the days they spent in the fast-food restaurant. Each day, the peak flow of the crowd varied and the workers had to go from relative inaction to action in a short amount of time. Interviews with workers, both off- and on-site, confirmed that pace of work was perceived by the workers as one of the more stressful aspects of the job. As the vignettes demonstrate, both a rapid increase in the pace as well as a sudden decrease were potential sources of stress. While the pace of work appeared to be most stressful for the crew shift workers (various job positions at the fast-food restaurant are described below in the section on role hierarchy), it also affected the assistant managers and swing managers because they had to monitor the production process. Workers in these positions had different educational achievements, although no one had a college degree. Crew workers and swing managers were paid hourly wages while assistant managers received a biweekly salary.

The only coping strategy workers could use to counteract this stress was to request shifts that were less likely to be as busy or as subject to irregular flow. This was the strategy used by Diana, one of our longitudinal participants. She worked as a cashier and lived with her 13-year-old son in a small apartment in a privately owned building. She had completed high school and was planning to be trained for a career in the health care industry. When she discovered she was pregnant, she requested specific shifts to avoid weekend work when the pace tended to be heavier. Because she was perceived by the owner managers of the fast-food restaurant (who were African American women) to be a reliable worker, and because they were sympathetic to her needs in pregnancy, they granted her request.

3.3.1.2. Office Site

The pace of work at the office site depended on the type and number of projects that were undertaken on any given day. The office site was at a public sector agency located in Harlem. The agency occupied three suites of offices and employed 52 full-time staff but also added consultants and temporary staff as necessary. About 19 people were employed as clerical workers, most of whom were African American women. Clerical workers were labeled as administrative personnel and were assigned to work either with individuals (the chief administrators) or to units. In addition to these were professional staff, also mostly African Americans (but there were more men in the highest positions) divided between project managers, deputy directors, and directors. Professional staff determined to some extent the projects to be worked on and assigned duties to the administrative personnel.

Administrative personnel had standing duties (such as answering phones, sorting mail, and typing correspondence) but were also assigned work on an unpredictable and irregular basis. For example, consider the case of Ms. Q, who was secretary to one of the supervisors at the agency. Her desk was located in a corridor along a row of desks. No cubicle walls separated her desk from the others, and her desk was right outside the director's office. The director worked on a variety of projects assigned by the chief administrator. The director did not discuss the scheduling of projects with Ms. Q, nor was there a policy that facilitated work being assigned in a standardized fashion to allow secretaries a certain fixed time to complete work. As a result, Ms. Q never knew if she was going to have a slow day or a busy day. On busy days, Ms. Q inevitably fell behind on her standing tasks and had to catch up on them on slower days. Ms. Q perceived her boss to be erratic and complained that the pace of work was stressful. Similarly, other secretaries and administrative assistants complained about the unpredictable nature of the pace of work and the lack of communication between themselves and their superiors. It should be noted here that the lack of control over pace was partly the result of a scarcity of resources, personnel, and lack of technical services in this public sector site. This site was consistently underfunded by the state government and (as is discussed later) was eventually eliminated when George Pataki became governor.

For this reason, the clerical workers were not the only ones affected by the pace of work. Professional staff also did not control the pace of work and were subject to flux in the workplace. For example, Ms. R, an African American in her mid-30s, was an independent consultant who was hired by the agency to work on a special project mandated by public sector officials. Ms. R was given a temporary office and a staff of three interns and was expected to produce a major report within 4 months. She was responsible for coordinating several commissioned studies, gathering data from other consultants and experts, addressing political and media concerns, and negotiating with city and state officials. An ethnographer stationed in her office observed that on any given day a "crisis" could arise in any one of these tasks. On one particular day, Ms. R, who had scheduled several meetings, was requested by the chief administrator to make herself available for a radio interview that could occur at any time. She had to reschedule her meetings so that she could stay in the office and prepare for the interview. Ms. R reported that this event was highly stressful, and she expressed frustration that she did not have control over her workday. Near the deadline for completion of the report, Ms. R reported that she stayed up all night for several nights in a row and practically lived at the office. The report was finished so close to deadline that it had to be hand carried to its destination to ensure on-time arrival.

In another example, Madeline, one of the longitudinal study participants recruited from this site, had a master's degree and was a project manager. She was responsible for overseeing projects related to economic development. Her pace of work was disrupted by crises in the projects she managed. Crises could result from late deliveries of material, failure of clients to meet appointments, and delays in work progress as a result of subcontractor error. Madeline viewed her inability to control these factors, and thus regulate her workload, as stressful. She attributed these problems in part to the fact that the agency she worked for was in Harlem and served a largely African American clientele; for this reason, she believed other state agencies did not accord her or her work the same respect they gave to organizations elsewhere.

These illustrations indicate that the pace of work for both clerical staff and professionals at the office site was a potential source of stress. While clerical staff had less control over the pace, professional staff were also affected because of larger structural constraints such as the location of the site in the public sector (which, as is described below, meant less access to resources and personnel) and geographic location in Harlem.

Ethnographers observed no real coping strategies developed at this site to counteract the stressful effects of the pace of work. Ms. R, however, eventually left this line of work to take employment in a less intense environment.

3.3.1.3. Hospital Site

Ethnographers undertook fieldwork at a large public hospital in Harlem at the recommendation of Community Advisory Board members and other participants in the Community Dialogue Group on site selection. This hospital was one of the largest employers in Harlem and employed a high percentage of Harlem residents. At the time of fieldwork, the hospital was under consideration for major budget cuts (see below). Fieldwork was conducted in several different obstetric clinics and the obstetrical ward (these choices were determined by hospital administrators based on their understanding of the study and criteria for minimum disruption for staff). The pace of work at the hospital was determined by the patient caseload and the conditions of the patients. Observation in both settings in the hospital revealed that the patient caseload and demand varied almost daily with little predictability of pace.

As part of the participant observation conducted at this site, an ethnographer observed an obstetric clinic on several different days. On one day, only 50 patients attended. Conditions appeared normal, and the staff was able to handle the load in a routine fashion. Staff working in the clinic included a registered nurse, physician assistants, nurse practitioners, nursing technicians, clerks, midwives, residents, medical students, and attending doctors. While pace appeared manageable on this day, on another day, conditions became "chaotic" because there was a larger-than-normal patient load. Patients had to wait a long time to be seen, and tension mounted among staff as they attempted to manage the situation. The ethnographer observed three cases of conflict that erupted among staff during this unexpected high-load period. In all three cases, the conflicts were between the nursing staff and resident or attending doctors. In one case, a doctor who was attempting to see a patient out of turn was berated by a nurse administrator for not following procedure; in the other two cases, doctors were criticized by nursing staff for making demands on them. On the obstetrical ward, the pace of work depended on the number of patients admitted for surgery or delivery. The ethnographer discussed the routine on the ward with a nurse, who reported that when it is busy, she never gets to sit down. Three of the EQ work site interviews were conducted at random with hospital workers in these sites. Respondents confirmed that patient overload and constant interruptions were perceived as stressors.

Conversely, when there were few patients, sections of the ward were closed and nurses' shifts were sometimes rearranged; thus, nurses might find themselves having to adjust to new routines. A section of the ward was closed for over 2 weeks at one point during the fieldwork. Several personnel expressed anxiety about when and if the ward would reopen. A nurse perceived this method of dealing with patient load (and hence work pace) as a function of the city government funding cuts to which the public hospital was subjected.

In sum, variability and unpredictability of the pace of work affected all staff, although a decrease in patient caseload probably had more impact on the nursing and technical staff than on attending doctors. However, the pace of work appeared to be a potential stressor across occupational level at all three sites.

3.3.2. Schedule Flexibility

Schedule flexibility refers to the ability of the women to regulate the number of hours and days that they work. Lack of flexibility in the schedule sometimes placed pressures on women when other aspects of their lives became problematic (such as a child becoming ill, a family crisis, or when the women were pregnant and felt ill or tired). Eighty-nine percent of respondents to the EQ who were employed reported that flexibility was a positive feature of work. Similarly, 93 percent of women who had previously been employed found flexibility to be a positive feature of previous jobs. Participant observation revealed that lack of schedule flexibility existed particularly at the hospital site, the office site (for the clerical workers), and two of the social service delivery sites (the child care providers and the social service providers). On the other hand, the fast-food restaurant employees and the self-employed women characteristically had more flexibility in how they could schedule their work time. Detailed ethnographic documentation follows.

3.3.2.1. Hospital Site

At the hospital site, the administrative workers were the ones who had the least control over their schedules. Ethnographers interviewed Ms. S, an African American in her mid-20s, who worked for the large hospital in an administrative position; she had little flexibility in her schedule. She had to work even though she was experiencing a high-risk pregnancy (she had diabetes and hypertension), and she worked during most of the pregnancy. She also delivered a premature infant. She described what she found stressful about her lack of schedule flexibility:

> [The job is] very stressful because in the operating room, you have to back someone up.... Because on the front desk, you have about, what ... six lines to answer ... the intercom [is] going ... they're sending for patients, they want blood. The doctors are yelling, "Where is my patient?" Nurses are screaming, "Where's this patient?" You have the supervisors down your neck, no one's picking up the phones, it's just you. It's a madhouse.... It's a madhouse. It was a real madhouse. I remember one day I was up there and my blood sugar, I felt it dropping. It went down to 40.... By the time I got off that desk ... oh, you start shaking, you get the trembles, you go into a cold sweat and you're just crazy. You just can't deal with anything. I called my supervisor and told him [to get] somebody out here to relieve me now. And to me, it felt like it took forever for someone to come relieve me, right.... I felt like he didn't move fast enough, because in the process of all that moving, my sugar was already low. So, the more you work, the more it drops. So, you know, being in a position like that, you're constantly working, you know, this is like around 10 o'clock in the morning and my sugar just took a sudden dive.

While administrative jobs had the least flexibility, nurses were affected because their shifts could be changed on short notice. For example, Anita, the longitudinal participant recruited from this site, was called in to work on short notice. As a result, she had to quickly find child care because her regular arrangements were not available. This was often a problem because most child care centers and after-school programs closed at 6 pm.

3.3.2.2. Office Site

Similar to administrative and clerical workers at the hospital site, clerical workers at the office site had to work fixed hours and did not have control over setting their schedules. If a personal emergency arose, they had to use sick leave. In one case, Ms. T, a middle-aged clerical worker with cancer and multiple sclerosis, still had to work to make ends meet. On a particularly hot summer day, she had to come to work even though heat exacerbated her symptoms. She told the ethnographer that she tired easily and that this made her irritable and anxious. On the other hand, the ethnographers observed that this office site permitted some flexibility with respect to the presence of children at the office. Thus, a secretary was able to bring her son to work when he had a school holiday and she could not arrange for child care. When interviewed, the personnel director of the agency, an African American woman, stated that she encouraged a worker-friendly environment. Other workers appeared to welcome the child. Thus, at this site, the largely African American staff and the more informal attitude about workplace regulations may, to some degree, have counteracted the lack of flexibility in the schedule for clerical workers.

3.3.2.3. Family Child Care Providers

Another group who had little schedule flexibility was the family child care providers. These women worked through a subsidized, nonprofit agency that contracted them to provide child care for infants and toddlers in their homes. They were certified by the agency and met requisite state criteria (including an inspection of their homes). The ethnographers met and talked with these providers during a 5-week continuing education course offered by the contracting agency. Twenty-five women, all either Latina or black and of a wide range of ages, attended the course. Most of the providers lived in Health Area 12, where the offices of the agency were located. During the course, the women discussed their perception of problems experienced by child care workers. A major issue was parents' tardiness in dropping off and picking up children. This disrupted their schedules, either delaying the routine at the start of the day or preventing the providers from doing their own business at the end of the day.

Elizabeth, a longitudinal participant recruited from this site, discussed the difficulties entailed in always having to be there for her clients. She was in her early 60s, and she had emigrated from the Caribbean to New York as a young woman. She had completed high school and lived in a public housing development. Her first husband died, and she remarried in later life. She stated that the nature of family child care required the child care worker's constant presence. Some of her clients worked for up to 12 hours and counted on her to be available. However, Elizabeth had some strategies to cope with this problem. First, she sometimes took the children under her care with her if she had to do errands on weekdays. She made it into an outing for the children, adding in a stop at a playground. At other times, if she had to be absent, she recruited a friend (a woman who lives in the same building) to substitute for her. Elizabeth usually paid her friend, so she herself lost income at these times. Occasionally, she relied on her husband, when he was unemployed, to watch the children during their nap time while she stepped out. Other women providers recounted that they drew on family or close friends to help if they had to go somewhere during the day.

3.3.2.4. Fast-Food Restaurant

It is interesting to note that most of the fast-food restaurant workers had some control over their shifts. Discussed above is the case of longitudinal study participant Diana, who chose shift hours that were likely to be not as busy. Diana also took advantage of her days off to schedule clinic appointments for prenatal visits. This flexibility allowed shift workers some autonomy and, in interviews, some of the workers discussed that flexibility as one of the advantages of this type of job. Some workers took advantage of the flexibility to attend college or general equivalency diploma (GED) programs while they were working. Shift flexibility, however, was limited to some extent by scheduling constraints. Once workers agreed to the assigned shifts, they had to report for work on time or risk being fired. Workers recounted to ethnographers several instances when people were fired for failing to report on time. In one case, a swing manager was fired because she failed to report on time: she had to be away on family business and made arrangements with a coworker to cover her shift. However, the coworker failed to show up, so the swing manager was fired.

3.3.2.5. Self-Employed Women

Finally, self-employed women had perhaps the most flexibility in their schedules. This was perceived to be a major advantage. The sample of self-employed women came primarily from participant observation with street vendors who, at the time of fieldwork, were located along 125th Street. The vendors sold a range of goods, including books, tee-shirts, African arts and crafts, health care products, and textiles. They generally sold their wares from small tables set up on sidewalks. In addition to these vendors, the ethnographers recruited three middle-stratum, self-employed women to participate in the longitudinal study (Noma, a performance artist; Billie, an entrepreneur; and Celine, a consultant). Other self-employed women in the neighborhood were also interviewed.

Self-employed women took advantage of their schedule flexibility by adjusting their work hours to accommodate other aspects of their lives, such as caring for their children, supporting family members, and attending medical appointments for themselves and their children. This type of flexibility made vending appealing to Aurora, a longitudinal participant. She was a street vendor in her mid-30s who had recently separated from her husband after many years of marriage. A practicing Catholic, she had eight children ranging in age from 1 to 17 years and became pregnant with her ninth child during the course of the study. When she found herself in the position of having to earn an income (after separating from her husband), she chose to try vending so that she could combine generating income with her child care responsibilities. Similarly, 37-year-old Ama, the Senegalese cloth vendor, set her own hours for vending and decided to skip days during her pregnancy when she was unwell.

Among the middle-stratum, self-employed women, flexible schedules permitted travel (Celine took trips out of state to visit family members; Noma traveled both for pleasure and for her profession), combining work with other activities (Billie spent time volunteering at a nonprofit youth program in Harlem; Celine researched her great uncle's role in the spread of vaudeville and minstrel shows during the early 1920s; Noma combined performance with teaching), and efforts devoted to improving their communities (both Celine and Billie were active members of their neighborhood or block associations).

Like the self-employed, women we met in the neighborhood sites who were in school also had some flexibility. The young women who were in high school stayed in school during their pregnancies, although they did not attend on days when they did not feel well. Among the respondents to the EQ, no women with less than a high school diploma reported that they went to school either full-time or part-time; 13 percent of women with a high school diploma reported that they went to school full-time, and an additional 21 percent reported that they went to school part-time during their most recent pregnancy. Only 7 percent of women with more than a high school diploma reported going to school either full- or part-time during their last pregnancy. This finding was not surprising because they already had advanced degrees.

In sum, clerical and administrative workers in structured job environments were least likely to have schedule flexibility, and they perceived this as a stressor. Professional staff at the hospital, the office site, and the social service delivery site were able to exert greater control over their schedules. However, some workers at lower-wage jobs, such as those in the fast-food restaurant, also had flexibility, and they used this to their advantage to counteract other stressors.

It seems clear that, in weighing the overall degree of stress presented by degree of schedule flexibility, it is important to consider other sources of stress and mitigating factors. It is also important to note that the ability to control schedules affected women's ability to manage their prenatal care, both as self-care and from the medical system. Women with less schedule flexibility had more difficulty with long clinic waits, taking rest periods, or finding time to eat proper meals.

3.3.3. Physical and Environmental Strain

Physical and environmental strain, as a component of overall job strain and its relationship to pregnancy outcome, has been the subject of numerous studies, whose results are somewhat ambiguous (see McLean et al., 1993). Nevertheless, most working women among the participants continued to work during pregnancy. For instance, none of the longitudinal participants quit her job when she was pregnant. In the EQ, overall 37 percent of women reported that they worked during their most recent pregnancy. Work during pregnancy was more common among women with more education, however; 47 percent of women with more than a high school diploma reported working during pregnancy compared with 33 percent of women with a high school diploma and 18 percent of women with less than a high school diploma.

Of those women who worked, women reported different exposure to physical job strains by level of education. While 41 percent of women overall reported that most of the time their job required them to stand, 18 percent of those with less than a high school education and 20 percent of those with more than a high school education reported standing. Only 8 percent of those with a high school education reported that they spent most of their time standing. Twenty-nine to 33 percent of those with a high school education or more reported that most of their time was spent sitting, while only 9 percent of those with less than a high school education reported that most of their time was spent sitting.

A compelling example of the impact of physical strain of work on pregnancy was observed during ethnographic fieldwork at a neighborhood site. A young pregnant woman of African descent, originally from St. Vincent, was very concerned about the effect of her work on her pregnancy. Although in St. Vincent she earned $900 a month in a clerical job, when she came to the United States (as an undocumented worker) she first worked as a live-in domestic and babysitter for only $350 a month. However, soon after she became pregnant, she began working at a retail commercial establishment on 125th Street, where she continued to work throughout her pregnancy. She recounted to ethnographers that she was compelled to work 11 hours a day, 6 days a week. She reported that she stood the entire time and was not given a lunch break. She complained of problems with vision and pain in her pelvis that was diagnosed as round ligament pain.

The fieldwork was not intended to provide any data specifically correlating such strain with pregnancy outcome, but observation of people at work illustrated their perceptions of and reactions to physical labor and to the environments in which they worked that have implications for future research on this issue. For example, at the fast-food restaurant, there was an informal ranking of jobs with those with greater physical strain being the least preferable. Thus, bun toasting and sandwich preparation or frying were least desirable while crew or station chief (a job that involved tracking demand for menu items and regulating production to meet demand) was most preferable because it was slightly more varied and allowed movement throughout the cooking area.

3.3.3.1. Fast-Food Restaurant

The fast-food restaurant was the site where we observed women engaged in the most physically stressful jobs. All the jobs at the fast-food restaurant (except for the general manager's position) involved a great deal of standing and working in cramped conditions with constant exposure to strong odors and noise. The fast-food restaurant had an attractive decor and clean dining area. However, the bulk of the work was done behind the counter in an area that was divided into rigidly circumscribed stations. Once assigned to a station, workers spent the entire shift standing and doing their part of the food processing. For example, one station involved toasting the buns. An ethnographer spent several days at this station. The station was a 3-foot area in front of the bun toaster, which was a large oven with racks. To one side was the storage area for the buns, and on top of this was the counter where the toasted buns were placed. The ethnographer spent an entire shift standing in one place putting buns in and out of the oven as required. This job placed physical strain on the feet and leg joints. The cooking area was always permeated by a strong (although not unpleasant) odor of food, particularly from the fryers.

A small lounge area behind the cooking area was available to the workers where they could take their break or eat a meal (workers received one free meal during their shift). The lounge had two chairs, a video player (for showing demonstration and training videos to new employees), and a small shelf where workers could put personal items. The workers' bathroom was in the basement (next to a large garbage can) and here also were small lockers where they could store their clothes (all workers wore uniforms during operating hours). In addition to having a small, circumscribed space to work in, workers in most of the jobs performed highly repetitive tasks. Sandwich preparation, for example, involved doing the same thing in a rigidly specified order over and over.

During her pregnancy, Diana, mentioned above, worked as a cashier, which was technically a less strenuous physical job. About 5 months into her pregnancy, she told the ethnographers that she had good days and bad days and that she found the odors and general environment of the site to be stressful. In general, however, Diana thought that her coworkers were very supportive of her. They did not allow her to pick up heavy objects, and they praised her for working so diligently.

Another worker interviewed by ethnographers, Ms. O (mentioned previously), recounted that she was afraid of falling because sometimes the floor had wet or greasy spots. The owners of the franchise, when interviewed, indicated that they tried to place their pregnant workers in the less strenuous jobs. They also increased their liability insurance for the pregnant workers. Ethnographers also observed workers using a number of coping strategies to relieve physical strain, including squatting briefly during lulls in the work, prayer, encouragement, and friendly words to each other as well as joking and laughing about their aches and pains.

3.3.3.2. Hospital Site

The hospital site also involved physical strain, especially for the nursing staff and orderlies, who were often on their feet all day lifting loads or pushing heavy gurneys. The doctors were also under physical strain at the hospital, spending much of the day on their feet or walking the corridors, and, in the case of residents, often getting little sleep. Among the four staff members interviewed for the EQ at the hospital site, two responded that they considered physical burdens to be a stressor.

While this type of strain is typical of these staff positions at all hospitals, it may have been compounded at this site by the poor physical environment that resulted from chronic underfunding and lack of resources at this public hospital. The obstetrics ward, for example, was cramped and crowded or dimly lit in some areas. Patients admitted for delivery sometimes had to wait in semipublic areas until a bed was available. Doctors, nurses, and administrative staff had to crowd into small work stations with little room for proper storage of charts and medications. Sometimes walls had not been painted for years and presented a dingy appearance. The media frequently reported on the lack of basic supplies such as wheelchairs and stretchers, cleaning supplies, detergents, mops, and brooms. The doctors and nurses informed the ethnographer that, at times, there was no toilet paper. At another point, delivery room gowns were not available. The ethnographer noted that an anesthesiologist was wearing scrubs from another hospital and asked him about it. He responded that they were not available at this hospital, so he brought his own.

One ethnographer recorded a notable instance of the compounding effect of this type of resource shortage on the physical strain associated with hospital work. She saw a doctor, who was attempting to inject a blood sample into a vial, accidentally squirt blood onto the counter and the floor because the needle was defective. The ward was out of alcohol, which the nurse needed to clean up the blood. She called the adjacent ward to see if alcohol was available there but was told she had to bring a container because they had only one bottle. In other words, she had to walk extra distances around the hospital merely to get a standard supply item.

3.3.3.3. Self-Employed Women

The vendors at the informal economy site were also exposed to a certain amount of environmental strain because they worked outdoors and were subject to fluctuations in the weather. For example, Rose, one of the adolescent longitudinal participants discussed previously, was working as a vendor in the summer while she was pregnant. She continued to work during a week-long heat wave when temperatures reached 100 degrees. She spent time walking up and down the street hawking tee-shirts. Because Rose was a "subcontractor" (i.e., she worked for another vendor who actually purchased the goods from a downtown factory and then hired others to hawk them, as well as manning his own table), she generally did not have a place to rest (some vendors rent space from store owners and can go inside the stores if necessary). Some vendors did not vend in inclement weather, but others, like Rose, vended at all times because they needed the money.

Vendors were also subject to physical strain. For example, Ama, who continued to vend while pregnant, complained of shoulder, neck, and arm pain from having to carry heavy loads of the African cloth she sold. Random interviews with four vendors for the EQ also indicated physical strain associated with this work. Respondents mentioned "lifting heavy loads" and "running from place to place" (to pick up supplies and deliver sold items) as physical demands they found stressful.

We found then that physical strain was a large component of the job strain at the fast-food restaurant, the hospital, and among the vendors. At the other sites, workers were not subject to a great deal of physical strain. It should be noted that at the hospital site, physical strain affected staff at many levels of the hierarchy—from orderlies to doctors. However, administrative staff, who were not involved in direct patient care, had fewer physical stressors. At the fast-food restaurant, physical stress primarily affected the shift crew workers. Managers were more able to move and sit down and were not as affected by the physical demands of the job.

In summary, our ethnographic results suggest that women in the public and service sectors of the economy, where African American women are disproportionately concentrated, are more likely to be exposed to chronic strain from physical and environmental sources and from unpredictability of the pace of work. However, schedule flexibility afforded by shift work may allow a certain degree of autonomy. Thus these factors have both positive and negative aspects that interact in complex ways to structure both experience and perception of stress.

3.3.4. Role Hierarchies

The structuring of jobs into hierarchical relationships at a job site and the degree to which relationships between workers are highly regulated may be a source of acute stress and chronic strain. Previous research has indicated that role hierarchy may be a stressor for workers at lower positions. Ethnographic research in this study indicates that there are also stressors for women at the top of the hierarchy, which may be mediated by gender and race. Here again, fieldwork identified general patterns, which may merit further research.

3.3.4.1. Fast-Food Restaurant

Jobs at the fast-food restaurant were rigidly hierarchical, and every position was defined as it related to the other positions. People in different positions wore different uniforms to clearly mark their place in the hierarchy. The position hierarchy was determined by age and experience. In order of status from low to high, the positions ranged from legal minors who were always part-time shift crew and could work only certain hours; regular shift crew who worked the cooking stations, did cleanup duty in the back area, and removed garbage; cash register workers, who were given the position after they gained experience at the work stations; hosts/hostesses who bussed tables and greeted visitors; crew or station chiefs responsible for supervision of the work stations; swing managers; shift managers; and finally, the general managers (one for each restaurant). The owners of the fast-food restaurant franchise were at the top of the hierarchy and usually were in the restaurant every day.

Participant observation at the site indicated that there were few tensions between people in adjacent positions in the hierarchy (between shift crew and station chiefs, for example); rather the sources of tension were between personnel near the top of the hierarchy and those nearer the bottom (the shift and general managers and the crew, for example). These tensions arose over issues of pay, hours of work, and general perceptions of unfair treatment.

For example, several workers interviewed by the ethnographers claimed that managers sometimes tried to cut crew members' pay by altering the hours worked on the workers' time sheets. Other workers complained that managers did not assign them to desired shifts or let them work longer hours; still others indicated that they had been let go for unfair reasons. On the other hand, the ethnographers observed many instances of good-natured exchange, support, and joking between people in the various roles in the hierarchy. Some of the shift and swing managers were particularly praised by crew members for their ability to be supportive. As ethnographers participated in the crew work, managers kept a friendly eye on them and gave encouragement and advice. Managers, all of them African American or Latina (about half were women), recognized that they had to both meet the demands of the job and be supportive of the crew workers as well. One man indicated, for example, that he would like to see the "girls" (referring to crew shift workers) do well, but they needed to be more diligent in completing their tasks. Another swing manager, a woman, mentioned that she liked to help the crew stay upbeat and positive. Sandra, a longitudinal participant and single mother in her mid-30s, who had been successively promoted from shift crew to swing manager, stayed close to the shift crew workers and tried to mediate at times between them and higher level staff.

The owners of the fast-food restaurant presented an interesting example of potential sources of stress for women at higher levels of role hierarchy. They were perceived as supportive of the pregnant workers; all the pregnant women at the fast-food restaurant interviewed by ethnographers reported receiving positive support from the owners. The owners provided encouragement and, at times, material support. In Sandra's case, they gave her furniture for her new baby and helped her find an apartment. The owners, two African American women, had both worked in the private corporate sector before they decided to become entrepreneurs. In several interviews, they discussed at length the difficulties African American women face in starting and operating a business. Their start-up difficulties included applying for and going through rigorous training required by the franchise corporation, finding access to credit, establishing business relationships with banks and other financial entities (for example, the first bank they trusted with their account lost about $3,000 worth of sales receipts), and undertaking extensive renovation of the sites of the restaurants. They perceived that some of their difficulties stemmed from being women franchise owners and some occurred because their franchise was in Harlem. The franchise corporation extracted a certain percentage of sales revenue in the form of rent and for purchase of the franchised supplies. The owners stated that because they were in a poor community, they set lower prices, and therefore their profit margins were smaller.

In addition to these types of business difficulties, the owners expressed feelings of conflict about their desire to, on one hand, support both the community in general and their workers and, on the other hand, make a profit to maintain and expand their business. They joined a support group of African American women entrepreneurs and worked with other Harlem business leaders to support community-based economic development. They also hired workers from prison work-release programs and tried to be supportive of generating a career path for workers. However, they often had to fire workers for a variety of reasons. They stated that they deliberately hired workers who lived in other parts of the city (such as the boroughs of the Bronx and Brooklyn) because they would not be tempted to slip food to friends or family members. The cash registers at the fast-food restaurant were under surveillance from video monitors. This negotiation between monitoring workers and enforcing business practices on the one hand and providing support and opportunity on the other at times was perceived as conflictive and stressful.

3.3.4.2. Hospital Site

Hierarchies at hospitals are well documented and similar to those found at the fast-food restaurant, made visible by marked differences not only in roles and duties, but in uniform and other outward indicators. In our study, tensions between people in different roles were clearly evident and could erupt into vocal conflict. Some of the tensions between staff were a direct result of the shortage of supplies and resources at the hospitals. Several staff at the hospital commented on interoccupational, race, or gender tensions that may have been exacerbated by difficult conditions. A nursing supervisor noted that the biggest challenge was "treating people as individuals, with respect and dignity ... and this is hard when people are stressed and overworked."

Although most African American women in the health care sector are concentrated in the lower echelons, the hospital site in our study offered some insight into potential sources of stress for middle-stratum and professional women. There were racial and gender issues at each level. Some nurses expressed resentment about the wage differential and hierarchical relationship with physicians, which some suggested were aggravated by ethnicity, race, and gender issues often exacerbated by the presence of a significant number of graduates of foreign medical schools. Nurses commented, "They still have the power and the bucks," or "They're the ones making the big bucks," and "The doctors think what they have to do is more important than what you have to do."

On the other hand, several African American women professionals thought they did not get the service and respect accorded to their male counterparts. An African American woman nurse practitioner, for example, commented that, though it varies with individuals, "African American women professionals have a particularly difficult time." She reported that sometimes nurses and clerks "will quickly fill the orders of male practitioners, but I have to insist in order to get procedures scheduled for my patients." A young African American female resident noted that she frequently was unable to get her questions answered by nurses and nursing technicians, and the ethnographer observed her after unsuccessful attempts to get her question answered saying to the nurses, "This is a question you are supposed to answer."

An attending white physician commented on the tensions between doctors and nurses. She thought it was variable, depending on the individuals involved, but that "tensions and prejudgments" were more overt at this institution than in other places. She suggested that, in this situation of resource scarcity, people's shortcomings and prejudices were "unmasked," and they may express themselves without "social civility."

3.3.4.3. Social Service Site/Child Care Site/Self-Employed Women

In contrast to the two sites where role hierarchy was rigidly defined were those where there was minimal or no hierarchy. Thus, at the social service delivery agency and at the family child care site, as well as with the self-employed women, autonomy and consensus style decision-making procedures were prevalent and generally perceived by workers as a positive aspect of the work site. At the social service agency, for example, the entire staff, from the director to case workers to clerical help, informally gathered together to discuss agency business or to make decisions. The site director's office door was often open, and program managers' desks were in the same rooms with their staff. The self-employed women perceived the advantage of working in nonhierarchical settings.

For example, Billie, a self-employed woman recruited from a neighborhood site, who was a partner in a production company, compared working for herself with her previous employment as a bartender. She stated, "I was making $800 a week [at bartending].... And then I realized [the relatives of her husband] were looking down on me.... The best-paying job is the one that you control and make your own salary. That's the bottom line." Additionally, Celine, an independent consultant, considered a career in media production but decided to freelance because of the autonomy this avenue provided. In the EQ, respondents frequently listed having their own business or working for themselves as an ideal job situation.

In summary, although the ethnographic evidence did not reveal strong patterns of coping strategies to counteract the stressors generated by role hierarchy, it did suggest that, for certain women in managerial or professional fields, considerations of gender and race may cut across divisions fostered by hierarchy. Hence race and gender may interact to produce conditions where African American women in managerial and professional positions are exposed to a unique type of job-related stressor. This stress may stem from the ways in which these professional women sometimes experience conflictive tensions between their status in the occupational and class hierarchy on one hand and race and gender solidarity on the other hand. Second, stress may stem from well-documented constraints of race and gender discrimination despite achievement. Further research is needed to investigate whether women in these strata are able to draw support or offer support across hierarchical boundaries and whether their actions and emotions protect them from stress or in fact increase their level of exposure to stress.

3.3.5. Provider–Client Interactions

In sites where a major part of the work involved interacting with customers or clients, these interactions could be tense or conflictive and thereby serve as specific sources of chronic strain. To our knowledge, little research has been published on the potential stressors and strains related to service provider–client interaction. Because African American women are concentrated in the service sector, the impact of this potential source of stress on their reproductive health should be further investigated. Fieldwork identified two different ways in which these interactions were perceived as stressful. First, interactions with clients were stressful when clients were erratic and unpredictable in their behavior; second, interactions were stressful when service providers attempted to cope with clients who were deeply stressed by chaotic economic conditions. The first type of interaction occurred frequently at the fast-food restaurant, and the second was more of a stressor in the social service delivery sites.

3.3.5.1. Fast-Food Restaurant

At the fast-food restaurant, the women who worked at the cash registers reported to ethnographers their difficulties in interacting with customers who could be rude, demanding, or hostile. An ethnographer observed an incident involving Diana, who was about 4 months pregnant at the time, working at the cash register. A customer, instead of placing her entire order at once, made Diana go back and forth for each item. When the customer noticed that Diana was getting annoyed, she asked, "Why? It's your job," to which Diana replied "Yes, it's my job, but you could make it easier if you tell me the whole order instead of me going back and forth like this." The disregard and condescension of the customers upset her, and on her break Diana called her boyfriend in tears. He suggested she leave early, but Diana did not want to do so because she was worried that her shift manager, whom she liked, would get in trouble.

Another worker described the cash register position as the most difficult because workers were not allowed to talk back to the customers. Ethnographers observed behavior on the part of the customers that included making loud complaints, demanding money back, and even throwing food at the worker. In addition to difficulties that arose from interactions with the erratic or unpredictable behavior of angry clients, there were difficulties related to having to enforce rules although the worker's sympathies might be with the client. For example, an ethnographer observed an incident in which a school child came in with a group of classmates during their lunch hour. Although the classmates had money to buy food, the child had brought her own lunch, which she planned to eat with her companions. Unfortunately, there was a rule that no outside food could be brought into the fast-food restaurant, and the security guard, on observing that the child was eating her own food, told her she wasn't allowed to do that. The girl had no money to buy food and broke into tears, ashamed at having broken the rule. The guard relented, but by then the girl refused to eat. The workers who observed the incident felt the tension of this episode. At times, very poor people wandered into the fast-food restaurant hoping to obtain a little food or use the bathroom, and they had to be turned away because the rules were strictly enforced.

3.3.5.2. Social Service Sites

Ethnographers observed that social service providers often appeared to be caught in the bind of having very limited resources at their disposal with which they could offer services to a low-income clientele who were experiencing escalating pressure from strained and diminished incomes, lack of opportunities, and punitive policies generated by budget cuts in federal, state, and city social welfare programs. The family child care providers were an illustrative case. During the 5-week continuing education class observed by the ethnographers, the most frequent topic of discussion among the participants was sources of tension around relationships with the parents who were their clients. Topics included worries about parent competence (providers commented that they were seeing more younger parents who were unsure of themselves), parents' lack of resources (a provider recounted how parents often did not send enough diapers), and communication difficulties because parents were always in a hurry when leaving or picking up their children. At the end of the course, the facilitator asked the providers to list the sources of stress, and concerns about interactions with parents were mentioned 7 times in a list of 11.

It appeared that relationships with parents were stressful for family child care providers because they could not be easily contained within the boundary between professional duty and personal relationships. The ethnographers observed that the family child care providers were generally committed to the profession and to the welfare of the children. They enjoyed their work and found it satisfying. Yet they also had to adhere to professional regulations, and they had to adopt measures to protect themselves from potential liability. Providers discussed their attempts to assist parents by taking on tasks such as toilet training or offering advice about child rearing (particularly to the younger parents), but these activities could become problematic when parents sought too much assistance or perceived the providers' efforts as intrusions. Difficulties and tensions in domestic work have been discussed extensively in the anthropological and sociological literature (Sanjek and Colen, 1990; Ruiz and DuBois, 1994), but the discussion has largely addressed domestic and child care workers who work for affluent clientele and thus are in unequal status positions. In the case of the family child care providers discussed here, the clientele were largely low-income themselves, and as one of the project's Community Advisory Board members commented, tensions between the providers and the parents often stemmed from general pressures on everyone that resulted from diminishing resources.

3.3.5.3. Legal Services Provider

The lawyers at the legal services provider site presented another example of potentially stressful conditions. The legal services agency observed by the ethnographers was a branch of a citywide organization that provided legal assistance to low-income clientele. At the time of the fieldwork, the agency had a contract with the city to defend indigent clients and also received some private sector support. There were 17 lawyers on staff at the Harlem branch office, and they handled about 5,000 cases per year. The largest division dealt with housing, particularly prevention of homelessness. The agency had been subject to severe cuts and had been unable to service most of the people who requested help, the majority of whom were women (more details about the impact of budget cuts is provided below). Of the 90 families who might come to a weekly legal clinic, for example, only 10 might be represented. The director described the situation as follows: "Because [in] this kind of work, one of the features of providing services to poor people is that the caseloads have always been enormous, the resources have always been meager, and what it means is that people get stressed out and they burn out. And so, attrition is very, very high."

In addition to the normal stressors of litigation, and the fact that there were "enormous caseloads with voluminous, challenging work," the lawyers experienced stress because their clients were poor. Thus, attempting to get the kind of cooperation they required in order to try their cases could be difficult. Because their clients were juggling several different problems at the same time, one or another might take priority. Clients might fail to keep crucial appointments because they were involved in another, equally difficult problem.

The lawyers described uncertainty and time pressure as a source of stress, particularly when procedures had to be carried out in a short period of time or a family, for example, would be evicted: "Will a client have the money to get to court or to make a phone call that's critical? Why does a woman miss an appointment to do an important affidavit? ... When the court date is the next day, this is stressful." They described the "importance of understanding the feeling in the pit of your stomach as an adrenaline rush and activate the fight, rather than the flight [response]."

The lawyers reported that one of their coping responses to the conditions they described had been to get involved on committees to improve court conditions, particularly racial and gender discrimination. Lawyers worked with tenant and housing activists to establish a child care facility at the housing court, for example. They also assisted the Housing Court Tenants' Information Project, which was providing information to tenants about their rights. One of the lawyers also was appointed to the rent guidelines board. Interestingly, while the lawyers reported feeling highly stressed, the respondents to the EQ noted that most women reported having a positive experience in housing court (see Chapter 2). One reason for this may have been that the legal service providers were mitigating the effects of the difficult conditions encountered by their clients.

Sadly, during the course of the research, an African American woman who was a supervising attorney at this agency died of a brain aneurysm at the age of 39. She had joined the agency in 1986 and specialized in housing litigation, including work on federally subsidized and city-owned housing. She was a vocal leader in tenant protection activities and served on committees and task forces to improve housing court. She also taught courses at major law schools in the region.

In summary, the potential source of stress for service providers that resulted from interactions with clients appeared to be exacerbated in conditions where scarce resources and persistent discrimination structured the daily experiences of both the providers and their clients. In these situations, providers seemed to incur additional burdens of stress while trying to mitigate the impact of resource scarcity on their clients. Gender interacted with these factors in an interesting way. Because many African American women are concentrated in the service sector, they bear much of this burden and may be acutely affected by these types of stressors.

3.3.6. Perceived Stress

Throughout the discussion above, workers' perception of sources of stress has been reported (for a discussion of the relationship between perceived stress and adverse reproductive outcomes, see Zambrana et al., 1999). In assessing these statements, it appears that middle-stratum women in professional or managerial positions were more likely to vocalize perceived stress. Customary patterns of conversation in these settings frequently included discussions of being stressed or burned out. For example, stress was a topic of conversation for professional women at the office site who ate lunch together every day. Similarly, ethnographers overheard discussions of stress at the social service delivery site and among professionals at various meetings and conferences they attended during fieldwork. Perceived stress and the ability to vocalize feelings of stress may have been more prevalent as a coping strategy among the middle strata of women. The role this strategy plays in mitigating the actual experience of stressful events should be further investigated.

3.4. CURRENT SOURCES OF EMPLOYMENT AND INCOME INSECURITY

As discussed in Chapter 1, New York City has witnessed major changes in its economic structure as a result of continuing processes of global economic restructuring. Combined with historical patterns of racial discrimination, the immediate effect on Harlem was dramatically evident in the field research as ethnographers witnessed the downsizing, modification, budget curtailment, or outright elimination at all the work sites except the fast-food restaurant.

3.4.1. Office Site

The office site, as discussed, was in the public sector. It was created as part of a New York State economic development effort in 1971. In August 1995, under the newly elected Republican administration of Governor Pataki (elected in November 1994), the site was eliminated entirely, and 37 people were laid off. A small core of personnel were reassigned to other state agencies. The proposal to close the site was included in the early budget documents of the Pataki administration, and some of the office personnel had joined forces with community activists in an attempt to save the agency. Their attempts were unsuccessful.

3.4.2. Hospital Site

Before fieldwork was initiated, the hospital site was subject to persistent underfunding and shortfalls. In addition, the site was affected by the national transformation of the health industry as well as the increased competition for Medicaid patients with private hospitals, who began to accept them for the first time once the government encouraged Medicaid patients to enroll in managed care programs and changed their reimbursement policy. The public hospitals were at a disadvantage in this competition because private hospitals had more resources and were often perceived as offering better-quality care. By fall 1994 and early 1995, personnel were expressing fears about possible closings or downsizing of the hospital as the city government considered a plan to privatize some public hospitals. A licensed practical nurse, when told about the Harlem Birth Right study, suggested that when looking for reasons for high infant mortality we should look at "the stress involved in coming to work and not knowing whether it's your last paycheck."

In another instance, during a focus group session held in late 1994, an attending physician at the hospital said, "Morale. Morale is very low. Because you don't know where the ax is going to fall." Also at the focus group, a hospital administrator commented on stress among the staff:

I find that with my staff there are a lot of call-ins, hypertension, you know, people are out sick for, you know, injuries on the job, you know, things like that. Working under stress is very difficult when you're trying to provide a service that has to do with taking care of another person.... We've had to close some areas in my division ... and do some cross train-ing of staff. In other words, if they're not used to working in a certain area, we had to go ahead and cross-train them so that they can be comfortable, which means it takes time for them to sort of feel comfortable in terms of delivering the care. But, the stress level I find is very much up with the staff. Many of the staff live within the community, and they too are concerned with all the issues in the community, and there is an impact on that. Interesting enough, neonatal intensive care, which has been the critical area for the babies, is under renovation for over a year or so. I've been there a year and it's still under renova-tion, so you have these neonates in a very crowded area and, of course, there's this staff trying to deliver in terms of community care. But ... my staff says they recognize the fact that they are very much a part of the community and would like to do something to enhance the services and healthcare and so forth.

An attending physician also commented:

But, when they cut, all of the hospitals are affected. The public hospitals are affected more because the private hospitals ... have other means ... they have large endowments and all that. We don't have anything. But, it's going to impact on a whole health care system. It's got to. People are going to be sicker. They're going to be sicker ... sick longer. And when you're stressed, you're sick longer, I mean, your immune system drops and you're more vulnerable to disease. So, it's going to affect the whole [population], it may not affect the upper class, but it's going to affect the middle class, too.

In mid-1995, under new leadership, the hospital developed a strategic plan to increase revenues and reduce costs. They proposed structural changes that included improving the appearance of the facility, consolidating services, establishing relationships with community-based providers, expanding the primary care capacity, and streamlining the structure. However, the plan was not fully funded, and the staff size was significantly reduced.

3.4.3. Self-Employed Women

The Giuliani administration campaigned on a platform to improve the quality of life in New York City. As part of this platform, the administration planned to remove all unli-censed street vendors from the streets. Harlem's vendors were targeted as a priority, and on October 17, 1994, 500 police officers were mobilized to remove the vendors. Media accounts described vendors who tried to set up their wares and were removed in police vans. Over 50 vendors and their supporters were arrested. The ethnographers observed events over the next several days as police maintained a heavy presence along 125th Street. Barricades were set up on the sidewalks, and police were stationed approximately every 20 feet between Fifth Avenue and St. Nicholas Avenue. This situation lasted for 3 days, when the police presence was reduced, although some police remained stationed on 125th Street for several weeks afterward. Among the consumers and businessmen on 125th Street, there appeared to be mixed feelings about the event, although even those who supported removal of the vendors were taken aback by the enormity of the police presence and the siege-like appearance of 125th Street. Though it is estimated that about 1,000 ven-dors worked on 125th Street, the alternative site (a lot across from the Malcolm Shabazz Mosque on 116th Street) originally had space for only 200 vendors.

3.4.4. Social Service Sites

All three social service sites were affected by budget cuts. The social service agency's contracts with city agencies were reduced as programs for youth and family social services were eliminated. The family child care workers were informed that New York State had implemented stricter regulations, which would require these providers to pay income tax on the state-subsidized portions of their income. Perhaps hardest hit was the legal services provider, whose contract with the city was reduced by about 11 percent, resulting in many middle managers being laid off. Some of these were long-time experienced lawyers who had chosen to work in the agency instead of joining a private firm because they were committed to helping indigent clients.

In summary, at all six sites, budget cuts and personnel reductions had dramatic effects on the work sites and affected all strata. In addition to these events, general economic conditions such as stagnant wages, lack of employment opportunities, and cuts in public assistance programs also increased insecurity about income and benefits. The consequences of these economic factors are discussed next.

3.5. CONSEQUENCES OF EMPLOYMENT AND INCOME INSECURITY

The consequences of employment and income insecurity were evident in the economic histories of study participants from all social strata, who found themselves, at various times, having to piece together income from a number of sources, including combining state assistance with multiple jobs, losing access to benefits or struggling to maintain benefits, and searching for new jobs.

Almost all study participants (with the exception of one teenager) had worked at some point during their lives. Similarly, among currently unemployed respondents to the EQ, virtually all the women (96 percent) had held paid jobs in the past. Although only 29 percent of employed respondents to the EQ reported holding multiple jobs, participant observation leads us to suspect that such situations are more common. The following cases demonstrate how these larger forces affected the lives of individual women and shaped the nature of stressors. Examined first are the cases of low-income women. It is important to emphasize the real economic hardships of their lives. They often had to scrape together meager resources to feed and clothe themselves and their children. There were several occasions when, because of shortfalls in public assistance and other income-generating strategies, women had to rely on food pantries, church organizations, and charitable groups to make ends meet.

3.5.1. Low-Income Women

Susan, a longitudinal participant, was a 27-year-old mother of five children and lived in public housing. Her history demonstrated the ways women in our study moved serially through employment, informal work, training, and the search for new employment. She was employed at a fast-food establishment but left during the course of the study because of conflicts with her supervisor. She began selling Tupperware and working at a day care center during the day. Four days a week, she also worked the night shift at a bar on 125th

Street that was owned by a family friend. She went to work at 11 pm and worked until the early hours of the morning. She also received supplemental income through a public assistance program, although this income stopped when her income from the bar was reported. At the same time, she was taking GED classes and registered for training for certification to become a home health aide. This training was free for those on public assistance, and Susan had been on the waiting list. She was finally called after she was technically removed from public assistance. Susan had begun the program and purchased the uniform when the program was defunded because of budget cuts. She had attended several sessions and taken a series of tests on which her lowest score was 80 percent. After the training, she had expected to find a job paying $7.00 an hour. She told the ethnographer that the program offered no benefits but she was hopeful that, after getting initial experience, she would be able to find work with the "better" agencies, which do provide benefits. Susan was frequently short of money. In 1994, her children did not attend the first day of school because she did not think she had appropriate clothes for them; by the end of the study we lost contact with her because her phone was cut off.

Others who followed similar strategies among our longitudinal participants included Gina, who was on public assistance at the time she was recruited for the study and used her time off from work to enroll in courses at a 4-year college. Gina also worked in the informal sector; she had a series of odd jobs, including babysitting for neighborhood women. As the center of an extended support network (discussed in the next chapter), she spent much of her time helping other women procure resources. Another longitudinal participant, Sharon, in her early 30s and unemployed when we met her, also had worked a series of secretarial jobs before she resigned because of an episode of depression. Several of Sharon's neighbors, also single women, similarly tried to string together odd jobs, public assistance, and periodic training programs.

Other low-income women combined low-wage work with school and supplemental public assistance. For example, Reina, the 19-year-old longitudinal participant, worked at a number of fast-food restaurants after she dropped out of high school. She compared this experience with slavery and said they did not appreciate her hard work. When she became pregnant, she was seeking a job as a cashier but soon gave up and decided to return to high school. Because she was pregnant, she was able to enroll in the Special Supplemental Nutrition Program for Women, Infants, and Children (WIC), and she received health care temporarily through the P-CAP program for pregnant women. However, when she attempted to get public assistance, she was denied, and at the end of the study she was still attempting to get benefits. She enrolled the baby in Medicaid soon after her birth. Reina also completed high school but had made no concrete plans by the time the study ended.

Like Gina, Latoya, a 20-year-old longitudinal participant, combined attending college with low-wage work at a fast-food restaurant. She had worked at the fast-food establishment for 5 years, since the age of 14. She took 1 month off for childbirth and, as a young mother, attended college and worked at the same time. She stated that she had not had a raise from the fast-food establishment since she began work 5 years before. When we met her, she worked the afternoon shift 4 days a week and sometimes on weekends. After the birth of the baby, she was able to receive assistance from WIC, and she had access to Medicaid for the child's health care. Unhappy with the low wages she was earning, she undertook and passed an exam for a bank teller and was looking for a job in that area toward the end of the study period. She stated: "I want something better for myself.... I have an education and I'm proud of it." However, by the end of the study, Latoya told ethnographers she often felt tired, slept a great deal, and had been diagnosed with anemia. She quit the job at the fast-food restaurant and curtailed her college courses.

In addition, even women with relatively stable employment found that they had to supplement low wages to make ends meet. Sandra, a longitudinal participant who was recruited at a fast-food restaurant, was 32 years old and had worked at the fast-food site since it opened under new ownership. She was hired from a work-release program. By the end of the study period, she had been paroled. After working shift crew, she completed a management course and worked her way up to swing manager. A raise and promotion that she thought were due from the fast-food restaurant were delayed. As her baby reached about 6 months, she found her income was inadequate, so she worked some odd jobs after hours; she applied for another job as a cleaner/janitor in downtown offices. When this job did not come through, she found in another borough a restaurant job that included a promotion and raise.

The vendors in the informal economic sector represented a special case with respect to income security. The vendors, according to a partial census conducted by an ethnographer, exhibited a wide range of incomes. Some, who had long-established sites, could earn $30,000 or more annually, while others net as little as $20 a day. Some were well enough off that they could subcontract others to hawk their wares. However, most of these appeared to be males. The women vendors earned less income and worked more erratically. There was also some difference between the African vendors and the African American vendors. Some of the African vendors worked seasonally, traveling between New York and their home countries and sometimes Europe. Others, such as Ama, a longitudinal study participant, were more permanently settled in the United States but often were supported through kin and immigrant networks. The African American vendors, on the other hand, were more varied in their reasons for vending and in the way they pieced together income and benefits.

For example, Aurora, a longitudinal participant recruited from this site, began to work as a vendor after separating from her husband, a sanitation worker who contributed to the support of their children. She sold handmade picture frames on the street. She first began working when she was in high school at a state-run summer employment youth program. She worked with them for three summers at a day care center, a summer program for children, and a summer camp. After graduating from high school, she worked at an inventory company for 6 years. While doing that she also worked part-time at a temporary secretarial agency and attended college full-time. She stopped working when she got married, but for a few years did some "seasonal work" during the holidays to earn money and was employed again at the inventory company for several months. She said that while she was vending she was able to put together money for rent, but when she was unable to vend anymore after the vendors were removed from 125th Street, she had to apply for public assistance because her ex-husband did not make enough money to fully support the family.

The elimination of the vending site forced these women to reconsider their income strategies. When they were interviewed just before their eviction, many remained uncertain about what they would do. Aurora had been able to work out an arrangement to sell her crafts in two small stores. However, there was no guarantee that her wares would sell there. Ama decided to make and sell food to the largely African hair braiders who worked in small salons or from their homes throughout Harlem. Many of the vendors who agreed to relocate to the market provided by the Malcolm Shabazz Mosque were African. Thus, the unreliable income provided by vending and the uncertainty that it induces must be weighed against the advantages reported above from schedule flexibility and autonomy that vending affords. At least for those at the lowest income levels from this type of employment, the problems generated by its unreliability appeared to outweigh any advantages in autonomy or control of pace.

As low-income women pieced together income from these strategies, they also had to piece together benefits, including health care, public assistance, and child welfare benefits. The struggle to actually obtain benefits and the stress this entails were discussed in the preceding chapter. However, it is important to note here that piecing together benefits in this manner placed low-income women in a precarious position because they had to juggle different levels of income and potential loss of benefits if their incomes rose. Thus, Sandra had P-CAP health insurance (a city- and state-funded program) and private insurance while she was pregnant, but she lost both after the postpartum period. At that point, she was not eligible for Medicaid, although she was able to get insurance for the baby through the baby's father's job benefits. After she was cut off from P-CAP, Sandra applied for an insurance policy through a private carrier but was rejected. The owners of the fast-food restaurant offered the workers an opportunity to enroll in a program with a private carrier, but Sandra thought the program was too expensive and the benefits it offered were insufficient for her needs.

The most stable benefit women received was the Section 8 housing subsidy from the federal government, which has more flexible income requirements. However, there was a long waiting list to obtain Section 8 subsidies, and there was also a long waiting list for entry into housing. It is interesting to note that it was low-income, steadily employed women who had the most difficulty accessing health and other benefits because they were often ineligible for benefits available to poorer women who were already on other forms of public assistance. This phenomenon has been documented nationwide, and recent reforms in health care insurance provision (such as protection for those who change jobs and increased coverage for children) do not help these women. Because these women, as reported here, are subject to a variety of interrelated economic stressors, lack of access to benefits appears to be even more stressful.

Among the currently employed women who were EQ respondents, overall 74 percent reported health care benefits, 63 percent had paid vacations, 52 percent had maternity leave, 70 percent had sick days, 26 percent received child care, 52 percent received pensions, and 56 percent received social security. Certain job benefits differed by level of education, however, and ironically, women with more education frequently had fewer benefits. For example, 84 percent of women with a high school education or less had health care benefits, compared with 57 percent of women with more than a high school education. Seventy-one percent of those with a high school education or less had maternity leave benefits, as opposed to 29 percent of those with more than a high school education. Fifty percent of those with less than a high school education had sick days, compared with 20 percent of those with a high school education or more. Sixty-three percent of those with a high school education or less had pension benefits, compared with only 27 percent of those with more than a high school education. Eighty-four percent of women with a high school education or less had social security, compared with 29 percent of those with more than a high school education. Some benefits did not differ across education levels;

more than half of women had vacation benefits (63 percent), sick days (70 percent), and disability benefits (57 percent). Approximately half had pension benefits (46 percent) and disability benefits (54 percent). For the most part, women believed their benefits were adequate. Eighteen percent of women had other benefits, such as dental and retirement benefits. Forty-three percent of women with more than a high school education reported having no benefits, compared with 17 percent of women with less than a high school education and no women with a high school education.

Health insurance coverage was obtained in a number of ways by women across educational levels: 51 percent of women received Medicaid, and this was reported by women at all educational levels (42 percent, 52 percent, and 56 percent); 29 percent reported having a private insurance company (42 percent, 22 percent, and 0 percent); 33 percent reported an HMO managed care plan (17 percent, 41 percent, and 33 percent); and 18 percent reported paying out of pocket (33 percent, 11 percent, and 17 percent).

Nearly one-third (30 percent) of the women reported they had never taken a vacation. Of the women who reported they had ever taken a vacation, 15 percent of them have not had a vacation in more than 5 years. On average, the women who had taken a vacation reported that their last vacation was for 17 days.

Among currently unemployed women respondents to the EQ, job benefits differed slightly by level of education, with women who had a high school education being more likely to have benefits than those with either more or less education. For example, 85 percent of women with a high school education had health care benefits, while only 27 percent of women with either more or less than a high school education had health care benefits. Seventy-seven percent of those with a high school education had vacation benefits, as opposed to 50 percent of those with less than a high school education and 44 percent of those with more than a high school education. Sixty-nine percent of those with a high school education had maternity leave benefits, as opposed to 43 percent of those with more or less than a high school education. Seventy-seven percent of those with a high school education had sick days and social security, as opposed to 47 percent of those with more or less education. Other benefits did not differ across education levels: only 21 percent of women had child care benefits, although approximately one-half had pension benefits (46 percent) and disability benefits (54 percent). Eighty-five percent of women with a high school education had some type of benefits, as opposed to 50 percent of women with less education and 33 percent of women with more education.

In summary, for low-income women in our study, employment and income insecurity and the precariousness of access to benefits added a magnitude of stress, uncertainty, and unpredictability to their lives. Reasons for vulnerability included lack of access to adequate income from jobs, instability of jobs, and lack of employment opportunities. Furthermore, there was a lack of employment with secure, long-term benefits. The struggle to obtain benefits was a particular type of stressor, and the sudden loss of benefits may have acted as an acute source of stress. The direct impact of these stresses and strains on health must take into account both constraints on access to health care itself as well as stress that results from the efforts to piece together meager income, get access to benefits, and take care of children.

3.5.2. Middle-Stratum Women

The economic histories of middle-stratum women participants demonstrated that, while they may have had long periods of employment that enabled a certain degree of stability, they also faced income and employment insecurity because of structural factors that determined their positions in the national occupational structure. Several of our middle-stratum participants were located at sites that were subjected to downsizing and elimination. During the study period, all middle-stratum women at the office site lost their jobs and attached benefits, some of the legal service agency managers were laid off, and some of the hospital's staff, including nurses, were laid off. As with the vendors in the low-income group, the self-employed women in the middle strata were subjected to economic fluctuation as a result of factors outside their control. It is interesting to note that 72 percent of the respondents to the EQ reported that they lived from paycheck to paycheck. When their responses were examined by educational level, no significant differences could be found.

Middle-stratum women subject to downsizing or job elimination incurred significant problems, primarily because they had difficulty finding another job. Madeline, a longitudinal participant, continued to believe that the agency where she worked (the office site) could be saved despite rumors to the contrary. On the day the staff were told that the agency would be subsumed under another agency, Madeline told the ethnographer that she was so "devastated" she went home in a "catatonic" state. She reported that all she could do was go to sleep because she was so depressed and that she had been unable to leave the house. In the months before the closing, she worked with employees on petitions and letter-writing campaigns, although she reported that many of the staff had given up. Though she participated in actions to challenge this situation, she also seemed to internalize it. She reported to the ethnographer that she was "very disappointed in herself" because she was not prepared for the competitive nature of today's market. Furthermore, she believed the equipment, training, and technology at the agency did not allow its workers to be prepared for work elsewhere. She declined to go to a job fair, which she thought would not do any good, and when asked by a coworker what she would do, she replied that she felt suicidal. She borrowed money from her pension to pay bills, received 8 weeks severance pay, and applied for unemployment. At the end of the study, she was seeing a therapist and trying to start a business in flower arrangement and fashion consulting. The agency had provided full health benefits, including a medical plan, a dental plan, and mental health benefits. These benefits extended for only 90 days after the agency was terminated.

For middle-stratum women in professional and managerial positions, tensions and stress resulted from the uncertainty and unpredictability surrounding jobs in the public and service delivery sector. For months before decisions were made about the extent and nature of budget cuts, public discussion and rumors created high levels of anxiety and low morale for personnel in affected sites. At the hospital site, before the 1995 reorganization, the ethnographers observed a great degree of anxiety and tension on the part of the staff. One nurse commented on the possibility of privatization: "Buyouts mean that they fire you and give you enough money to buy a cup of coffee and a newspaper so that you can go and look for another job." Staff constantly discussed the possible effect of policy decisions. Some people described the tension they felt between their commitment to working at this particular hospital and the problem of "burn-out." An African American third-year woman resident told us that she came to the hospital because this was the population she wanted to serve. She added that she thought she was able to learn more because of the variety of problems, despite the inordinate amount of time spent on paperwork and scheduling tests instead of caring for patients. Anita, a nurse and longitudinal participant who had been working at the hospital for several years, described herself as "burned out."

Under these conditions, these middle-stratum African American women may have been caught between the commitment to serve needy people and frustration at not being able to control resources and decision-making processes. However, workers at all levels also reported things they liked about working at the public hospital. A frequent theme, which perhaps counteracted the negative stressors, was the feeling of esprit de corps. One attending physician who had worked at the hospital for many years said she continued to work there because they were "like a family to me." She noted that she knew people at all levels of the hospital, from janitors to administrators, and they all asked her about her children. She said that knowing people made "a difference" to her. She liked "the idea of fighting to make things better" and believed that things can be improved if one "pushes." A registered nurse who worked for this hospital from 1972 to 1977 went to work in another city and then returned in 1991; she described herself as "born and raised in [this] Hospital" and stated that she liked working there. During the discussions about budget cuts, unions and others initiated numerous demonstrations, and staff including physicians, nurses, administrators, janitors, and housekeepers wore buttons declaring "Save [this] Hospital."

Finally, although self-employed middle-stratum women enjoyed the autonomy and flexibility that this type of work provided, they also perceived stressors in the uncertainty of their ability to earn sufficient income. The owners of the fast-food restaurant recounted the enormous risks they had undertaken to open the business and how hard they had to work. Billie, a longitudinal participant who was a partner in a small business, discussed the uncertainties of the business: "It's just like last year when we went through it, it was scary enough, but the timing.... I still had other resources. I still had money coming in from somewhere else. And this year is not quite the same, and I've exhausted all my resources, and I've not paid my rent to pay certain things."

Some self-employed women combined a variety of jobs (much like low-income women) to insure income: Noma, for example, a longitudinal participant mentioned above, had a graduate degree but had an insecure source of income because she is an artist. Noma performed as much as possible and also performed at summer festivals. She also taught and had done odd jobs, such as working in a health food store and teaching nursery school, when she could not find performance jobs. Her husband, an artist, had an insecure source of income, too. Celine, another longitudinal participant described previously, did a variety of work, including graphic design, political consulting, and freelance writing. She also managed an economic development project.

In summary, while there were a variety of viewpoints about the meaning and definition of being middle stratum, many people in the study sample perceived this status to be precarious and subject to change at any time. It is interesting to note that young people in Harlem aspired to both achieve professionally and maintain a commitment to their communities. In a group interview held by an ethnographer at the office site, three young interns (two men and one woman), who were all from middle-stratum families and who were pursuing graduate degrees, discussed their aspirations and perceptions of middle-class life. Each of them saw themselves in 10 years as pursuing professional careers. One was in graduate school in architecture and urban planning and saw himself working in architecture, but for inner-city development. His role model was a prominent African American architect who works for community improvement projects. Another was pursuing a doctorate in public policy and saw himself in 10 years either practicing law or running for elected office. The young woman was studying urban planning and hoped to also get a degree in business administration and international affairs. She thought she would like to work in international business in Africa. All three discussed the importance for the middle class of staying close to community ties, and one expressed his desire to live in a black community.

3.6. RACE, DISCRIMINATION, AND WORK AS SOURCES OF INTERRELATED STRESS

Middle-stratum participants we studied felt that working with African American personnel was a protective factor that often was compared with experiences of discrimination people had experienced in job settings outside of Harlem. A young intern at the office site recalled working for a large architectural firm and disliking the highly competitive, egotistical atmosphere. Attorneys at the legal services provider discussed how race and gender discrimination was used by adversarial attorneys to intimidate them. One lawyer explained that the landlord attempts to intimidate the tenant and the landlord's lawyer attempts to intimidate the tenant's lawyer. "They see a woman, a minority and what do they say? I'm going to chew you up and spit you out." She described her feeling of being "stressed out" by the current case she was trying, in which a lawyer said to her, "I'm going to get all of your cases and fix your career."

A young professional couple who lived on Strivers Row stated that they worked around white people all day and that this could be very stressful, particularly because of the necessity of self-censuring. The husband, Mr. B, said that he liked to be able to talk about controversial African American issues without someone concluding he was a racist. They discussed their perception of the stressors of working with whites, which ranged from white colleagues wanting to discuss with them every crime African Americans have committed to white colleagues using the word "nigger" in their presence. The wife, Ms. T, said that during the trial of a group of young black men who were accused of assaulting a young white woman in Central Park, she wore a Walkman to screen out the insensitive comments from white people. The couple expressed the feeling that when they came home they could relax as part of a community.

Mr. B felt very strongly that the presence of the African American middle class was very important to communities such as Harlem and that the middle class had to get involved in grass roots activities.

In another instance, Mr. C, who worked at the office site, said that he liked working around black people all the time: "What could be better than this?" He compared his situation with that of friends who worked downtown and made much larger salaries, but "the psychic cost is too great." In the EQ, 80 to 90 percent of respondents reported that the race and ethnicity of their coworkers was a positive feature of their job, and 44 percent of the respondents thought discrimination had affected their employment.

In conclusion, the ethnographic findings demonstrated that multiple work-related stressors may have interrelated with each other, shaped the experiences of women in our study, and affected their well-being. The types of employment and income insecurities generated by these African American women's concentration in the public and service sectors of the economy were the greatest sources of stress and must be accounted for in relation to other stressors. While there were differences across strata for exposure to stress, unemployment and income insecurity had a broad cross-strata effect. Thus public health interventions not only must target specific components of job strain but must pay attention to the structural conditions of the gender and race hierarchy that place large numbers of African American women in severe conditions of income inequality. In the next chapter, we discuss the ways women in our study, particularly as single heads of household and especially when pregnant, coped with these stressors through the creation and maintenance of support networks.

NOTE

[1] It is interesting to note that the genealogical information collected on our longitudinal participants confirmed the larger statistical trends reported here. These data showed a decline over three generations (generation is defined as a category of matrilineal descent—grandmother, mother, ego) in manufacturing jobs held by the study population from 5 to 2 percent and an increase in professional jobs from 14 to 29 percent.

4

SOCIAL SUPPORT AND REPRODUCTIVE HEALTH

4.1. INTRODUCTION

The importance of social support in health and illness and in reproductive health (Boone, 1989; McLean et al., 1993) has been extensively explored. The literature suggests that support networks are important in recognition, compliance, and treatment during and after (cf. Helman, 1990) pregnancy (Boone, 1989). Though intervention trials to provide social support have found little evidence of increased birth weight or reduced preterm delivery, studies are needed to explore the definition, meaning, and differential effect of social support (Rowley et al., 1993).

Family, though often narrowly defined, has been viewed as a primary support system. Furthermore, the marital tie has been presumed to be a major source of social support, which suggests a strong relationship between marital status and reported well-being. For example, Schulz and Rau (1985) observe, "Perhaps the most powerful normative life-course supportive relationship, in terms of its health protective functions, is the marital relationship."

In Central Harlem in 1990, 69 percent of all households with children under 18 were described as headed by women. The decline of the traditional married-couple family found in Harlem is part of a national trend that now affects all racial and ethnic groups in the United States (Wilson, 1996). It is important to note that the precipitous increase in the number of households headed by women has developed largely in the past 30 years. Before the 1950s, the typical African American household consisted of a two-parent family with the father or both parents working (Gutman, 1976). This household form persisted throughout the periods of Jim Crow, the disruption of the "great migration" north, and ghettoization. For this reason, analysis of what has occurred in the past 30 years to produce such a rapid and devastating transformation in family and gender roles is a major issue among social theorists. Sociologist Wilson (1987, 1996) has persuasively demonstrated the role of larger structural forces, such as the flight of businesses from cities and the preference of employers for nonblack employees, in producing black male joblessness and low earnings. These findings have been widely discussed and debated (Wilson, 1996). In his recent book, Wilson argues:

> In the inner-city ghetto community, not only have the norms in support of husband-wife
> families and against out-of-wedlock births become weaker as a result of the general trend
> in society, they have also gradually disintegrated because of worsening economic condi-
> tions in the inner city, including the sharp rise in joblessness and declining real incomes.
> (1996:97)

Other scholars have explored the role of additional structural forces, including the
expansion of the criminal justice system as a means of social control and the simultaneous deterioration of the social welfare apparatus (Marable, 1996, 2000); the impact of the
proliferation of illegal drugs, particularly crack cocaine, in the mid-1980s (Hamid, 1993);
and the mass introduction and proliferation of firearms in urban areas (Canada, 1995).

In examining how women actually make decisions about their pregnancies, what
emerges is the importance of family both in women's discovery of pregnancy and in their
subsequent attitudes toward the discovery. This is true not only for adolescents but also for
older women, since "the family" includes a wide array of social relationships with parents,
partners, and affines. The nature of these relationships also has an important effect on the
course of the pregnancies and women's overall experience of their pregnancies, as well as
their long-term health status and that of their families. In this chapter, we examine the role
social networks play in decisions about pregnancy as well as the role of social support systems in maintaining reproductive health and in mitigating stress. We argue that though the
married-couple family form has declined, women frequently form networks, often woman
centered, that have a strong influence on economic survival and childbearing decisions;
that how these networks are recruited may vary with class; and that women relate to men
in a variety of ways, including through men's consanguineal kin networks.

4.1.1. Sources of Stress

We emphasize the ways woman-centered networks serve as a support system to allow
women to have and raise children without a steady income from men and to maintain their
households despite adverse circumstances. However, it is important not to romanticize the
cost of this to women, who have primary responsibility for supporting the household, often
on marginal incomes. Though the disadvantages for children in these households has been
widely discussed and debated, less emphasis has been placed on the consequences for the
women. This section presents, in women's own words, the major source of stress or chronic strain reported in a focus group of women heads of household.

Studies have found that persistently poor families tend to be headed by women (Edin,
1994). For low-income women, as well as for some middle-income women, the lack of
economic resources is a major issue. When asked what they perceived as most difficult
about their lives, single mothers who participated in our focus group on women heads of
household discussed financial difficulties and their attempts to deal with them. One participant commented:

> I would have to say ... basically ... finance.... Finances is a big part of it. Because, if you
> can't support them the way you want, or the way you think they should be supported, then
> it's very hard.

Another participant reiterated:

> Bills, and everything ... paying the bills by yourself. They might need something. They might need a coat. You've got to settle for a $29 coat that's like this thin when you really want something nice and warm so you don't have to buy another next year, you know. Things of that nature. The kids are growing constantly, then clothes cost. You can't buy one without buying the other, you know. My kids, their clothes cost the same as mine. So, try with a budget of $161 every two weeks, try clothing three people, cleaning the house, keeping the clothes clean and you know, things of that nature.

The women tempered the discussion of the stress of finances with a discussion of countervailing emotions:

> Yeah, but when you were talking about financially hard ... that's important too, but I think the main thing is having love, if you don't have love.
>
> Well, you can have love for your child that can't spoil.
>
> As long as he doesn't mind sleeping in his shoes and coats and stuff and like that.
>
> I'm saying that love comes with it regardless. I mean, raising a kid ... that's not ... I mean, that doesn't basically say what's the good part, bad part about raising a child ... I'm saying as far as raising a child ... the finances ... you know, it's like, you don't have it, it's hard. That's what makes it so hard.
>
> But, that's what's make you strong when you have to struggle, you know ... when you're struggling.
>
> If you want something good for your kids, if you have better outlook on life, then, of course, that struggle's gonna come along with a will to do everything within your power to make sure that the kids are well taken care of, you know, by any means necessary.

Other women discussed feelings of depression, guilt, anger, and self-blame, which can be responses to financial strain. One woman related, "I was really depressed, and my daughter is very perceptive, and she picked up on it. And I said that I don't want this kid to have to deal with my emotions because she's 3 years old ... I try not to take it out on her ... I haven't yet, but I'm very conscious of it."

As another source of stress, women in the focus group cited failed expectations and disappointments—specific things they wanted to do but were unable to do because of the constraints of being single parents. These included major goals, such as work and school, as well as personal care, self-care, and sleep. Comments were made such as, "I want to go out, maybe meet a man," "you just want some time to yourself," or "I want to go to work."

> For me, it would be school. That's something I haven't been able to do because of having my kids. I had ... I keep putting it off. The more ... I want to go, the more I can't go. I have to care for them, they come first, that has to wait. But, it's coming along because it's coming to a point where I'm almost in a position to get back and where I could get my diploma because I never finished high school and go further on in my life. I told my kids. I'm supposed to be going to school ... probably part-time or some of the time, so I can get a higher education where I can get a good job and really take care of either of you without having to depend on aid or people outside ... I could say I truly worked for this.

> I have about a year left in college, but it's not because I have my daughter. [It's] because I just got tired of being hungry when I was in college that I started working. So, I would like to finish that ... I used to go to the gym and I don't anymore. Sometimes it's easier going when it's light outside, but I don't think there's any reason for a kid to be out after eight o'clock. So, I just don't do it anymore. I'd like to find a way to get back into that.

> I don't get to go to the gym anymore. I don't have the money to go in there either. It's a long list of things. I would like to go and have myself beautified, I mean, from head to toes. Have my hair done. I'm tired of doing my own stuff. Shop for myself ... I would like to go to the gym, simply to do something, you know, to relax the mind.

> It's like things that I want to do, but I don't have the time. Like she said about being hungry, I'm tired of being broke. That's one thing, too, I want to get a job. She pushed me back a little further. My daughter's 5, and I couldn't wait for her to get into school and be there all day.

When asked about sleep patterns, though a few women (particularly those with older children) said they got enough sleep, most participants thought they did not:

> I sleep 2 hours and then I wake up for an hour, go back ... I never sleep straight through the night, you know. If I get up to go to the bathroom, I know I'm not going to get back to sleep ... I close my eyes, but I sleep in intervals ... Two hours here.

> It varies. Sometimes I worry a lot, and when I do, I don't sleep. And it doesn't matter how many hours I've been up ... it catches up with me. I get to sleep at like 12, because I work at home, so I have to wait for them to go to sleep to do what I have to do, you know, to get my problems together. And then, so I always sleep like 2 or 3 hours at a time ... I work in between or, you know, clean up, taking them to school. I got to take them to school, then I come home, and I lay down with the little one and get up in 2 hours and take another one to the half school program and then come back, and then I got to go pick them up from school, take them to the homework program, and then I lay down for a half an hour to sleep. Then I may get a half an hour sleep over here, so it's never any set time. But, then, after like 2 or 3 weeks, I do need that time to sleep for a whole day. That's when I shoo everybody off and then I sleep for a whole day, you know, and I catch up that way.

> I don't sleep. I might get a little bit or lay down for a little while, 2 hours and then I'm up again or something like that.

Finally, one focus group participant's comments summed up the general perceptions of most of the women:

> Okay, well I feel that being a parent, you should prepare yourself, and you should plan for it. Now, if you just happen to get pregnant, you have to deal with it the best way you know how. And as far as being a single parent, it is hard ... but, you just have to deal with it.... If the father wants to be part of it, or he's gone or whatever, you just have to deal with it, you know. I don't know ... I've dealt with it. His father's gone ... but, I don't really care about that, I just say life goes on and just deal with it and take care of your child, you know.

4.1.2. Coping: Individual Strategies

Clearly, women understood the consequences of raising children as single heads of household. However, they also had developed a variety of strategies to cope with the stressors generated by their circumstances. Women in the focus group referred to above also discussed their individual strategies, including those that were emotion focused, such as spirituality, or problem focused, such as support groups. Their comments included the following:

The only thing that I do is get on my knees and ask God, and He helps me find my way to take care of my daughter and do other things in life. That's the main thing.

Well, I'm a Buddhist and I chant. That helps me through a lot, you know. Because it makes me stronger ... helps me be more determined to change the situation. And other times when I just feel like being depressed, I just like give myself a day and enjoy it. You gotta do it.

I go to St. Luke's.... Every Tuesday they have ... a group where parents can get together. They have coffee and doughnuts and stuff like that. And we just sit there ... we exchange our situations and stuff like that. And I think it's good because, you know, you need some sense of the stuff that's inside of you.

I get on the phone or I write.

These strategies did not differ significantly from those of the respondents to the ethnographic questionnaire (EQ) who, when asked what they did to take care of themselves, responded that they spent time on the following: time for oneself (86 percent), religious/spiritual activities (65 percent), clothing (75 percent), exercise (60 percent), health behaviors (83 percent), medical care (81 percent), education (70 percent), music and arts (68 percent), and miscellaneous others. These varied somewhat by level of education (Figure 4.1).

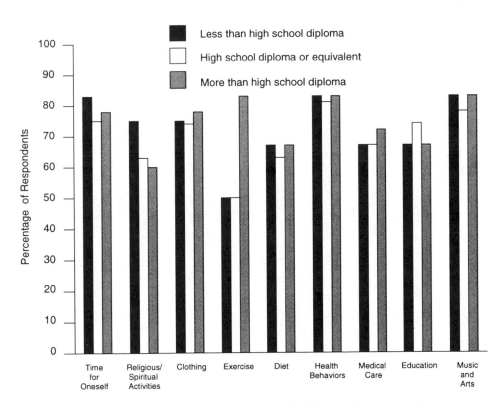

Figure 4.1. Respondents' Stated Methods of Self-Care, by Education Level

When women were asked to think about what went into feeling good about themselves, they responded in the following ways: personal qualities (98 percent), achievements (91 percent), appearance (95 percent), family (89 percent), community (68 percent), work (70 percent), and miscellaneous other qualities. Again, these differed somewhat by level of education (Figure 4.2).

Some individual strategies were less benign. When a mother of eight was asked by the ethnographer how she managed, she laughed and said, "I smoke," as she lit a cigarette. In addition to these individual strategies, women turned to their networks of family and friends as they made critical decisions, including decisions about pregnancy.

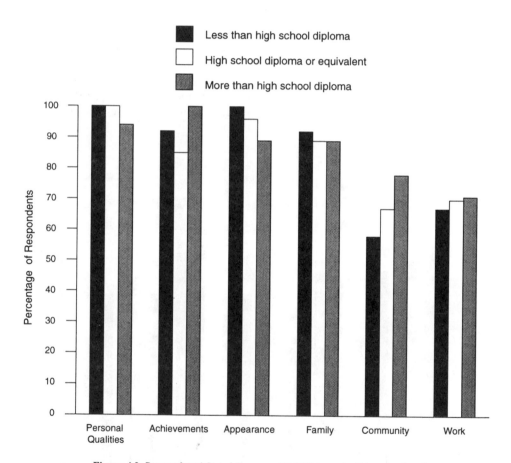

Figure 4.2. Respondents' Stated Sources of Self-Esteem, by Education Level

4.2. SUPPORT SYSTEMS AND REPRODUCTIVE HEALTH

In addition to seeking medical care (discussed in the next chapter), women continued to work, take care of their families, and support their communities—and throughout their pregnancies, they remained enmeshed in a series of social relationships. It was within this context that we examined the everyday practices women used to ensure a healthy pregnancy. Once pregnancy was recognized and its course determined, most women, on their own initiative, took active steps to try to secure a healthy pregnancy.

Just as social and physiological factors structured the range of feelings toward and experiences of pregnancy, so too did they influence the myriad ways women in this study coped with their pregnancies on a day-to-day basis. The degree to which women were able to care for their bodies and ensure their health depended on the circumstances of their lives (as we have documented in previous chapters), but all participants we encountered took some steps at some point to care for themselves. What constituted care, moreover, also was highly variable. It drew on a wide repertoire of knowledge that was not limited to the medical system and the doctor/patient relationship. Rather it also included advice from mothers, grandmothers, aunts, and other relatives; advice from friends; information available in public and commercial media sources; and women's own inventions. Hence, the medical prenatal care that women sought out and received may only have been part of a much wider set of strategies women actively implemented on their own. One of the most significant steps women took to improve their pregnancy outcome was to draw upon existing social support networks of family and friends.

4.2.1. Family Values

Previous studies in Harlem undertaken by one of the principal investigators as well as the participant observation in this study indicated a set of social arrangements involving both men and women that was more complex than the term "female-headed household" implies. Contrary to the culture of poverty model, which suggests deterioration of the family, we found that although economic conditions strained support systems, people perceived family to be important and were involved in a variety of flexible support systems. From these observations, we constructed the EQ to reflect our ethnographic findings instead of simply posing the "standard" survey questions that often are strongly influenced by traditional notions of family. Though policy and planning literature often describe the destruction of the African American family, the EQ found that almost all women (95 percent) commented about the importance of family ties. Overall, 90 percent of women reported that family relationships were most important to them (e.g., "if you don't have your family, you don't have anyone"); 74 percent reported that children were most important ("my children are most important because I birthed them"); 56 percent reported that partner relationships were most important ("always there for me when I need it"); and 58 percent reported that friends were most important ("they are reliable and pick me up when I'm down"). These various types of relationships were not exclusively most important, however, as reflected by the fact that many women reported several different types of relationships as most important. Only 11 percent of women reported that support groups were most important; 16 percent reported that other relationships were most important.

When asked what they meant by family, most respondents included blood relatives over a range of generations: "my kids, mother, and father," "children, mother, and grandmother," "immediate blood relatives," "mothers, brothers, sisters, nieces, nephews, and grandson," "your immediate family, people who are close to me even though they go their own way, it's still there, a phone call keeps that bond." In addition, others included partners, fiancés, husbands, and in-laws in their definition of family. Still others included a broader definition that included "church family," "a group of people getting along together—children, mother, partner, cousins," "the people you are close to," "togetherness, trustworthy, and a friend and the bond we have between us," and "the people that are close to you and that you love and be with the rest of your life and your dog." Respondents referred to relationship ties and support as a component of family as well as the complex relationships that underlie designations of sibling or friend: "being very close-knit, always being there for each other, children and nephew," "sometimes siblings can be more than just a relative ... and a friend is more family than siblings sometimes," and "it doesn't mean just blood relatives—the people I love and care about that love and care about me."

Again, though the literature often portrays the breakdown of family ties, almost every respondent reported maintaining family ties by telephone, and overall 80 percent reported either sending cards or letters. While 35 percent of women reported attending family reunions in the past year, this differed by level of education, with those with less than a high school education reporting a substantially higher rate (75 percent versus 16 percent versus 36 percent). Attendance at births and funerals in the past year was reported more frequently by women with the highest levels of education, however (births, 33 percent versus 20 percent versus 53 percent; funerals, 42 percent versus 48 percent versus 59 percent), while attendance at weddings showed a different trend (50 percent versus 28 percent versus 24 percent).

When asked about the good things that come from participation in family events, respondents reported an increase in closeness to family members: "people become more united," "feel closer to family," "camaraderie—the continued establishments of a relationship," "strengthening the bonds of the family," "gives us a sense of belonging and appreciation for each other," and "realize how much we love each other." Women also reported the benefits of finding out new information about family members, catching up on news, and learning more about family history: "you can catch up on things that have been missing and you could not find out over the telephone," "get to see family members that [you] may not have seen in a while," "get to meet people you did not know was family—or new family members," "learn about the past from older family members especially when we were little," "we get to see each other and find out what's going on in each other's lives," and "bring back memories."

Through participant observation, we found that, while support systems, which were often based on family relationships, were significantly strained by difficult economic conditions, there were a variety of social support arrangements. Hence, respondents to the EQ reported broad social networks. On average, women reported 5 or 6 network members (range, 2–24) who knew them well, whom they felt close to, and whom they could count on for everyday favors, rely on when they were sick, spend time with in social activities, ask to look after their children, talk to about personal matters, count on for a loan of several hundred dollars in an emergency, share happiness with, lean on, give help to, and share their most private feelings with. For example, only 15 percent of women reported having no one to help them when they were sick, only 11 percent reported having no one to socialize with, only 2 percent reported having no one to talk with about personal matters, only 2 percent reported having no one to lean on, and only 4 percent reported having no one with whom they could share their most private feelings. Furthermore, only 20 percent of women reported that there was no one they could count on for an emergency loan of several hundred dollars; interestingly, this did not differ substantially across educational level. All women reported they had at least one person in their network who knew them well.

Women reported that many aspects made them happy about their relationships with friends and family. Most commonly mentioned was a sense that family members were always there for the respondent and offered emotional closeness and understanding: "to share each other's thoughts," "that I can talk to them about anything," "the honesty and understanding," "we understand each other and [are] there for one another," "it's open and we can communicate well," and "they like me for me." Some women talked about the pleasure it gave them to help their family and friends: "I just enjoy doing things for people," "they can depend on me," "I'm able to make them laugh," "we get a chance to relax and not talk about problems," "I'm able to help them if they need me," "the ability to share with another person, to give and receive love," "if they call on me for some type of support, and I can assist, this pleases me," and "knowing that I could be a help to them when they are in need." What comes across clearly is the happiness and sense of security that friends and family relationships provide and the satisfaction the respondents derive from being able to help the people they care about in many ways.

Information from the EQ indicated the importance of various kinds of support from these networks. Overall, 74 percent of the EQ participants reported that they talked with family members about their pregnancy, and 60 percent talked with friends. Family members included partners, husbands, boyfriends, grandmothers, mothers, sisters, aunts, cousins, fathers, uncles, brothers, nieces, and daughters. The importance of family members as a source of information was more significant for women with fewer years of education. Over half the women with a high school diploma or less went to their family for advice, while only 33 percent of those with more than a high school diploma relied on family for advice. Of all family members, mothers were the most commonly relied on for advice, although sisters, cousins, a brother, aunts, and the partner's mother were also mentioned. Approximately 25 percent overall relied on friends for advice, and this did not differ markedly by level of education.

The extent to which women were able to draw upon their social support networks emerged from the EQ data. Overall, 83 percent of women reported help from family members, and 45 percent reported help from friends. Seventy-four percent received some kind of aid from the baby's father.

Though the EQ demonstrated that most women seemed to use support systems, how they recruit and use support systems as well as their effectiveness was influenced by a variety of factors, including the following: class, age, point in the life cycle, and available resources. The ethnographic data demonstrated 1) the variety of ways women recruited various kinds of support; 2) the ways resources available to members of support systems reflected the distribution of wealth; 3) for African American women, the complexity of the relationship between education, occupation, and income; and 4) the class heterogeneity of the families of African American middle-stratum women, who may have been the only ones in their family to attain middle-stratum status.

In the case material cited below, we provide extensive detail to illustrate the interrelationship of the occurrence of potential sources of stress and the use of social supports as a resource for coping strategies.

4.2.2. Low-Income Women

Among the low-income women, in most cases, we found support systems that included friends but were centered around matrilineal kin. This may have partly been a function of age: several studies have found that women in matrifocal households tend to be younger (Boone, 1989), and clearly co-residence may be a factor of age.

Reina, a 19-year-old whose support network of matrilineal kin facilitated her school attendance and care of herself and baby, was a clear example. Reina's immediate kin and her relationship with them played a key role in structuring her attitude toward her pregnancy. Her aunt and her mother supported her decision to keep the baby. Reina's aunt became a source of support for Reina throughout her pregnancy and after delivery. Reina also received support from other family members and from friends. Her mother helped her enroll in the high school for pregnant girls so she could continue her education. Her godmother was also very active in helping her stay in school.

After the birth of her child, the network of social relations remained critical. Reina received child care support from her aunt (who babysat while Reina was at school), her mother (who took care of the baby when Reina went out with her friends), and her cousins. Even though she no longer had a relationship with the baby's father (and he had not contributed any significant monetary support), he was present at the delivery and still visited the baby from time to time.

Similarly, in the case of Latoya we found a strong matrifocal network centered on matrilineally related women across generations. However, the young woman also reported feeling confined by these arrangements. Her case was an interesting illustration of the interrelationships of concomitant positive and negative aspects of networks. Latoya was in her early 20s and a mother of two children ages 4 and 1. When we met her she worked in a fast-food restaurant in Harlem, where she had worked part-time since the age of 14. She also was a student at a junior college. She finished high school while pregnant with her first child and continued as a college student through her second pregnancy. Her goal was to be a writer. She was raised in Harlem, where her mother still lived in public housing with Latoya's younger sister, although by the end of the study Latoya lived in an apartment in the Bronx. Her parents were separated, but they continued to be in contact with each other and with her. Latoya said, "My family taught me that my parents don't have to live together, and they can still love me." Even though she did not live with them, she talked with her family every night.

Latoya had received extensive aid from her consanguineal and affinal family. Her older son lived with her grandmother. During her second pregnancy, she lived with the baby's father and his sister. Her mother provided extensive child care; her father provided her with financial support when she was forced to stop working, and he picked her up from the hospital after delivery. When she was younger and ran away from home, she stayed with her grandmother and her father. With the help of her family, she was able to graduate from high school and begin college while she was a young mother.

Although family was her major source of support, Latoya also had friends. In addition to her family, Latoya's good friend and coworker provided her with emotional support ("I talk to her about my feelings"). They socialized together and her friend sometimes babysat when her babysitter was not available. She found emotional comfort in church. Her child's father and his family provided help. The baby's father, with whom she was still good friends, took the baby on weekends.

Despite her strong support network, in her attempt to work, take care of children, and go to school, Latoya frequently reported feeling tired and depressed. As mentioned previously, at the end of the year that we followed her Latoya was diagnosed as anemic and was sleeping a great deal. We lost contact with her when her phone was cut off.

In the third case, Aurora was older, but her matrilineal kin remained critical to child care assistance. Though Aurora had completed 2 years at a city college before she left to get married, she was primarily a housewife before she started vending several months before she was recruited as a participant in this study. Her ex-husband provided some support in addition to the money she made as a vendor. Aurora said her family was her primary support system: "I have a large family so I get a lot of support. I have eight sisters and I have eight kids, so each of them is claimed by one of the sisters." She reported that one of her siblings "adopted" each child shortly after he or she was born. While she was vending, the children stayed with her mother or a sister. The older ones also helped out with the younger ones. When Aurora delivered her ninth child (which resulted from the pregnancy observed by the ethnographers), one sister stayed with Aurora's children until the oldest child came home from school, and then each of her sisters took a few of the children home. The father of the baby also was very helpful.

A fourth case was that of Gina, who was a nodal point of support for an extended network of kin. At the time of fieldwork, her household included two foster sons (one was her mother's uncle's son, and the other was her mother's sister's son); Ms. U, a 20-year-old woman who was a sister of a partner of one of Gina's cousins; and also, from time to time, Ms. V, a distant cousin also in her mid-20s. Ms. V and Ms. U gave birth to premature infants during the course of fieldwork. Both were living with Gina at the time they were pregnant, and Gina provided emotional, instrumental, and financial support for them. She often accompanied them to their prenatal care visits and to a Healthy Start Program in which they had enrolled. In addition to spending a great deal of time at the hospital with them when they gave birth, Gina also helped take care of their babies when they returned home. Ms. V periodically lived in the Bronx with the baby's father but, because their relationship was unstable, she did not want to permanently reside with him. Ms. V worked part-time, and she was able to help Gina pay the rent on her apartment. Gina and her relatives held a baby shower for Ms. U, which was attended by about 50 people with gifts for the baby. In addition, Gina maintained a close relationship with her own mother, who lived in an apartment in the same building. Her mother worked and provided Gina with emotional and financial support. In addition to these relationships, Gina maintained relationships with a wide circle of cousins, aunts, and uncles. Finally, Gina had over 15 stepsisters and brothers, most of whom lived in the South, but she did not have close relationships with them.

Other cases in which low-income women relied on kin included Rose, an adolescent vendor who ran away during her pregnancy and lived with her grandmother temporarily after the baby was born. Eventually, her grandmother obtained custody of the baby. Additionally, Ama, a Senegalese street vendor, received help from both her sister and her husband in caring for her children throughout her pregnancy.

At times when some mothers were not always supportive, other matrilineal kin often stepped into the breach. Such was the case with Ivory, another pregnant high school student in our longitudinal study, whose mother lived on one of the poorest blocks in Harlem. As mentioned earlier, her case was unusual in that her mother, who was traumatized by the sudden death of Ivory's brother in a hit-and-run accident, had become a heavy drinker and was not available to help Ivory or accompany her on clinic visits. One cold winter morning, an ethnographer received a collect call from Ivory, who was crying and said that her mother had thrown her out of the apartment. Ivory had spent her only quarter on a call to her sister, but the answering machine had picked up. When the ethnographer rushed over, she found Ivory outside wearing only a nightgown. The ethnographer took her to Ivory's sister's house. Ivory stayed there for the rest of the pregnancy, and she planned to stay with her mother's relatives in Philadelphia after the delivery.

To a lesser extent, friends, "other mothers," and other fictive kin were also active in the networks of low-income women. Such was the case with Sandra, a longitudinal participant from the fast-food restaurant site. Sandra had a cesarean section and developed a post-operative infection, so she had to remain in the hospital after delivery. She was able to call on her friends to care for the newborn when the baby was discharged after 3 days. When Sandra came home, everyone was very supportive. Her girlfriends had organized a well-attended baby shower for her, and she received baby clothes, a stroller, and other parapher-nalia. Joe, the baby's father, was also supportive. He gave her gifts, paid for the television in the hospital, and bought her food. With the help of the owners of the restaurant where Sandra worked, she found a new apartment. As previously mentioned, these owners also bought furniture for the apartment, and she and Sarah, the baby, settled in. Early on in her pregnancy the restaurant owners had also advised Sandra about her prenatal options.

4.2.3. Middle-Stratum Women

Although these woman-centered support systems have been documented primarily among low-income women, the middle-stratum women studied also recruited support systems. The ethnographic work pointed to the complexity of the situations of many middle-income women and the variation of women so categorized. Though most included both family and friends, there seemed to be a tendency for middle-income women to have support networks composed more of friends than of family, while family was more important for less-privileged women. This tendency was verified by the EQ, where we found that women with less than a high school education and those with a high school education were more likely to report that family relationships were most important (92 to 98 percent), while women with more than a high school education were most likely to report that their friends were most important (78 percent). Furthermore, the EQ revealed that the higher the level of education, the more fre-quently family was reported as the main source of stress. Family was reported as a main source of current stress by 25 percent of women with less than a high school education, 22 percent of those with a high school education, and 44 percent of those with more than a high school education. As we examine the cases of middle-stratum women, it is also important to note, as discussed earlier, the complexity of the interaction of factors such as education, income, and benefits and the heterogeneity of middle-stratum families with respect to class status.

Three cases (Billie, Anita, and Robin) illustrated the variation within the social net-works of middle-stratum women. None of the three was pregnant when participating in the study. Billie presented an example of an unusually strong support system composed of both family and friends, which allowed her access to emotional, material, and informa-tional resources. Though Billie could be characterized as relatively privileged based on income, occupation, and lifestyle, she had only a high school education.

Billie was in her late 30s. She had lived in various parts of New York City and at the time of the study lived on a block of brownstones in Harlem. She had been divorced from the father of her 23-year-old son for many years. After finishing high school, she had worked as a clerk and in the recording and broadcasting industries; she finally became co-owner and vice president of a small company. She had disposable income and was able to travel abroad on vacations.

After her marriage dissolved, she and her then-young child had lived with her mother and sister. She had since remained close to her family, and the year we were in contact with her she cooked Thanksgiving dinner for 23 family members. However, she also had a fairly strong network of friends and colleagues. She said of her women friends, "Sisterhood is real; I have friends who are as close as sisters." She remarked that should she lose her housing, she could always find a place to stay.

She also had people from whom she could borrow money. She had borrowed money from her son's godfather to send her son to college and had paid it back over several years. She also had a platonic male friend to whom she was very close: "I know that he would take a bullet for me." She described him as a remarkable individual who himself had raised his three daughters in public housing after his wife committed suicide, and he was able to give them each $15,000 to get started in life. Billie reported that she could borrow money from this friend as well as from her oldest sister. She described times in life when she was "struggling," and her friend had left blank checks for her to pay her phone and other bills. She did not borrow money from her girlfriend, but her girlfriend employed her for services, such as interior decorating, that could pay several thousand dollars. The ethnographer commented that Billie often seemed to be straddling two worlds with her networks: her working-class family and her middle-stratum friends.

Anita, on the other hand, whose family demonstrated the heterogeneity frequently found among African American middle-stratum women, primarily relied on friends and neighbors. Anita was in her early 40s and was a registered nurse who worked at a large public hospital in Harlem. She had been divorced twice and had two children, who were 16 and 7. She had had a difficult life and for a time was on welfare before she trained to be a nurse. Anita's father, who died when she was a teenager, was a politician and community activist. Her mother did not attend school beyond high school. Her younger sister, a medical doctor, was married to another doctor. Her younger brother did not attend college and worked as a vendor. In the course of discussing family, Anita remarked on the stratification that characterized two branches of her family; one branch did fairly well financially, and another branch had low income. Though she gave financial assistance to her brother and godmother, her primary support consisted of friends and neighbors. Her older child and neighbors helped with child care. For example, one day when she had to work unexpectedly, her neighbor downstairs, who had four children, watched her youngest daughter for her.

Though Anita had friends with whom she socialized and neighbors who helped with child care, she bore the full responsibility of work in the home. When asked if she had anyone who would help her with housework, she said, "No. No, no, no. I wish I did; I'm kind of angry about it, actually." When asked about help when she was sick, she replied, "No one offers, and there is no one I would call. I just try to grit my teeth and get through it ... not that I don't want to have someone to call. If I was in Miami, I could call my mother and she'd help me out.... I just put my life in the hand of the good Lord and He carries me through, I guess." She stated that she did not have anyone she would feel comfortable borrowing money from in an emergency. She said that she "couldn't ask because folk don't have it." When pressed, she thought that perhaps she might ask her sister, since she and her husband were both doctors; but because her sister had told her they didn't have any money, Anita had never asked them for anything. She noted that she had worked hard not to be in the position of having to ask anyone for anything and had not had to do that since moving to New York.

Third, Robin represented perhaps the clearest case of middle-stratum woman who relied principally on friends for support. As previously mentioned, Robin lived with her husband in a brownstone they owned in Harlem. Robin had made friends with several of her neighbors, all of whom appeared to be middle stratum. They provided each other with emotional support and, occasionally, instrumental support (as when her friend, Ms. W, relied on Robin for babysitting). Robin also was friendly with elderly people on her block, who watched her house for her.

Two other middle-stratum women, Noma and Fatima, illustrated the operation of support systems specifically during pregnancy. Noma presented an example of a more solid family with middle-stratum/professional status based on education. Her income, however, was sporadic and episodic. She was able to address this disadvantage in part by calling on a fairly wide network of family and friends, which she was able to draw on during her pregnancy.

As noted earlier, Noma was a young performing artist. She had recently moved to a rented apartment in Harlem. She lived with her partner, who was a musician, and her 7-year-old daughter from a previous marriage. She was recruited into the study when she was about 7-1/2 months pregnant, held a master's degree, and had irregular income because both she and her partner worked in the arts.

Noma had strong relationships with her family. Both her parents were college educated; her older brother was an entrepreneur who had a master's degree, and she described her teenaged half-sister as Ivy League bound. Her mother traveled from Washington, DC, to visit her, and Noma visited her father in Florida. Other than her partner's sister, however, Noma had no kin in the immediate area. She emphasized that this was particularly a problem for child care. Nonetheless, during the time when we followed her, we observed that Noma was able to recruit far-away relatives for relatively long-term, rather than immediate, child care. When she had to go on tour, she sent her daughter to stay with her mother's mother in Los Angeles or to her father and stepmother in Florida. Her partner's friend and that man's girlfriend also babysat occasionally.

Noma stated she did not like to borrow money but could borrow from her father in an emergency without being expected to repay it immediately. A few years before, when she borrowed $4,000 from him, he said, "Pay me back when you can." She said that she did not like to ask her mother for monetary aid because her mother did not have as much money as her father did. Despite the fact that her brother was relatively well-off, she did not like to ask him for money because she considered him "very tight with a dollar."

Though Noma described herself as isolated, the ethnographer observed that she was consistently able to call on a wide network of friends and young women colleagues to help her with babysitting, when she was rehearsing and performing as well as in other emergency situations. Her friends donated money to buy her a washer and dryer, and they donated furniture. She was also able to call on her friends for rides (picking up kin from the airport) and for babysitting. When her car was impounded in Washington, DC, friends and family helped her pay to reclaim it. She said that her partner's mother, father, and step-mother would also help them out in an emergency. Despite her extensive network, Noma frequently was short of money to buy food. As we discussed, she encountered bureaucratic difficulties trying to sign up for Medicaid, and when she received a $3,500 medical bill for the birth of her baby, she said she had no idea how she would pay it.

Fatima's situation was similar. Fatima was a social worker at a nonprofit social service agency in Harlem. Together she and her partner looked into alternative care facilities (discussed in the next chapter). Her partner accompanied her to the Lamaze classes and attended the delivery. In fact, he was her main source of support during her pregnancy. Fatima's family had lived for an extensive period in Africa. At the time of the study, her siblings were scattered; one brother lived in Paris, and other siblings lived in the South. Her mother had remained in Africa for a time, but had returned to New York and was living with Fatima while going to school to learn accounting. Fatima relied mostly on friends for instrumental support. She was on good terms with several of her coworkers, and two of them visited her within a few hours after the baby was born. She also brought the baby with her to work on her first day back. Fatima characterized herself as very self-reliant. She did not seem to solicit support from siblings or friends except at a minimal level.

4.2.4. Differences and Continuities by Class

That cross-class differences and continuities in our study were not always clear-cut gives some insight into the vulnerabilities of the African American middle class. Clearly there were significant differences in the support available to such women in our study, reflecting differential access to financial, informational, and other resources. However strong a support system, it cannot offset the consequences of scarcity, though it may serve important functions in mitigating these effects. At the same time, for certain sections of the African American middle class, because of their precarious situation with respect to resources and employment, an expense such as having a baby may create a crisis situation that cannot be addressed by support systems. We suggest that middle-stratum women may be more likely than other groups to recruit support systems in which friends are more important than family. The following two examples of women we encountered in fieldwork demonstrate the tensions of middle-class women who are trying to juggle child care and work.

Ms. N, as we discussed earlier, worked as a television producer. She had lived in a rented apartment in Harlem for 5 years; she stated that the cost of the rent had become difficult to handle, and she sometimes rented out one of the bedrooms in her apartment.

As a single mother of a 5-year-old daughter, she reported that she often had difficulty making child care arrangements. She frequently had to work late and had not been able to make arrangements for someone to pick up her daughter after school and keep her until Ms. N returned from work. These difficulties led in part to school officials referring her to the child welfare authorities, as discussed earlier. She stated that it was very taxing not to have family in the region and that she did not feel she could ask for help with child care from most of her friends. When we interviewed her, she was facing the prospect of eviction for nonpayment of rent as well as the possibility of being laid off from her job. In discussions with the ethnographer, she described the tensions and difficulties of balancing child care, job demands, and the problems of an inadequate support system as "extremely taxing and stressful."

Though Ms. T was not a single mother and appeared to have a more stable resource base, child care was still difficult. Ms. T lived with her husband (both were in their 40s) and 18-month-old son in a house on a brownstone block in Harlem. She was a nurse. Her husband grew up poor, had been with the New York City uniformed services for many years, and now held a law degree. Ms. T said she slept an average of 5 hours per night, which she did not consider sufficient. Having returned to work when her baby was 4 months old, Ms. T had a fluctuating schedule. She and her husband employed several babysitters who could provide care at various times and thus could provide backup service for her and her husband's erratic schedules. When asked whom she could turn to for help in an emergency, Ms. T said that most of her family was not in New York City. Though her father's sister lived in the Bronx, she had not turned to her for help because she had 13 grandchildren. She said that "hypothetically" she could get help from her husband's family (who lived in Harlem), friends, or church-group members, but she had not used these contacts because she and her husband were both "proud." They were also dubious about the qualifications of these potential babysitters.

We have suggested that middle-stratum African American women may be more likely to recruit support systems in which friends are more important than family. Undoubtedly a complex set of issues influence this situation, including age, mobility, and distance. It may also reflect the class heterogeneity of the African American family and the demands on those with presumably better access to resources but whose situation may be insecure.

That friends may be especially important in middle-class support networks may have implications for African American women in their reproductive years. Infant and child care is an arena in which class differences may affect relatively privileged women in unexpected ways. While middle-income African American women may have greater material resources for child care (though frequently these are not adequate), they may have fewer family resources. They are less likely to be co-resident, and family members may be unavailable to them because of distance, mobility, or conflicting obligations. To the extent that it is deemed inappropriate to call upon friends for certain types of help with infant and child care, middle-class African American women may find themselves in difficult circumstances.

A reluctance to ask for assistance from friends is not limited to middle-stratum African American women. For example, Newman discusses isolation among middle-stratum white women, for whom "the cultural emphasis on nuclear-family independence constrains middle-class, divorced women to rely on their families of origin for help, and makes it difficult for them to extend ties to individuals outside this narrow range" (1986:242). To the extent that this is true for middle-stratum African American women, and to the extent that their families of origin are not easily available as part of their support network or that they have replaced family networks with friends, their financial insecurity may have special consequences.

4.2.5. Kinwork

It is the case, across class, that women are responsible for recruiting and servicing support networks (Rapp, 1987). It may become particularly complicated to create, manage, and sustain cross-household kin contacts in situations where relationships with men are tenuous.

Only one respondent to the EQ reported that no one came to her for help. This reflects the strengths of reciprocal relationships within networks but also reflects the costs of network membership. About half the respondents reported that they thought they had to give something back if someone helped them, and this finding differed somewhat by level of education (33 percent versus 52 percent versus 56 percent).

Anthropologists have described this activity as "kinwork" and noted that, unlike housework and child care, it is generally unlabeled (di Leonardo, 1984). Some respondents to the EQ reported problems with family relationships. Those that did included disagreements, envy ("little jealousy sometimes"), not being able to help ("seeing them go through changes and not being able to help"), lack of understanding ("them not understanding me and what I am coping with," "wondering if it's a sincere appreciation"), family intrusiveness ("family wants to take away your life"), and heavy expectations ("sometimes they expect too much. I am a good person but sometimes I can't help"). Further studies might explore the ways kinwork may be simultaneously stressful and protective and how this might vary with class.

As was clear from our ethnographic material, family and friends were available not only for advice and comfort, but they also accompanied women to the hospital, aided financially and with gifts, and helped out with household tasks, child care, and moral support. One woman described her support network: "They got me what I needed and stroked the ego." The importance of networks, which was evident in the ethnographic data, is congruent with a large body of literature on African American families and other support systems. This literature not only emphasizes the social importance of such networks but also clarifies how features such as the transformations in family structure and function respond to changing historical conditions (see, for example, Collins, 1991; Mullings, 1997; Stack, 1974; Wilson, 1987). Our ethnographic research supported other findings in this literature concerning the fluid and dynamic nature of families and support networks, the importance of recruitment of nonblood kin ("blood mothers and other mothers") that are called upon during pregnancy, the central importance of woman-centered networks despite varied roles of men, and the continuing importance of consanguineal kinship.

4.3. FAMILY, MARRIAGE, AND FEMALE–MALE RELATIONSHIPS

Among African Americans nationally, better-educated African American women are more likely to marry than African American women with less education (Wilson, 1996). However, it is also true that highly educated African American women have substantially lower rates of marriage than comparably educated white women (Wilson, 1996). We asked EQ respondents to describe their current relationship status, and they were not restricted to choose only one category if they thought a combination of categories were a better reflection of their current situation. Overall, 21 percent were married, 11 percent were separated, 11 percent were divorced, 7 percent were widowed, 35 percent had never been married, 5 percent were dating, and 12 percent were in a romantic relationship. With respect to current relationships, 73.7 percent of the women reported currently being in a relationship with a partner. The distribution of marital status/partners was examined across level of education. Among women with less than a high school education, 17 percent were married, 8 percent were living with a partner, 17 percent were divorced, 8 percent were widowed, 42 percent had never been married, and 8 percent were dating. Among the women with a high school education or general equivalency diploma (GED), 22 percent were married, 4 percent were living with a partner, 4 percent had a sometime partner, 11 percent were separated, 15 percent were divorced, and 11 percent were in a romantic relationship. Among women with more than a high school education, 22 percent were married, 11 percent were living with a partner, 17 percent were separated, 6 percent were widowed, 22 percent had never been married, 6 percent were dating, and 22 percent were in a romantic relationship.

Current relationship status differed by educational status. Only 42 percent of women with less than a high school education reported having a current partner, while 74 percent of those with a high school education or GED and 95 percent of those with more than a high school education did. Although 56 percent of women overall reported that their partner was more important than family and friends, women with more than a high school diploma were most likely to report so (25 percent for women with less than a high school education, 56 percent for women with a high school education, and 78 percent for women with more than a high school education).

The social context we have described above and in previous chapters results in a severe shortage of marriageable men (Wilson, 1987, 1996). The issues of employment and unemployment seem to be a consideration in making decisions about marriage and affect the course of the relationship for women of all strata. In the context of high unemployment among males, marriage may result in a loss of benefits for women. For example, Elizabeth, a 63-year-old family child care provider in our study, had lived in public housing in Harlem for 20 years. After the death of her first husband, she raised her son, who was in his 20s at the time of the study. She also helped raise her nieces and nephews and was currently babysitting her cousin's young baby. Elizabeth met her second husband soon after her first husband died. She did not want to remarry but reported that he finally "wore me down," and she married him in 1990. She stated jokingly that she regretted having remarried because it resulted in the loss of her social security payments from her deceased husband. Though her second husband was employed when she met him, he was laid off soon after that and was currently unemployed. She and her husband made dinners to sell every Friday and Saturday.

Underemployment and consequent involvement in the informal/illegal sector may also be issues in decisions about marriage. During the course of fieldwork, longitudinal participant Susan, whom we met when she worked at a fast-food restaurant, reported to us that her male friend, with whom she had had a relationship for a number of years, had signed with a record company and wanted to get married and "move me and my kids out of the projects." However, Susan was hesitant to "marry for money," and she wanted to go back to school. A few months later she and this man were no longer living together because she did not think he was stable enough, and she needed "stability in her life, for me and my children." Susan urged him to get a job at McDonald's or Wendy's, but he had completed 2 years of college and said he refused to work for minimum wage and did not want his friends to see him in that type of job. He became involved in the illegal sector, which Susan found unacceptable.

Given the larger social forces conditioning the high rate of unemployment of men, the women in our study expressed the need for self-sufficiency. To clarify this issue, respondents to the EQ were asked how they were raised to think about being a woman. The theme of self-respect and independence was consistent across levels of education: "respect yourself and be independent," "being responsible, not to depend on no one but themselves," and "learn to stand on your own." These images may have been operationalized in decisions about relationships.

Longitudinal participant Diana reported that her baby's father was delighted by her pregnancy and wanted to marry her. They had difficulty finding affordable housing where they could set up an independent household. She said that she had decided not to say "yes" yet because she wanted to be independent and self-sufficient before marrying Jack, an independent mover who owned his own van. Diana began to feel that Jack was "too laid back" and was not aggressive enough about finding jobs. After the child's birth, she and Jack continued to live together.

Billie poignantly reported her struggle for self-sufficiency and the advantages and disadvantages as she perceived them:

> It's amazing things you can do with two incomes. I've never had two. I've never been involved or lived with anybody ... that brought in another income. So, I look at the things I've been able to do by myself. And I just ... it astounds me what people can do with two incomes.... But, you know what? When it [her marriage] didn't work out, that was the first indication. It was like okay, people do not get married and live happily ever after. So, what it made me know is that I was going to have to go outside of my norm and do things to make extra money ... So, I started waitressing and I started bartending. I taught myself some skills that would allow me to make extra money and provide for the things that I thought were necessary.... I just don't feel that there's anything I won't or can't do in order to support me or mine. You know, you do what you have to do even if you don't want to do it. And I think women are subjected to so many images put on them if they do this. Because I remember getting a phone call from my husband and his family saying that you're working all these jobs, maybe Alex (her son) should come live with us. And that was their judgment on my being a bartender. When I settle down and whoever I marry, it's going to be because I love them ... So, I would really like to have a second income because I've never had one. I've never had anybody say, I'll pay the rent and you pay the rest of the bills. I've never had the advantage of whatever money I have, using it to do different things, other things outside of duties. And I would really like to know what that feels like. And so ... just thinking about those women who became homeless ... it may have been a one-income household, but it was a man's income. And it's very bad. A lot of times, men don't want you to work because they want that control. But, you should never ever assume that something can't happen to somebody. All of those men could have died. They didn't have to get divorced. They could've died and there could have been no insurance. Because a lot of times, women don't even know if there is insurance. They don't look into those things because they think he's supposed to take care of everything. I've had the advantage of nobody ever being responsible enough.

Not surprisingly, some women in our study expressed ambivalent feelings about marriage. Among the respondents to the EQ, some women reported qualified and negative opinions about marriage: "I don't want to be around married folks," "don't care for marriage, long-term commitment is OK," "marriage is life time, didn't like to be tied down, long term without marriage is OK," "I think they are nonexistent, theoretically it's a phenomenal concept," and "I felt more relaxed in the [long] term commitment without marriage rather than marriage." One young woman we encountered during fieldwork was studying for a master's degree in urban planning at a major New York university and working on the Empowerment Zone in Harlem; she hoped to go on to business school. She asserted that women do not want the pressure of marriage and that she herself wanted children but not a husband.

Participants in our focus group on women who head households were not sanguine about the possibilities of a long-term relationship:

> I want to get married, but I'm not rushing it. I'm single. I don't have nobody right now. I'm chilling. I'm trying to get my apartment, job, take care of myself so when a man does come, you know, he's going to look out for me.

> I met this man on the train one time and he started talking to me. He was a business man from out of town and we were talking and he asked me how old I was. I said, "I'm thirty-four." He says, "You've never been married." I said, "No." He was like, "Too bad." And it was like ... what I felt like is that he meant it as if, "Oh, you're thirty-four and you've never been married. You ain't never gonna get married. You'll have more luck falling out of an airplane or something, right?" And I thought about it for awhile after he said it and I thought, maybe he's right. You know, I've been on my own since I was twenty, and sometimes I feel like it would be nice to have somebody ... do everything. Boy, that would be fun.

Despite the circumstances described here, we found that many women continued to adhere to the traditional goals of marriage, which must itself be a source of stress in these circumstances. Most respondents to the EQ, despite ambivalence about its benefits, reported positive views on the "ideal" marriage and long-term commitment. Positive comments included the following: "marriage is wonderful, you have to give a little and take a little," "I want to get married once for the rest of my life," "I think it's the greatest thing since apple pie, some make it and some don't," "marriage is very sacred to God, it is a very serious thing," "marriage is wonderful," and "marriage is a compromise." A number of women compared marriage and long-term commitment: "marriage is more responsible—because your partner will not just walk out and leave you. Don't agree with long-term commitment [without] marriage," "I think it's good, I believe in long-term commitments and marriage if need be. You don't necessarily have to be married, to each his own. Too many people who get married are not together," "long-term commitment is good as long as it's good, if it's bad you can get out of it," "I don't see the purpose of being in a long-term relationship without marriage like I am," "I don't really believe in marriage, the legality of it," "long-term commitment is really a scapegoat with no commitment. Marriage is a covenant through God.... It is the highest form of compliment you can give to a lover because it is for life," "I think that marriage is the optimum way of being, but not necessarily the most practical or the most viable," "it's important for the community and done one time, taken seriously. Takes two very responsible people to give and exchange and care for each other. It's not what it's cranked up to be, can be fun and painless and stressless," and "marriage is a partnership, it's caring, it's a friendship, it's a bond and a commitment. Long-term commitment should be the same."

A participant in the focus groups on women who head households commented, "I would like to be married, because I'm a good woman. I can be faithful to a man." Another participant elaborated:

> I would love to be married, because I know I could be a very good woman to any man that kisses my fanny. But ... I think guys are just afraid of the challenge and the commitment ... because women are very set in their ways ... when they put their foot down, they mean business. I think God might have made a mistake because we are just so ... firm about things. Where men, they think they are firm, but ... I'll analyze a man in a minute. I'll read 'em.

Anita, a nurse and a divorced mother of two daughters, in describing the consequences of her own marriage said, "I feel like a bird whose wings were both blown off and it fell to the ground and was all bloody and floundering around and couldn't fly again. And then it tried to heal itself and then it kind of did, and it grew new wings, but it never went up in the sky again." Yet when asked what she wished for her daughters, she gave expression to the themes of realism and idealism that seem to inform the perceptions of many African American women:

> Definitely a college education.... Because we have to keep learning or you'll become stagnant. Not even for financial reasons, of course, that's important.... So they can support themselves. They have to know how to make money just to support themselves, but I hope they'll be able to earn money in a creative way.... And I want ... I definitely want them to get married. I want them to have good husbands; that will support them.... People were meant to be married ... I think people were made to be in pairs. I definitely want both of them to have husbands. I've learned some hard, rough lessons. I've made some mistakes. I'm an old cow now going out to pasture ... and I want them to have husbands. I do ... I want them to have a stable setting and to have one man ... I think that's important. I think it's important because I think that's the way it's meant to be. For a man and a woman to be together. And to have a family. It's easier financially. It's easier emotionally. It's easier in all kinds of ways. With the right person I'm saying. Once each for a lifetime. Yes.

While the literature and public policy often assume that men are absent, participant observation indicated that although many women were not formally married, although the traditional married-couple/nuclear family was not dominant, and although the financial support was often limited, women related to men in a variety of roles. In other words, choices about marital status did not necessarily limit networks. For this reason, we asked the EQ respondents about men in their lives.

EQ respondents reported that men in many different types of kin and partner relationships were important in their lives; some of these responses differed by level of educational achievement. For example, although 56 percent of women overall reported that their partner was most important, women with more than a high school diploma were most likely to report so (33 percent of women with less than a high school diploma, versus 56 percent of women with a high school diploma, versus 72 percent of women with more than a high school diploma). Approximately 40 percent of women across all levels of education reported that a brother was the most important man in their life, 50 percent overall reported that a son was most important, 20 percent reported an uncle in that role, and 30 percent reported a nephew as most important. Of all men named as most influential, most women reported their father to have been the most influential man in their lives. Others included were uncles, brothers, husbands, ex-partners, grandfathers, and "a friend of my mother's." Only 6 of the 57 women did not name a man who was influential in her upbringing.

When asked why these men had been influential, women spoke of being loved and of receiving life-long encouragement, support, advice, mentoring, teaching, and moral guidance. Across educational levels, women described men who were caring, thoughtful, and supportive. They also described men who stepped in to be helpful after the death of a father or to create a father relationship. Women described the important influences of these men in many ways. Regarding fathers, women had the following comments: "he had good morals, standards. He stayed home and took care of us, talked to us. I could go to him with any problems I had. I was lucky," "he always wanted the best for me," "because he helped my mother shape me to be the person I am," "nurturing me and teaching me the do's and don'ts and support," "father taught me self-worth, respect people," "because he taught me to manage—he has his own restaurant," and "because he was always there for me, and I could tell him anything." The influences of uncles and grandfathers were also described in similar ways: "he taught me right from wrong," "my father died when I was three, Uncle Charles was right there for me," "uncles, like father figures to me," "because I grew up without a father. He passed away, and my uncles were the men in my life," and "I lived with him [uncle] when I was very young. I developed work ethics and schooling from him. The big part of who I am comes from him." Brothers were also critical influences for many women: "he always gives me good advice and is always there. Like my father's image—he is the oldest," "because he was the oldest and used to help me with everything," and "after my father got sick, I could always look to my brother for help." One woman spoke of the important influence of two of her mother's coworkers: "I can call them, and they try to help me. I can talk with them."

One woman spoke of a long-lasting relationship with a man she met through the Fresh Air Fund and who she said had "been a father figure to me." Many women spoke about their partners: "he taught me a lot of things that I didn't know about life. He respects me and wants to see me happy," and "he was older than me, and he made sure I did what I should be doing. When I was about to make a decision, we talked about it, and he gave his honest opinion, which was very good." Only a few women reported negative influences, and those were described in general terms: "all of them [men] has some negative influence," and "[brothers] have been a negative influence because they're not there."

Women reported as well that many different types of men provided assistance in various ways. Again, women mentioned partners, husbands, boyfriends, brothers, sons, uncles, fathers, cousins, godfathers, male friends, pastors, and grandfathers. They reported multifaceted types of assistance, including financial—"gives me money," "will give me a loan," "helps me financially, he is my son's godfather"; instrumental—"helps with money and children and problems," "gives money, cooks, helps with appliances," "he cooks, mops, and everything," "they build things for me," "helps me with food and transportation to get me where I need to go"; child care—"babysits," "he helps me with the kids and round the house, also repairs and goes grocery shopping with me"; and a broad range of emotional support—"supports, talks, encourages," "is encouraging me and giving me spiritual nourishment," "give me guidance," "gives massage and drives me around and listens to my problems. He's my best friend and he understands my individuality," "supportive and nurturing." Most women reported global support—"everything and anything," "whatever I ask," "looks after my well-being," "do for me, they make me feel good," "anything I need done," "support system."

As we have noted, the lack of formal marriage did not mean men were absent from households. Women frequently continued to have some contact with the fathers of their children, as did the children. Among the EQ respondents, about 36 percent of women reported that their child's father helped with clothing, 42 percent reported help with money, 45 percent reported help with discipline, and 27 percent reported help with homework. These responses did not vary greatly with level of education, although women with less than a high school education were more likely to report that their partners helped with discipline (66 percent of women with less than a high school education versus 44 percent of women with a high school education versus 36 percent of women with more than a high school education). Over half the women with children reported that their child had a relationship with the father's family, and this response varied slightly by level of education (50 percent of women with less than a high school education versus 75 percent of women with a high school education versus 64 percent of women with more than a high school education). Among our longitudinal participants, most of the women who had children continued to be in touch with the fathers of their children.

Partners and affinal kin generally played some role in the pregnancy as well. While only one of our longitudinal participants, Ama, was legally married to the father of her child, most were in touch with the father and/or the father's family during the pregnancy and delivery, but the relationship sometimes ended shortly after the birth of the baby. Participants in the birth experience focus group joked about how they enjoyed attention from their partners during pregnancy: "When I really started craving I sent him out about 5 o'clock in the morning. He had to go to work. I wanted me a hero. I sent him to the store!" Overall, women received a range of emotional and practical support from partners and their kin, and this again cut across educational levels. For example, the partner of Noma, the performance artist, was with her during the delivery (described in the next chapter). Noma's affines were supportive of her during the pregnancy. In the case of Diana, a cashier at a fast-food restaurant, the baby's father was actively involved throughout the pregnancy. He and his mother attended the delivery, and Diana stayed with her partner's mother and grandmother throughout the pregnancy and after she gave birth. Similarly, Sharon, an unemployed clerk typist, received support from her affines: her partner's brother and his wife agreed to be the godparents of her child and visited and brought her groceries. In Sandra's case, her partner attended the delivery. Even though he discontinued the relationship when the baby was 2 months old, he continued to be in touch and make contributions. Despite the rupture with her partner, Sandra maintained a close relationship with her affines. Her mother-in-law was quite supportive, and Sandra regularly took the baby to see her paternal grandmother.

It appeared that women adapted to the fragility of female-male relationships by making alliances with the matrilineal kin of their children's father—by relating to men through the woman-centered networks of their children's father's consanguineal kin. Thus women sometimes received support in the form of shelter, financial help, or child care from the matrilineal kin of the baby's father, and this support might continue after the relationship with the baby's father dissolved.

Relationships with fathers and brothers sometimes became important and were a source of critical assistance. For example, Sandra, a manager at a fast-food restaurant, was in her early 30s. Although the baby's father was very supportive throughout the pregnancy and at the delivery, they broke up soon after the delivery, and his visits and support became erratic. On the other hand, Sandra's male consanguineal kin, particularly her father and brother, were very supportive financially. When she was in need of money one of her father's brothers gave her $300. Her mother's brother lent her money in emergencies, and she believed he was someone she could lean on. She described her father similarly. Her father agreed to match whatever she spent to buy a car. Furthermore, as we have noted in several case studies, many women had very supportive male friends who, although they were not partners, assisted them financially and emotionally.

4.4. PREGNANCY, MOTHERHOOD, AND THE SOCIAL IMPORTANCE OF REPRODUCTION

In the course of fieldwork, it became apparent that views about motherhood, its responsibilities, and the social importance of children also shaped decisions and experiences of pregnancy. For this reason, we asked EQ respondents a series of questions about modeling womanhood. When asked how they were raised to think about being a woman, they frequently mentioned taking care of family: "a woman is the head of the household, really the decision maker, responsible for the upbringing of children," "the head really," "act like a woman and do all the things women should do, take care of your husband and family," and "a woman is the backbone, she does all the cooking, sewing, everything."

When asked what they believed was the most important thing about being a woman, some respondents spoke about childbearing: "being able to raise a family, my children," "to have children and raise them correctly," "we have the power to give birth. We are blessed with that, our mothering instincts, caring for people," "we can have kids and men can't," "that we can experience labor (not the pain), but having the baby inside of you," and "getting to be a mother—to give birth."

Other respondents stressed responsibility for others, capacity to do many things, and the ability to pass values on to future generations: "being able to carry the burden of society on my shoulders, black women are supposed to be strong like a Timex—takes a licking and keeps on ticking," "being able to handle a variety of things at a time, work better under pressure," and "being responsible, caring for family."

Discussion in the focus group on households headed by women reinforced the comments of the EQ respondents. One focus group participant said:

> I'm proud because I'm a damn good mother. And I love my child, and I'm always going to be there for my child, and I'm just happy because I'm with my son. I can't be deprived of my son. I'm just so happy. I'm happy.

Another woman stated:

> Well, I'm proud that I have come a long way. My mom kicked me out when I was pregnant with my son, and I went to live in the shelter, and they were so nice to me. That's why now when I see people like crackheads and people, you know, derelicts, you don't look down on them, because you never know, it could be you. Living in that shelter, to me was my rock bottom, and from the shelter they put me into a small kitchenette apartment. Now, I live on 115th Street, in a two-bedroom apartment, from the front all the way to the back of the building, and I have good son. I'm trying to hang in there. You know, sometimes I want to tell him that I want to quit, but I really don't quit being a mother. Because it's hard, but I hang in there even though you go through lows sometimes.

The importance of motherhood and the responsibilities of raising children have been noted in several studies (Ladner, 1971; Collins, 1991; Boone, 1989). In this study, while there were clearly exceptions, and despite ambivalence about particular pregnancies, awareness of the importance of motherhood and the responsibility of children cut across educational levels. Noma, a professional artist, and Ruth, a welfare recipient, were both extremely concerned about their children's well-being and were assiduous in their attention to their children. Noma, who reported having very rich childhood experiences, gave extensive thought to child care, as the ethnographer remarked, "working to keep them informed, happy, creative, confident, spiritual, and entertained (without television)." Ruth, despite her many personal difficulties, still made sure both her sons were always neatly dressed and took time to find opportunities such as after-school programs and special summer camps for them. Reina, the young woman who relied on maternal kin for support, appeared to the ethnographer to be transformed after the birth of her baby, apparently not minding the long nights and the curtailment of her social life. She assumed full responsibility for the care of her child.

The importance of motherhood and children and the ways some women sought to rise above their circumstances was perhaps best illustrated by the case of Sandra, a woman in her early 30s who carried herself with self-assurance and confidence. When we first met her, as we recounted earlier, she was working as a shift manager at a fast-food restaurant and living in a private building that housed women who were trying to improve their circumstances. She was on parole from prison after serving time for a minor drug offense. At first, Sandra was unsure whether to carry the pregnancy to term, but her age and her partner's desire to have a child convinced her to continue the pregnancy.

After the birth of her daughter, Sandra became immersed in her child's well-being. Her partner terminated their relationship a few months after the birth of the baby. After trying unsuccessfully to revive the relationship, Sandra continued to take the child to visit the father but reported resignedly, "We are a team now, Sarah and me—it's just us." Sandra spent months trying to find a good day care facility. Thinking of her daughter, she carefully planned her budget and job schedule. Having previously been in trouble with the law, she had become a role model for younger women on her block, who asked her to help them find jobs.

4.4.1. Social Support and Pregnancy Decisions—"Wantedness"

One of the factors that influences a woman's decision about a pregnancy is her view of the social world into which the child might be born. The process of determining whether a child is wanted takes place in a social context and changes over time. Thus, asking a woman if the child is "wanted" at the time of delivery or in the postpartum period (as is currently done in epidemiological surveys) may be misleading if it obscures the process women go through in determining the course of the pregnancy.

Given that pregnancies are often unintended (as discussed in the next chapter), women commonly feel a great deal of ambivalence about their situation. What to do once pregnant is not always a clear-cut decision for women; instead, they weigh a variety of factors to decide whether the pregnancy is to be continued or terminated. This process is complex and seems to involve both time and a degree of emotional strain. While medical interventions are largely based on the physiological aspects of conception and pregnancy, for study participants, this dimension formed only one aspect of a larger concern with a web of social relationships within which the child once born would or would not and could or could not be nurtured. These concerns focused not only on what we might call first-level relations of personal networks of family and friends but also on second-level relations in terms of the impact of wider structural forces on the life chances of the mother and child, as was described in the previous chapters, as well as cultural attitudes toward children and motherhood.

The processes involved in decisions about pregnancy have clear implications for early intervention in prenatal care. To understand this, it was important to explore how participants described the discovery of their pregnancy, their reaction to that discovery, and their decision about the course of the pregnancy. Asked how they felt about their pregnancies, EQ participants responded with emotions that ranged from straightforward—"good, because I wanted a small baby to hold"—to more complex—"I felt good. I was shocked," and "I was miserable. After 3 to 4 months I was elated and then I had my girl." One woman described her response to a pregnancy loss: "I felt like I lost something very grand that I am going to miss for a long time." A few women commented on their desire for the pregnancy: these ranged from wanting the pregnancy, to not wanting it, to feeling that it was "unexpected but OK."

The longitudinal participants' experiences revealed that the range of reactions and emotions reflected the variety of situations in which women discovered their pregnancies. One of the critical factors involved in women's decisions about pregnancy is the point when the pregnancy is "discovered." Recognition of pregnancy occurs only partly in a medical setting. Before this, awareness depends in part on the woman herself and to a lesser extent on those from whom she seeks advice. The case of Celine illustrates some of the issues and their complexity. At age 16, before going abroad on an exchange program, Celine had a sexual relationship with a man for the first time and only once. "Just experimental stuff," she said. Celine's menstrual cycle was still irregular, so she did not worry when she missed her period. She described the process of discovering her pregnancy as a teenager out of the country:

> I began to gain weight and I thought it was being there, the food, you know, my face was getting round. And in fact, people I was living with, who were mostly Spanish-speaking, would tell me in Spanish, "Gosh, you eat like you're pregnant." I was like, "No, you're just kidding." I said [to myself] there is no way anything could have happened. It's not possible, my friends told me. And at that point in high school, I was with a group of ladies who pledged virginity throughout high school and wait 'til you get married and that whole thing. So ... I didn't tell them about it.... No one ... knew, and the way I carried myself, I don't think they suspected anything. So, I'm gaining weight over the year and after about three or four months, I think it was must have been five months then, I began to feel some serious changes in my body. I knew something was happening, I wasn't stupid, I wasn't totally naive.

Celine's denial of her pregnancy and her reluctance to talk about it with family and friends was similar to the experience of three other longitudinal study participants who first got pregnant in their teenage years. Because of their inexperience and sometimes fearing parental reaction, they ignored or hid their condition for some time. Also important in a few cases was the irregularity of the menstrual period. Thus, all these women at a young age were faced with a situation that would clearly have a major impact on their lives, and they took time to decide how to proceed. However, as Celine's case further demonstrates, family members, once they come to know of the pregnancy, often supported the young woman. Celine described how her middle-class family overcame their dismay at her pregnancy and offered support:

> And then my brothers and sisters ... I told (my mother) not to tell anyone. Maybe they even thought that there wasn't a kid in there. And when my son was born, my mother was real-

ly happy ... she was like overjoyed and oh boy ... so wonderful ... so interesting, you know, sort of like a combination of wonder because of the whole circumstance. To me to have survived that is just incredible when I think about it. So, my son was born.

Similarly, Ms. X was a 22-year-old African American college student who was 10 weeks pregnant when we met her. She said she had become pregnant because she changed her birth control medication. She had planned to finish school, begin a career, and get pregnant when she was around 30. Though she was not happy about being pregnant, she said she did not believe in abortion: "It's not the child's fault." Her family agreed to help with child care while she finished school.

How a woman felt and the course of action she took, however, did not always coincide. For example, Gina, a longitudinal participant, who had three foster children in her care when we recruited her, decided to terminate her pregnancy when it became clear that her relationship with the baby's father was not going to work out: "He's not really going to be there for me."

In contrast, Fatima, a social worker in her early 30s, had three children from previous marriages. When we met her, she was 19 weeks pregnant with her fourth child. She lived with Abraham, the baby's father (another social worker), for a few years. He had no children, and Fatima decided to have this child because Abraham wanted one. They planned to get married after the birth of the baby, and Fatima referred to Abraham as her husband.

In each of these cases, women considered the attitudes of their partners, who thereby influenced their decisions indirectly. In other cases, members of a social network participated more directly in decisions about a pregnancy, pressuring a woman in a given direction. While in some cases the pressure was to terminate, in other cases it was to complete a pregnancy. For example, in the case of Rose, one of the longitudinal study participants, the young girl's father wanted her to terminate the pregnancy, but she resisted and ultimately had the baby and received assistance from her grandmother after her delivery. In two other cases, family members exerted pressure on the young women, both of whom were initially ambivalent, to keep the baby, and both complied.

In addition, a series of life circumstances were important in determining the course of pregnancy for women in the study sample. Which factors came into play at any given moment differed throughout the life cycle of each woman as well as across educational levels. Such factors included work, school, housing, resources, women's view of their own opportunity structure, and age. It must be emphasized, however, that the interplay of factors was never a simple matter, as was demonstrated by the fact that women who had been pregnant several times did not take the same course of action in each pregnancy. For example, Sharon, who had recently separated from her husband of 16 years, had been pregnant several times. Of those pregnancies, two were brought to term; one she lost to fetal distress, another was an ectopic pregnancy, and another she terminated voluntarily. When we met Sharon, she was 5 months pregnant and had recently broken up with the baby's father. She was depressed, smoked frequently, and had little appetite. She was ambivalent about the baby and had made several appointments to have an abortion, but had not followed through. She did not think she could afford to have a baby right then, but neither could she bring herself to terminate the pregnancy.

On the other hand, several women in the study sample also decided almost immediately to continue the pregnancy, even though they did not intentionally "plan" to get pregnant. For example, Noma, the performance artist, wanted the baby as soon as she realized she was pregnant because she thought it was the right time to have a second child. Similarly, Ms. S, whose husband worked in a fast-food restaurant, decided to go through with the pregnancy even though she had diabetes. She and her husband carefully monitored her health.

As we can see, changing conditions and feelings led women to take different courses of action in their pregnancies. Indeed, in each of the cases described above, the women expressed some ambivalence about their pregnancies, and the direction in which to proceed was not clear-cut. Often it is not until women go through this process of decision-making that they actually seek prenatal medical care. Therefore, research is required to develop a more nuanced understanding of the difference between unintended and unwanted pregnancies and the implications of this decision-making process for public health intervention.

4.4.2. The Role of Support Systems in Shaping Attitudes Toward Pregnancy

Just as women's decisions about their pregnancy are influenced by a complex array of factors, so too is their perception of the experience of pregnancy itself. Again the physiological dimensions of pregnancy, while important, must be placed within the wider framework of social relations and conditions that structure the pregnancy experience and how it is viewed. Although fieldwork was not designed to provide correlative data on the relationship between emotion and pregnancy outcome, the findings suggest that positive feelings about being pregnant did improve attitudes toward self-care. Such attitudes may be an important variable between pregnancy-related stressors and adverse pregnancy outcomes.

Participants in the EQ reported many positive experiences of pregnancy; again, these did not differ by level of education. Many women reported that "just knowing that I was having a healthy baby" and knowing that it was "a good pregnancy" were positive experiences. For some women, "it was my first pregnancy, I did not think I could get pregnant." Others described "the thought of having a baby and the husband," "no pains, no stretch marks," "it was exactly what I wanted," "an easy pregnancy," "I really wanted the baby," and "the baby showers."

EQ respondents reported that positive assessments of pregnancy often had to do with the specific support received from family and community: baby showers, celebrations with favorite foods, gifts, and support from family, friends, coworkers, and others. One woman said, "I enjoyed being pregnant. My family and friends spoiled me. People gave me seats on the bus." Latoya, one of the longitudinal participants who, though she had not planned to be pregnant with her second child, was happy about her pregnancy, told us, "Everybody treated me like normal, it's just that I had a baby on the way. Everybody treated me better. They helped me with things, they tell me not to look down, they tried to take the work load off me. They were very nice."

Again, longitudinal participants' experiences validated the EQ data. For example, Reina's pregnancy experience spoke to the importance of social support in possibly mitigating the impact of a range of stressors during pregnancy. When she was about 7 months pregnant, Reina went to Chicago to visit relatives and friends; in the 8th month, her friends and cousins gave her a baby shower. She received baby clothes, a stroller, and other baby items. Reina was confident she could raise the baby because she helped take care of her young brothers and some of her relatives' children. Thus, although she was a young woman still in school, having the support of her family facilitated a positive experience of pregnancy.

Just as support from social networks could help shape positive pregnancy experiences, so too, the absence of such support, or tensions within relationships, could have a negative effect on these experiences. Data from the EQ revealed that, although the vast majority of women received help from family during pregnancy, the absence of such support could not be considered negligible; 17 percent reported no help from family, 26 percent reported no help from the baby's father, and 65 percent reported no help from friends.

Support-weak situations may form part of the overall sources of pregnancy-related stress that conditions women's pregnancy. Among respondents to the EQ, about 41 percent reported specific things they found stressful when they had their last babies. These frequently had to do with lack of social support: "I had to do it alone." Women of all educational levels reported such difficulties, including "the father of my kids was stressing me out," "my husband was having an affair," "the father of the child abused me while I was pregnant" (15 percent of women in the EQ reported that they had experienced physical violence during their previous pregnancy), "me and my husband were breaking up," "I was in a bad marriage," and "my husband and I separated when I was 5 months pregnant."

Focus group participants also discussed problems with relationships as well as problems that prevented their partners from being good fathers. One woman said, "Sometimes men are just so selfish. They don't think about ... what they do." Another concluded that her partner was supportive in some ways, but not in others: "Sometimes you feel that you want somebody to hold you, I would like to have somebody to hold me, and sometimes he wasn't there. Most of the time he worked nights, and in the daytime he was sleeping." Others reiterated their unmet need for partner support: "I was stressed because he didn't spend enough time with me, so I guess that I wanted to be near him, and he was always out to this, out to that, and outdoors. And I would just cry, I don't know why, I would just cry."

The impact of these conflicts is illustrated by the experience of longitudinal participant Sharon, a woman who, as noted previously, contemplated abortion, in part because of termination of the relationship with the baby's father. Sharon expressed bitterness toward the baby's father, emphasizing his specific behavior and its impact on her well-being. She was not alone in this, as many of the women interviewed expressed similar dissatisfaction with partners. In addition, however, Sharon's sense of loneliness during her pregnancy also reflected what she perceived to be an extremely sparse social network. Her parents were dead, and she was not close to either of her siblings. Sharon specifically told us she was "tired of struggling" and lacked support from family members. She stated that she was very unhappy and stressed about being alone with the pregnancy. One of her major concerns was about childbirth, because she had no one to be with her during the delivery. She was also worried that she did not have anyone to watch her other children while she was in the hospital. She explained that her ex-husband had first agreed to take them, but then refused, while her sister's life was so disorganized that she was not a good candidate. A female friend offered to look after the children but only in exchange for money, and Sharon did not see her as a viable option. Eventually, her ex-husband agreed to care for the children at his residence in Staten Island.

In summary, we have demonstrated here that the experience of pregnancy and pregnancy loss must be understood within the wider context of women's social world, their networks of support, and other social and individual resources on which they draw to ensure positive outcomes. The data reported in this chapter suggest that, in order to understand how women conceptualize pregnancy and the ways they care for themselves during pregnancy (independent of the medical health care system), it is important to consider these larger systems of social relationships in which women are embedded. Interventions that focus only on single factors (e.g., get women into prenatal care early or get women to "plan" their pregnancies) or isolate physiological or behavioral risks (for example, risk of vaginal infections or substance abuse) may not be effective, because women may be unable to comply unless social factors are also altered. More effective interventions might begin with the social relationships of women and build on their positive experiences and their own strategies for ensuring care.

At the same time, our ethnographic data indicate the importance of participant observation as a methodological research tool. Not only did it allow us to examine the importance of these networks, it also allowed us to reveal the social and psychological implications of when these networks are not available, as was the case with Sharon, discussed above. Moreover, by enabling us to document what people actually do, as well as what they report, participant observation suggests the need to consider how approaches to social support analysis may not adequately account for the disparity between what Barrera has termed perceived social support—"an individual's perception of the availability and adequacy of supportive others"—and received social support—"supportive activities engaged in by others in response to a stressful situation" (cited by McLean et al., 1993). For example, although Sharon felt alone and abandoned throughout her pregnancy, the ethnographer was able to document various forms of support from family and friends, such as a baby shower attended by 20 adults and 10 children as well as support from her in-laws after the birth of the baby. This disparity between support perceived and support actually received cut across educational levels. Noma, for example, also told the ethnographer that she had "no one in this area she could turn to." Yet we were able to document extensive help from friends and family. Finally, participant observation graphically demonstrates the dynamic nature of social support networks. While longitudinal approaches have examined support systems over time, participant observation allows direct analysis of the processes and events that lead to change.

Having examined how social support shapes women's decisions and coping strategies with respect to reproductive health, in the next chapter we turn our attention to the issues that surround medical interventions in pregnancy.

5

HEALTH CARE DELIVERY
AND REPRODUCTIVE HEALTH

Since the turn of the century, the health care delivery system has promoted prenatal care as the single most important way to manage pregnancy and prevent poor pregnancy outcomes (Wilcox and Marks, 1994). Extensive studies have verified a relationship between prenatal care service and birth outcome: adequate care is associated with improved outcomes and inadequate care is associated with poor outcomes, including infant mortality.

Medical and epidemiologic studies show that the United States, in general, has lower rates of women who seek early prenatal care (i.e., in the first trimester) than its European counterparts. Within the United States, married white women are most likely to seek early prenatal care. Black, Hispanic, and Native American women have lower rates of early pre-natal care and significantly higher rates of late or no care. As women attain higher degrees of education, early prenatal care rises significantly (Wilcox and Marks, 1994).

Measures of the adequacy of prenatal care have concentrated heavily on the use of formal health care delivery systems to provide such care. Most studies have focused on the significance of early entry into medical prenatal care and the continuity of care, while some have proposed a series of composite measures (such as the Kessner index) to look at both month of first prenatal visit and total number of visits (Wilcox and Marks, 1994). Principal sources of information include national health surveys, birth certificate reg-istries, and the Pregnancy Risk Assessment Monitoring System (PRAMS) survey of the Centers for Disease Control and Prevention, established in 24 states.

On the basis of these studies, national health policy has continued to emphasize efforts to get more women into prenatal care in the first trimester, setting a goal for the year 2010 of increasing to at least 90 percent the proportion of all pregnant women who receive prenatal care in the first trimester. States and cities with large populations of low-income people have undertaken special initiatives. The Healthy Start Program is a con-certed federal effort to improve engagement in prenatal care in high-risk areas nationwide.

Nevertheless, the underlying premises of these studies and their findings have not gone unquestioned. Questions have been raised about the validity of prenatal care studies because of the bias represented by the self-selection of women who seek early prenatal care (Wilcox and Marks, 1994). Of equal importance is the fact that the question of precisely how prenatal care works to bring about a good pregnancy outcome remains largely unanswered beyond the obvious fact that continuous prenatal visits allow medical personnel to monitor women for conditions that will put them at high risk, such as preeclampsia, toxemia, and diabetes. These studies, however, have not addressed the causal link between prenatal care and pregnancy outcome. Ethnographic inquiry suggests that the questions surrounding prenatal care provided by the health care delivery system must be situated within the broader social context that structures women's experience during pregnancy. In the previous chapter, we described the way family and support systems play a critical role in the decisions made about the course of the pregnancy and the experience of pregnancy (outside the medical system). In this chapter, we first consider how recognition of pregnancy and decisions about its course occur within a social context. We demonstrate that how, when, and in what manner women engage with medical prenatal care form only a part of that wider process of the interplay of individual and social behavior, social relations, and social conditions. We then turn our attention to the interactions of women with the health care delivery system.

5.1. PREGNANCY INTENDEDNESS AND RECOGNITION

To understand how the participants apprehend and manage pregnancy, it is necessary to explore their attitudes and experiences not only about pregnancy, but also about birth control and decisions about pregnancy. Although fewer than half the women (49 percent) surveyed on the ethnographic questionnaire (EQ) reported using some method of contraception, all the participants in the longitudinal study reported that their pregnancies were "unplanned"—that is, they were relatively surprised when they found out they were pregnant. The only partial exception was Robin, a middle-stratum woman[1] who worked for a publishing company in midtown Manhattan. Robin finished high school and was nearly 40 years old and childless; she was actively trying to get pregnant and thus, in a sense, was "planning" for pregnancy. This overarching social fact of conception as primarily unintended has clear implications for medical models of prenatal care and risk prevention and speaks to the need to understand pregnancy within the wider flow of social life.

The understanding of pregnancy as unplanned must necessarily begin with an examination of women's attitudes toward and practices of pregnancy prevention. As reported in both the longitudinal cases and the EQ survey, the most common contraceptive practices were the condom and the rhythm method. All the longitudinal participants relied primarily on condoms or rhythm for birth control, while in the EQ these two together accounted for 61 percent (condoms, 48 percent, and rhythm, 13 percent) of contraceptive use.

Among all EQ respondents, 33 percent of those with less than a high school diploma were using a method to prevent pregnancy, while 52 to 56 percent of those with a high school diploma or more were doing so. Among those with less than a high school diploma, 25 percent reported using condoms, while 50 percent of those with at least a high school diploma did so. Fifty percent of respondents with less than a high school diploma reported sterilization, while 42 percent of those with a high school diploma and only 20 percent of those with more than a high school diploma did so. Ten percent of respondents with more than a high school diploma reported using an intrauterine device (IUD); none of those with lower educational levels reported using this method. No one reported using Norplant (contraceptive implants). Interestingly, 20 percent of respondents with more than a high school education reported using other methods, 25 percent of those with less than a high school education reported using other methods, and 35 percent of those with a high school education used other methods. Other methods included foam, mind over matter, celibacy, and over-the-counter suppositories.

The prevalence of condoms and the rhythm method is not surprising, since they represent the most readily available forms of birth control, and they are among the least costly. However, the ethnographic data clearly demonstrated that use of contraceptive methods cannot be reduced to a question of market availability. Rather, how women actually make decisions about contraceptive methods necessarily takes into account a complex array of social, emotional, and practical criteria. The results of the longitudinal study demonstrated that participants selected specific contraceptive methods based on their attitudes toward, knowledge of, and previous experience with contraceptive methods in general. Several women reported that they disliked various methods of birth control—they considered them to be uncomfortable, unreliable, or dangerous. Some women, for example, distrusted oral contraceptives because of their side effects (one woman recounted that they exacerbated her asthma, and another woman said they gave her dizzy spells). Some women believed that methods such as the IUD or Norplant injections were not foolproof and therefore were untrustworthy.

When other methods of birth control appear to be ineffective or difficult, sterilization may be an option. For example, one longitudinal study participant, Aurora, was considering a tubal ligation after the birth of her ninth child, even though she was a practicing Catholic, saying that "God will forgive me." Another woman encountered during the fieldwork, Ms. Y, reported that she had decided to have a tubal ligation after she had been with her partner for 6 years and they had had two children.

Sterilization, however, is not always so freely chosen. Lopez (1987), for example, documents sterilization abuse and the constraints within which women may select sterilization as a form of contraception. The case of Reina, a young woman mentioned in earlier chapters, demonstrates the nuances between choice and coercion. She decided to continue her pregnancy because her aunt told her that if she went for another abortion, the hospital might sterilize her. Determining the extent to which sterilization is truly a method of choice is particularly important when we consider that 36 percent of respondents in the EQ reported sterilization as the method they used.

Among participants in the longitudinal study, three did not use contraceptive methods because they doubted their ability to conceive, frequently because of prior illness. Two had experienced ectopic pregnancies (one of them had to have an ovary and fallopian tube removed), and the third lost a baby because of fetal distress. One woman was in her early 40s and the other two were in their middle to late 30s.

These findings indicated that while the vast majority of pregnancies in the longitudinal study were described as unplanned, clearly this outcome was not synonymous with an absence of efforts to prevent pregnancy. Participants' accounts revealed that pregnancy prevention was not a simple question of adequate planning, medical prescriptions and advice, and availability of methods. Although the availability of contraceptive measures was clearly key, pregnancy at times was the result of the failure of the contraceptive methods used, at times the result of fear and mistrust of available contraceptive methods, and at times the result of misconceptions about the role of illness and age.

The accounts women give of their pregnancies have critical implications for the feasibility of early medical intervention as the principal strategy for ensuring optimal reproductive health. Our ethnographic research suggests that 1) pregnancies often are not intended; 2) as a result, women often are ambivalent about their condition; 3) in making a decision about the pregnancy, and whether they want the baby, women often weigh a series of social, cultural, economic, and psychological factors, seeking advice from others; 4) this process often takes time; and 5) often it is not until after this process is completed that women seek medical care. This study thus implies that preventive care for healthy pregnancies should begin significantly before the medically defined state of pregnancy.

5.1.1. Seeking Out Prenatal Care: Barriers and Strategies

The women of Harlem we interviewed and followed over the course of a year actively sought prenatal medical care and established a routine of medical visits for the remainder of their pregnancies. Along with seeking advice and support as well as changes in routines and nutritional strategies, their concern for prenatal medical care formed part of their own efforts to have healthy babies.

It was clear from the ethnographic data that these women—regardless of income level, type of occupation, and educational background—went to great lengths to obtain what they considered quality care. Their efforts to obtain prenatal care were constrained, however, by a number of factors, including whether a hospital accepted Medicaid patients and whether the women had insurance. What is equally important to note, however, is that at the time of the research, the options available to our study participants as New York residents were perhaps somewhat unusual. First, New York received over 11 percent of Medicaid funding nationwide (New York Times, 1997), and thus a greater percentage of women in New York had access to Medicaid (and to P-CAP or MOMS program) insurance. In addition, because of the number of medical schools and training hospitals in the New York City area, the health care infrastructure was much greater than in other parts of the country. Finally, with the increasing trend toward managed care in New York City, many hospitals were more willing than elsewhere in the country to accept Medicaid patients. It also should be noted that these circumstances could easily shift with changes in funding and legislation.

A critical element for women searching for quality medical care is the facility where they receive prenatal care. We found that, for the most part, women in our study were willing to travel out of their community to find a satisfactory facility. The exception was longitudinal participant Claire, who was in her mid-20s and lived on a poor block in Health Area 15. A welfare recipient, as was previously described, she had not graduated from high school and had two sons, ages 5 and 3; she was about 4 months pregnant when recruited. Her choice of facility was based largely on proximity, because she lived close to the public hospital and her child care schedule limited how far she could travel.

In general, study participants either selected the public hospital because there were things about the care they liked, or they went to relatively inconvenient facilities to get what they perceived to be better care. For example, Ruth, who was taken to the large west side hospital to deliver after she waited more than an hour for an ambulance, had traveled across Manhattan to go to a hospital on the east side for her prenatal care. Fatima, who lived in the Bronx and worked in Harlem, also went to the upper east side, while Ivory, a shy teenager and Harlem resident, went all the way to the Bronx. That Harlem residents were willing to travel extensively to find satisfactory facilities was also documented by a study of families who experienced the death of a child during its first year of life (Phillips, 1996).

Facilities available to women in our study could be categorized into three types: ambulatory clinics, in-hospital clinics, and alternative care (Figure 5.1). We had only one case of a woman who went to a private doctor; in her 5th month she switched to a hospital-based clinic. Respondents to the EQ relied almost exclusively on in-hospital clinics for prenatal care (25 of 29 women who responded to the question). Two women delivered in other countries, and one woman delivered out of state. One woman went to an ambulatory clinic.

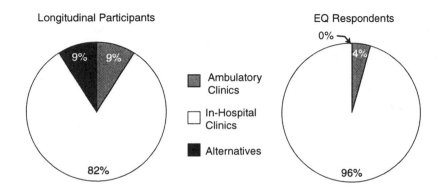

Figure 5.1. Type of Prenatal Care, by Facility

The type of facility women selected for prenatal care, moreover, did not seem to correlate with occupation or educational attainment. Ruth, although unemployed and poor, sought one of the most "exclusive" hospitals in the city. Diana, Sharon, and Sandra, all of whom had some postsecondary education, went to large city hospitals. In the EQ, respondents with a high school diploma or more selected large city hospitals over smaller, private hospitals (only one woman who had completed high school chose a private hospital). However, among the longitudinal study participants, the two women with postcollege degrees selected alternative care.

In the ethnographic research, the reasons women gave for using any given facility varied, centering on their perception of the quality of care they would receive within the context of existing constraints and options about insurance and financial circumstances. The two women who used alternative care facilities, Noma and Fatima, were most explicit in stating that they had given considerable thought to their choice. Fatima, who had delivered her previous three children at a large hospital, decided to use a birthing center because she liked the idea of the more "down-to-earth" approach to childbirth provided there. Noma chose to have a home delivery with a midwife. Sandra and Reina, who used the ambulatory care clinics, did so because those places were less bureaucratic about their insurance arrangements and had flexible hours. The remainder of the women interviewed used in-hospital clinics because they perceived the care to be more comprehensive, because the clinics accepted Medicaid, or because they thought the quality of care was better. Women were familiar with hospitals' reputations, although opinions varied greatly about each (some thought a particular public hospital was a good place to go for care while others avoided it at all costs).

However, women faced difficulties and barriers in finding an appropriate medical care facility. We have discussed in previous chapters the difficulties women face in obtaining public assistance and that many women in Harlem, across social strata, do not have access to secure benefits. Here we examine specifically how these difficulties intersect with other barriers to obtaining prenatal care. Although these problems affect primarily low-income women, middle-stratum women are not immune.

Longitudinal recipients recounted how their initial attempts to obtain early medical care were hampered by bureaucratic processes, as in the case of Noma. She attempted a home delivery, but she eventually delivered in a hospital. Noma spent a lot of time trying to get Medicaid. She said she was "tired of the red tape and lying" she had to do to get coverage and said the experience "diminished her spirit" without making any progress. She discussed how much better things were in Paris, where she once lived, noting that there anyone who worked had health coverage, which was a great deal "more civilized" than in the United States, which she described as generally "fucked up." When she received the hospital bill for $3,500 for childbirth, she could not pay, because neither she nor her husband had health insurance. Eventually the hospital suggested she apply again for Medicaid and offered to help her work through the bureaucracy.

Other women described the difficulties they faced, with or without Medicaid. Reina was unable to sign up for care at two different hospitals and eventually settled on a clinic near her home that was an outreach center operated by a large, private hospital. Even after choosing the clinic, she had to wait several weeks for her first appointment. Because of these initial difficulties, Reina did not go for her first prenatal exam until her 11th week of pregnancy. Sandra, the manager at a fast-food restaurant, discovered that her earned income placed her just above the Medicaid eligibility line. As a result, she had to search for a pre-natal care facility that she could afford without insurance, a process that took some time. Finally, she found an ambulatory clinic that was part of a network of clinics affiliated with a large, public hospital. Latoya, who had no insurance when she became pregnant, had to search to find a clinic that would accept her. Women at a Healthy Start Program meeting also discussed their difficulties with insurance. Two thought they had been arbitrarily cut from Medicaid and another reported she was cut from Medicaid and food stamps as soon as she started working at a low-income job. The latter woman delivered prematurely.

These problems were not limited to women with less education. Another woman, Ms. Z, currently a licensed practical nurse, recounted that she initially tried to enroll at "Morningside" Hospital and was rejected because they claimed they had filled their quota of Medicaid patients. She went to another large public hospital, but she did not like it, so she returned to Morningside and demanded that they take her, which they did. In this case, the ethnographer commented to the woman that she had a lot of courage to stand up for herself. The woman responded, "After a while you just get hard ... when you have to deal with city agencies, you have to get an attitude...."

Such bureaucratic barriers not only delayed initial care, they were also a source of continual problems. Several women who started out at one clinic or hospital later switched because they were unhappy with the treatment they received, and this delayed care as well. Rose, the street vendor who had run away from home, first attempted to get care at a west side hospital. There, Rose felt the need to lie about her age and living situation for fear she would be reported to child welfare authorities. In fact, the social worker threatened to report her baby's father (for statutory rape); in the end, Rose left and went to another hospital, where they accepted her without asking a lot of questions. By this time, she was 4 months into her pregnancy. Again, it was the hospital's nonmedical, regulatory procedures rather than Rose's lack of concern for her baby's health that delayed Rose's care.

In other cases, circumstances unrelated to the pregnancy interfered with care. Ivory, mentioned earlier, initially went to the clinic of a large, public hospital. However, her brother, who had recently died from a hit-and-run accident, was pronounced dead on arrival at that hospital. Traumatized by the memories of her brother's death there, she switched to a private doctor. Later, because the doctor had admitting privileges only at the same hospital, she left his care and went to a clinic in the Bronx.

What was clear from the ethnographic data was that the women in Harlem, like women elsewhere, wanted to have a healthy pregnancy and child. They actively sought care and took other actions to try to ensure such an outcome. Delays in obtaining such care, though at times due to personal ambivalence, were more often the result of the time and effort required to find the care they needed; this, in turn, was structured by the limited options open to these women.

5.1.2. Types of Prenatal Care

Although women in the study may not have engaged with the medical system until toward the end of the first trimester or later, almost all eventually did get prenatal care. All the women in our ethnographic sample were in prenatal care at some point in the second trimester, and 91 percent of women surveyed in the EQ said they had prenatal care. Women in the EQ reported an average of 11 prenatal visits. About 63 percent of women went to talk to a doctor about their pregnancy, and 50 percent talked with a nurse. It is interesting that in the EQ, most respondents reported being well treated at the hospital or care facility, and 67 percent delivered at the same facility where they received prenatal care.

The accounts of women interviewed about their experience of prenatal care varied widely. Although the different types of care facilities provided similar services, what tended to vary was the way services were provided. To better understand these similarities and differences as well as how the Harlem women in this study experienced and responded to them, let us examine the various settings where the women received their prenatal care.

5.1.2.1. Experiences with Ambulatory Clinics

Two of the women in our longitudinal study, Sandra and Reina, obtained their prenatal care in ambulatory clinics. In both cases, as we noted, they chose the care facility because staff were willing and able to smooth over insurance problems. In Reina's case, staff provided services even when she was not fully enrolled in Medicaid; in Sandra's case, they provided her with the P-CAP program. Reina chose an outreach center operated by a large private hospital located in East Harlem where the patient composition, though mixed, was largely Latina. Sandra chose an outreach center that formed part of a network of clinics affiliated with a large public hospital. The health care network was initiated under Mayor Dinkins to provide preventive health care to Harlem's residents. With six sites throughout Harlem, it provided outpatient care and referred people with serious problems to the hospital.

Both outreach clinics provided a clean environment. The clinic Sandra attended was well lit, clean, and well staffed. The East Harlem office, though worn, was also clean. Posters on the wall in both Spanish and English encouraged breastfeeding. Each clinic had various educational videos and published materials in the waiting room, although they were not offered to the women in a consistent manner. Sometimes the videos were running, and sometimes the waiting-room television set was turned on.

Both clinics had comprehensive services including postnatal and pediatric care, pharmacy, and social work services. In both clinics, nurses and midwives provided most of the care, which involved routine prenatal services. Sandra and Reina both received a regimen of prenatal vitamins and nutrition counseling. Both were tested for diabetes, and both had sonograms. Beyond that, however, it did not appear that the midwives were able to spend more than 10 to 15 minutes per visit with the women.

One of the ethnographers accompanied Reina to several of her prenatal and postnatal care visits and was able to observe the extent and nature of services provided. She provided the following account:

> At her first visit, Reina was given a routine exam and left blood and urine samples. The nurse/receptionist recorded her medical history and calculated her due date. Reina told the nurse she did not smoke cigarettes or drink. She also reported that she had asthma. Reina was not given a prescription or recommendation for prenatal vitamins because the results of the blood tests were not yet available. The nurse simply gave her an appointment card, and she was free to go. It took 3 hours to do the exam, have her blood drawn, and do the patient history.

> At her second prenatal visit, about 3 weeks later, Reina again had a routine exam. The midwife told her everything was fine and gave her a shopping bag full of vitamins, other health care products, and educational pamphlets. Reina scheduled her next appointment and was told she would see the same midwife throughout her prenatal care. The midwife was a young Latina woman who seemed very caring and gentle. After she finished with the exam, Reina went down the hall and began the process of enrolling in the Special Supplemental Nutrition Program for Women, Infants and Children (WIC). She was given a date for an interview with a WIC officer. Then she saw her assigned social worker at the clinic and obtained a letter that allowed her to get into the high school for pregnant girls. Finally, she left a urine sample. Again she was there 3 hours.

> A couple of weeks later, Reina went back to see the WIC officer and formally enrolled in the program. She also had a tuberculosis test, which was negative. At later prenatal visits, she was tested for diabetes and had a sonogram. The diabetes test was negative and the sonogram showed healthy fetal development. Reina had a matter-of-fact attitude toward her prenatal care and her pregnancy. She was not overly excited about it, but she followed the standard regimen of prenatal care. At most, she missed one of her prenatal visits.

> Although Reina was diligent about her medical care, she chose not to attend Lamaze classes because she did not think she needed them. Her general attitude was that she knew what to expect from the pregnancy, labor, and delivery. Her aunt, her mother, her cousins,

and her friends who recently had babies gave her extensive counseling, so she did not think she needed a class for help.

For her delivery, Reina went to the clinic-affiliated hospital. Her mother and aunt, along with the baby's father, accompanied her to the hospital, and her aunt was with her in the delivery room. The birth was problem-free and the baby, a girl, weighed 6 pounds, 5 ounces (2,863.3 g). Reina was very matter-of-fact about the delivery, as she had been throughout her prenatal care. The delivery went as she had expected, and was "not a big deal."

In contrast to this matter-of-fact attitude about her prenatal and birth experiences, Reina was radiant with the baby. She named her Akee, a name she heard somewhere and liked and which she thought of as African. For pediatric care, Reina took the baby to the same clinic she went to for prenatal care. A young doctor who worked for the Commissioned Corp of the U.S. Public Health Service provided the care. The pediatrician was very gentle with the baby and took ample time to answer Reina's questions and encourage her. Reina was uncomfortable with breastfeeding and never initiated it. At 6 weeks, she was feeding the baby half a tablespoon of cereal three or four times a day in her formula. Even though Reina had not been able to get a proper Medicaid card for Akee, the clinic continued to provide care for the baby.

As is clear from this account, overall the clinic staff provided a friendly and supportive atmosphere for Reina during her pregnancy. With the help of staff, she was able to get through the web of bureaucratic entanglement and gain access to care for both herself and her baby. In addition, she was able to enroll in the WIC program, which allowed her to maintain a healthier diet. However, as is also clear, Reina's average prenatal visit lasted about 3 to 4 hours (as was also the case for Sandra). Most of the time was spent waiting between weight checks, urine and blood tests, and checkups. In each case, the actual birth of the baby took place in the affiliated hospital under the care of the resident staff. The midwives who provided the prenatal care were not present at the delivery. Although Reina's delivery was routine and unproblematic, Sandra was not happy with the course of her delivery. She had a cesarean section and developed a postoperative infection. At the time of her delivery, none of the hospital staff on duty was among those who had seen her during her prenatal care.

5.1.2.2. Experiences with In-Hospital Clinics

Most of the women we followed through their pregnancy experiences used in-hospital clinics for their prenatal care. These clinics, like the ambulatory centers, offered a range of services from social work to pharmacy in conjunction with the health care exams, and women's experiences with them were not markedly different. Those who went for prenatal care to in-hospital clinics had longer waiting times for prenatal visits and had different perceptions of support from medical personnel than did the women who went to ambulatory centers.

Although all the hospitals provided an array of services, each put its own touches on the routine of prenatal care, so the types of care varied widely. Even within hospitals, clinics varied in the services they offered. For example, one hospital had a special clinic for teenagers where there was a concerted effort to educate young women. A trained midwife offered Lamaze classes during clinic hours (thus ensuring a captive audience). However, the clinic for adult women did not offer equivalent classes.

The extent to which women used the services provided at the in-hospital clinics also varied. Women sometimes chose to take advantage of these services; at other times, they avoided them. For example, Rose, as we noted, was not interested in taking advantage of the social work services; in fact, she wanted to avoid them for fear of being sent back to her father. All the women used the in-hospital pharmacy services, even though they experienced lengthy waits to receive their medications.

One of the most frustrating aspects of the hospital clinics was the length of time required for each prenatal appointment. While visits to the ambulatory clinics lasted 3 to 4 hours, hospital visits often filled an entire day of a woman's schedule, and most of the time at the clinic was spent waiting between procedures.

Rose's experience was a case in point. Rose was very concerned about her baby and faithfully went to all her prenatal visits at the clinic for teen mothers at a large hospital. The hospital had three procedures for the early prenatal visits: nurses took the patient's weight and checked the urine, and a physician did the routine prenatal exam. These procedures added up to a total of about 15 minutes of care. Between each procedure, however, was a long waiting time, so the young women spent virtually the entire day in the clinic. During this waiting time, the only program offered was a Lamaze class taught by a midwife who worked with the hospital. Rose attended this class and received her certificate but was dissatisfied with the information she received. She stated that she would have liked more information about different breathing techniques and other tips for delivery.

The ethnographer accompanied Rose to several prenatal visits. One day, the clinic was crowded and people sat in a large room waiting for the clerk to call out their names. Some women were accompanied by male companions. Rose and the ethnographer sat with another young woman, Monica, who was with her baby's father. She and Rose had developed a friendship during their clinic visits. During this visit, there was no Lamaze class and Rose and Monica played cards, as they often did on clinic visits. They sent Monica's partner, Jorge, to the fast-food place down the street from the hospital; the young women knew the menu by heart.

The ethnographer accompanied Rose to the exam room for her prenatal exam. Rose's regular doctor had not been there for the past two visits and the doctor who saw Rose this time was brusque and clearly in a rush. The exam took less than 10 minutes. But Rose enjoyed listening to the baby's heartbeat. The doctor gave Rose a refill of her vitamin prescription, and then she and the ethnographer went to the pharmacy, which was located in a dingy room with hard plastic chairs. There they waited for the prescription to be filled. By the time Rose finished in the clinic and the pharmacy, it was six o'clock. She had been there since noon.

Ama, the Senegalese vendor, developed a strategy to address the long waits. Ama tried to combine her prenatal care visits with pediatric appointments for her daughter, Aso. She had befriended one of the hospital aides, who liked to purchase goods, such as purses, from Ama. This aide helped Ama get through the various prenatal stations—urine check, weight and blood pressure check, and obstetric exam—which allowed Ama to complete her visit more quickly. Nevertheless, the day the ethnographer accompanied Ama, she spent 6 hours at the hospital. At this visit, Aso was very congested. Although Ama finished her visit in about 2 hours, she had to wait for Aso to see a doctor and then went to the pharmacy for Aso's prescription. There were only three people in line in front of her, but it took an hour to have the prescription filled.

For patients who worked at jobs that did not have flexible hours, missing work almost invariably raised issues of how they could continue to work and keep their prenatal appointments. Ms. X, the college student in her last year, who expected her parents to help care for the child while she finished college, said she attended the public hospital because she could not afford to go elsewhere and because she heard they gave good care. She was working for the summer as a supervisor at a swimming pool, a job she has had for several summers. She expected to be finished with her appointment by 11 am and was upset when she had to call and tell her supervisors she would have to take the day off. She expressed great concern about the length of time she would have to spend in the clinic and whether she would have to leave her job. She had hoped to save money to help support herself when she had to stay at home to take care of her baby.

Diana's story provides another dimension of how women responded to their prenatal care in the hospital setting. The clinic where Diana went for care was bright and well lit. It had a waiting room with about 40 chairs. Almost all the walls were covered with informational signs and posters. Most of the patients were black or Latina. There was a television that the clinic staff used to play educational videos on car safety for babies, baby care, and breastfeeding. Diana knew that her prenatal visits were all-day affairs, so she scheduled her appointments on her day off from work. Moreover, to better take advantage of the day, Diana prepared questions for the doctor ahead of time because she knew from experience that doctors respond better when the patients are well prepared. She reported that she had seen Latina women at the clinic come out of their doctors' offices looking confused because they missed much of what the physicians told them. She had seen them asking the janitors questions (in Spanish) because they were perplexed. She said that sometimes she had seen Latinas go back to the doctor's door to clarify something after speaking with the janitor. In comparing these cases with her own, as she herself put it, "when I leave out of there, I am complete."

While doctors' attitudes and those of patient care staff at the clinics varied tremendously, even in the best of cases, they were rarely able to spend more than 10 to 15 minutes talking with each patient. Staff in the clinics, pressured by heavy caseloads, sometimes were not able to fully address the patient's concerns. Rose, for example, was quite upset to learn, 7 months into her pregnancy, that the doctor she had been seeing regularly was no longer at the clinic. When Rose tried to inquire about what happened to this doctor, she was not able to get a satisfactory answer. On another occasion, when Rose went for a visit, the resident appeared not to have read Rose's history and asked questions that Rose considered irrelevant. Rose also said that when she complained of dizziness, the resident was unresponsive.

To some extent, the practices described above reflected structural problems in the public hospitals caused in part by inadequate facilities, lack of resources, and shortage of staff (increasingly also characteristic of HMO settings). At one large, public hospital clinic, for example, there was only one electronic fetal heartbeat monitor for the whole clinic. As a result, any time a doctor needed it, she/he had to knock on the doors of all the examination rooms and interrupt patients' exams in order to retrieve the monitor. Practitioners, including doctors, also had to fill out numerous forms, locate test results, and often even schedule tests for patients themselves. These tasks took away time that could have been spent with patients. The ethnographers noted that a significant portion of the time spent in long waits for medications at the pharmacy was due to the fact that the pharmacist spent a great deal of time typing labels and instructions by hand. These problems appeared to have increased with the 1994 city budget cuts. Patients at a public hospital clinic observed, for example, changes in services, noting that education classes and videos were no longer offered.

Pressure from understaffing sometimes occurred in conjunction with problems of either miscommunication or lack of communication between staff and patients. In one instance, we observed a patient trying to communicate to the nurse-midwife that she thought the vitamins she had been prescribed were making her sick and that, consequently, she had stopped taking them. The midwife, although otherwise thorough, patient, and solicitous, did not seem to hear the complaint until the ethnographer (who was also a registered nurse) intervened and asked if something could be done to change the vitamin prescription.

In other instances, ethnographers observed that although doctors and other staff were respectful of patients, they often ignored or did not seek information about their social circumstances, data that might have helped staff understand their patients' ability to comply with medical advice. This lack of communication or miscommunication might be partially attributed to medical training, which emphasizes "treating" symptoms and "managing" problems, at the expense of situating the patient in a more holistic context (Martin, 1987).

In other cases, however, we observed positive attempts to remedy some of these problems. Recently, for example, one hospital revised its procedures so that nurse-midwives followed the same patient throughout the prenatal care period. This arrangement facilitated patient care and as one practitioner put it, held midwives accountable for the patient. Before these changes, patients saw any practitioner who was working on the day of their appointment and thus often "fell through the cracks." Even so, however, patients at this hospital were not guaranteed that their midwife would be with them for the delivery.

5.1.2.3. Experiences with Alternative Care

Two women in our study chose alternatives to the prevalent practice of using medical clinics and hospitals. Noma, the performance artist, wanted to have a home delivery attended by a midwife, and Fatima, the social worker, opted for a birthing center on the upper east side. In both cases, the women were attended by midwives who provided the same type of prenatal care (fetal monitoring, blood and urine tests to monitor for potential problems, and weight checks) the clinics provided. Both women thought their experiences of prenatal care had been positive.

In Noma's and Fatima's accounts, two elements seemed to differentiate their prenatal care experiences from those provided at other clinics. First, in contrast to traditional, Western medical practice, alternative care seemed to approach pregnancy and childbirth within a wider, holistic framework. As a result, Noma and Fatima thought they received much greater support from the midwives, who in both cases spent a great deal of time with them, answered their questions, and provided advice on nutrition and general health as well as emotional support. In addition, the midwives who provided their prenatal care were present during the delivery. Second, both Fatima and Noma thought they were able to maintain much greater control over their own pregnancy experience than they would have in a traditional clinical setting. These differences can best be understood by examining the two cases in greater detail.

Fatima had delivered her previous three children at a large hospital. She shifted to the birthing center so she could have a more natural birthing experience. The center was located in an old mansion, and its interior resembled a house more than a clinic. The staff was friendly and caring, and the clientele was diverse. The center accepted Medicaid patients as well as those with private insurance.

Fatima explained that in a normal prenatal visit, she saw the midwife who was on call that day. Although she had a permanent physician, generally she saw the midwives and midwives' assistants. She described the procedure as follows:

> First you get your own chart. Then you go and urinate. You collect your own sample. You get a swab and collection bottle in the bathroom, where there is also a scale. You weigh yourself. You check your urine with a thing that changes colors, there is a color chart on the bottle and you enter the results and your weight on the chart. The urine check tells you how many ketones, how much glucose, and how much protein is in your urine.

She showed the ethnographer her chart and the indications of protein traces in her previous urine samples. After she completed the chart, the midwife tested her blood pressure and monitored the fetal heartbeat. One of the most striking aspects of Fatima's prenatal care was the extent to which she was able to participate in the activities as well as the knowledge and experience she gained from this participation.

These elements of support, participation, and control were equally or perhaps more evident in Noma's prenatal, and especially birth, experience. The midwife who attended Noma was part of a small group of health practitioners in Harlem who were combining Western medical practices with alternative healing strategies drawn from an extensive body of knowledge and experience. This group had been active for some time in Harlem health politics and particularly in widening the scope of services offered to Harlem residents. In addition to providing services from storefronts and from their homes, this group also sold and distributed literature on the streets.

The following is Noma's experience of labor and birth as witnessed by the ethnographer. When Noma went into labor, she called the midwife, who came to her home. The midwife helped Noma find a comfortable position, and Noma turned on a jazz station on the radio and held a crystal in her hand, which she squeezed during contractions. When a contraction began she got on her hands and knees and breathed through it. In addition to the midwife and the ethnographer, a friend of Noma's was there, who massaged her back during contractions. Noma's partner, Phil, who was away on tour in San Francisco, arrived later that day.

As Noma was having a home delivery, she was able to prepare her surroundings to meet her needs, which were social, psychological, and cultural as well as physiological. In the living room, she had set up an altar with a candle, a jar of water taken from Senegal, a picture of Frida Kahlo (a Mexican artist), baby moccasins, some fruit, incense, and photos of family members. Next to Noma's bed was a chest covered with fabric and an assortment of supplies such as lubricating jelly, alcohol wipes, gauze sponges, and disposable gloves. On the other side of her bed was the ultrasound jelly and Doppler used to hear the baby's heart rate. At the foot of the bed was another table with more gauze, clamps, and scissors. On the bed, wrapped in white fabric, was a silver ankh (the Egyptian symbol of life) with a crystal in it.

The day wore on, and between contractions Noma rested on several pillows and seemed to go into a light sleep. The day was very quiet and a bit hot. In the background were street noises. Periodically, the midwife measured the baby's heart rate, took Noma's blood pressure, and continued to monitor Noma's progress and the extent of her dilation. The midwife also encouraged Noma to get up and walk around. Throughout the day, a number of people called to check on Noma and inquire about the baby. Most of the calls were from friends, although Phil's sister and brother also inquired about her condition. Friends dropped by and helped out by bringing in food and playing with Noma's daughter.

Noma continued to experience contractions for the next 2 days, but she did not dilate beyond 4 to 5 centimeters. The midwife remained with her at all times and was joined by an assistant. On the third day of labor, Noma's mother arrived and worked with the midwife to support Noma through this difficult labor. The midwife gave Noma some tea made of ginger and alfalfa, which is thought to ease the labor, as well as a dropper of echinacea, which is used as a natural antibiotic. People continued to call, drop by, and bring food.

Toward the end of the third day, the family and the midwife became concerned that although Noma had dilated to 7 centimeters, she still was not ready to deliver. Noma still wanted to stay at home; her mother, Phil, and the midwife supported her decision. However, on the fourth day, all decided that the labor had not progressed and Noma should go to the hospital. She chose to go to one with a strong midwife program. At the hospital, the midwife was able to attend to Noma throughout the delivery. The hospital staff administered Pitocin (oxytocin) and an epidural (anesthetic). After that, labor progressed more rapidly, and she had a normal vaginal delivery. Noma had a healthy baby girl who weighed 6 pounds, 3 ounces (2,806 g).

Noma's childbirth experience evolved over 4 days. Throughout that time, she received continual support from family, friends, and the midwife, who remained with her the entire time. She was able to arrange her surroundings to meet her varied needs. Noma maintained a highly nutritional diet, and when conditions demanded, she was willing to forego the home delivery and go to the hospital for her child's benefit. This was also the case for Fatima. Although Fatima was a practicing Muslim, her religion exempted her from the Ramadan fasting because of her pregnancy. Thus, cultural differences and alternative approaches may be successfully combined with what is traditionally considered appropriate prenatal care.

In summary, the three types of prenatal care facilities chosen by women in the study were similar in the type of care offered but different in the way the care was provided. In all instances, women seemed to be relatively content with the system they had chosen, although those who attended clinics (whether ambulatory or in-hospital) had more complaints, especially about the waiting time and the bureaucratic entanglements, than those who used alternative care. In view of the fact that women in this study were willing to go to different types of facilities, removing any barriers of access to any facility by means such as insurance reform and provision of universal health coverage would be an important intervention.

5.2. DOCTORS, PATIENTS, AND DIFFERENT PERCEPTIONS

As women in Harlem told their stories, it became increasingly clear that they, as women elsewhere, were interested in having healthy babies. This concern for a healthy pregnancy and a healthy child cut across educational levels. What these women considered quality and appropriate care may have differed among individuals; it also may have differed in some respects, but not all, from that considered appropriate by medical professionals. Nevertheless, most women implemented routines that they considered appropriate prenatal care. They sought help and advice from a variety of sources, including, but not limited to, medical personnel. They implemented, where possible, changes in their daily routines and dietary practices. However, circumstances often did not permit them to make the changes they knew were necessary. They generally took responsibility for their pregnancies, and they sought to put into practice what was within their power to do.

The pregnancy experiences that the women in this study allowed us to see contrasted sharply with perceptions often held and expressed by medical personnel. In most cases, staff seemed to be concerned about their patients, but in many instances, staff members appeared to be judgmental of the women, often on the basis of their understanding of lifestyle choices and individual behaviors as explanations for poor pregnancy outcomes. For example, a West Indian nurse at one of the public hospital clinics talked about how the lifestyle and behavior of poor women was the major reason for poor pregnancy outcomes. Similarly, an African American pediatrician with a practice in Harlem stated that the problems of teen mothers and out-of-wedlock births were largely problems with the poor. He claimed he had not seen this problem in his middle-class African American clientele:

> ... and unfortunately, that is a cycle which is condoned and supported by the state. So, there's no onus to having a baby out of wedlock. When I was a child, there was a big onus to having extramarital ... or premarital relations.... Or you know ... a teenage girl having a baby when she's 14, 15, 16. But at this juncture ... there is no onus to that.... Then, on top of that, they have the problems with smoking and drugs and alcohol.... So, these external things, beside the genetic things, will provide more of a problem for that group having babies...

While lifestyle issues are certainly important, patients may perceive such attitudes from medical personnel as indicating a lack of respect for them, and this may restrict their attendance, compliance, and communication. One respondent to the EQ reported that a major stressor during pregnancy was what she considered to be a negative perception of patients by physicians, and she ascribed it to race: "The white doctor ... said something I've never forgotten: 'I'll see you next year.'" Similarly, a vendor we encountered on 125th Street told us that she always started her medical visits by telling doctors that she is not married, has never been pregnant, has never had an abortion, and does not use drugs, in order to "deter that line of questioning" and let them know that she is "an intelligent woman."

These perceptions of the poor also influenced the way doctors and other staff treated patients under their care and how they understood their patients' lives. For the most part, we found that staff maintained a professional and courteous attitude toward their patients, sometimes informally expressing their negative views privately to the ethnographers. However, sometimes they communicated their perceptions of their patients through verbal and nonverbal behavior. This problem was discussed by one of the nurses, who remarked that sometimes staff narrowly limited themselves to tasks such as scheduling because "they dislike patients and do not treat them with respect" (as ethnographers observed from time to time). She attributed these attitudes to the fact that "because staff hold steady jobs, they believe what they hear in the media and distance themselves from people who are not working."

The different perceptions held by pregnant women and staff, and their impact on pre-natal care, can perhaps best be understood by examining more closely the problem of missed appointments. Medical personnel frequently considered missed prenatal care appointments to be an indication of women's lack of concern about their pregnancies. During the course of our study, we came across this view on several occasions and found that such views could even come to form part of the information passed on to new staff. For example, a white obstetrician at the large public hospital told the ethnographer that she taught residents that even if a patient said she missed her appointments because of child care or work difficulties, the patient should still be held responsible for missing the appointment. When the ethnographer suggested that women might face real difficulties in keeping prenatal appointments, the doctor stated that there are always solutions for women (such as letters to their employers) that allow them to keep their appointments.

The ethnographic data, however, indicated that solutions might not be so simple. The research indicated that once enrolled in prenatal care, most women tried to keep their appointments, and the reasons for missing them were diverse. In only a few instances did women actually "skip" an appointment deliberately. Longitudinal participant Diana's rea-sons constitute a telling case. Diana, a worker in a fast-food restaurant, was diligent about her prenatal visits with the exception of two visits, which she deliberately missed. The doctor had been insisting on her having an amniocentesis, which Diana did not want to have. She said that she would love her child whether or not she/he had Down syndrome. Her grandfather, with whom she was very close, told her that she would not be the first person "to open her door" to a Down syndrome baby.

Feeling under pressure, Diana simply avoided the clinic during that period to "beat those tests," as she put it. She said she would be furious if the doctors and nurses contin-ued to hound her. She also said she would lose her temper and "the next thing you know, they would say crazy black woman needs to be put on evaluation." When she returned for her prenatal care, the doctor told her she was "very crafty." Diana believed that either she would have been pressured into having a test she did not want, or her understandable anger would have been misconstrued based on existing racial stereotypes.

In other cases, women missed appointments because they were out of town, as was the case for Reina, who visited relatives in Chicago. Sometimes women missed appoint-ments because they stayed up late the night before at parties or with their boyfriends. Given that this was true only of the younger women (under 25), our study suggests that age, rather than level of educational attainment or income, is at the root of this behavior.

Often, however, missed appointments were the result of circumstances beyond the women's control; this was particularly true for women with a limited income. For exam-ple, a child care arrangement could fall apart, and as a result, the woman could not go to the clinic; in some instances, women took older children out of school to watch the younger ones. In other instances, a family member was sick or in trouble and needed atten-tion right away, or women could not get off work at the last minute.

For example, Ms. U, who lived with Gina, missed prenatal appointments because her mother demanded that she babysit her younger siblings. She gave birth prematurely to a low-birth-weight infant. In another instance, Ms. V, a relative of Gina's who had graduat-ed from high school and worked part time, missed appointments because she was juggling a job with constant travel to and from the Bronx, where she resided temporarily with the baby's father. Her baby was born prematurely. Finally, Ivory, the adolescent who lived in a tenement, missed appointments because someone stole her school bus pass, which deprived her of transportation. On other days, when her mother's apartment had no heat or hot water, she was ashamed to go to appointments or to school "unwashed."

Because all the agencies required different paperwork, sometimes women missed appointments because they arrived at the clinic with the wrong papers. Again, this was true especially for the low-income women, who had the most bureaucratic entanglements, and for the younger women, who tended to be more disorganized with their papers. Low-income women had an additional difficulty in trying to reschedule missed appointments: they lacked telephones at home, and the pay phones on the street were usually out of order. This was the case with Claire, who was in her mid-20s and had previously been homeless. A variety of circumstances prevented Claire from keeping all her prenatal appointments: tasks for her other children, staying up late at night, and misplacing her paperwork. She did not have a phone in her apartment and could not easily reschedule appointments.

When staff were unwilling or unable to recognize these circumstances, the quality of care was clearly affected. This was exemplified by one of the events our ethnographers observed in an in-hospital clinic: a young, teenage woman was in some distress, and when a fellow patient asked what was wrong, the young woman said she had missed her sonogram appointment, but no one would schedule another one. The patient counseled her to walk into the head nurse's office and explain her situation. The teen emerged moments later and burst into tears because someone had been short with her. She said, "They don't care about anyone in this place."

In other instances, hospital staff, who otherwise might have acted differently, were subject to the impact of these misperceptions about poor people and the hospitals that served them. During the research period, for example (especially after Rudolph Giuliani became mayor), city officials and others frequently criticized public hospital management and staff. One staff member commented that she loved her patients but increasingly felt she could not deal with the hospital. She noted that the hospital itself was in a subordinate relationship with a large medical school that "looks down and denigrates" staff's actions and practices. She stated that this attitude told people, at every level, that they were at this hospital because they were not good enough to be elsewhere: "It destroys talented people who want to contribute to the community. The dedicated young people who want to work with poor patients try to stick it out, but after 5 years they go elsewhere, and poor patients are the losers."

5.3. BETWEEN ENGAGEMENT AND DISTRUST

The patterns that emerged suggest that women in our study actively sought prenatal medical care and maintained a consistent routine of care. At the same time, however, they did not necessarily use the available services to their full extent, and sometimes they appeared to consciously maintain a degree of distance. This simultaneous engagement and distrust of the medical establishment suggests that we must move beyond simple dichotomies about attitudes and behaviors. Rather, we must construct a more nuanced picture of women's relationships with the medical system, analyzing in greater detail what women accept and what they do not, how they respond, and what alternatives are available to them.

In examining what women had to say about their pregnancy experiences, it becomes clear that, to some extent, they selectively used the medical care facilities according to their own expectations and views of appropriate prenatal care. Once they selected a medical facility, how they specifically used the facility and what they used it for was placed within their own wider framework of appropriate prenatal care. This framework included the existing social world, social networks, and social views within which their pregnancy evolved, as well as alternative practices.

Most eligible women took full advantage of access to the WIC program and vitamin prescriptions to improve their diet. Similarly, women generally accepted blood and urine tests as well as obstetric exams and fetal monitoring as part of their standard medical care. In contrast, very few women we observed in the course of fieldwork actively sought or took Lamaze or other formal childbirth preparation classes, although some attended classes when they were available. This was true across educational levels.

Rose, for example, received childbirth preparation classes from the midwife at the clinic for pregnant adolescents as part of her regular clinic experience. However, she expressed dissatisfaction with the material covered in the class. In another instance, Diana, the fast-food restaurant worker, also went for preparation classes, partly for her husband's sake and partly because she thought that because there had been such a long interval between pregnancies, she needed to go to the class. Clearly, Noma, who chose to have a home delivery, received extensive preparation instructions from her midwife as an integral part of her prenatal care.

Fatima and her husband also took the classes at the birthing center. In general, they were satisfied with the classes but found some aspects disturbing, including a video about the birthing process, which showed nude women. As practicing Muslims, the couple considered public displays of undressed women immodest and inappropriate; they believed the women in the video should have been wearing clothes. Even though some of these women were black, Fatima and her husband suggested that nudity during birth was "a white thing."

In other cases, participants chose not to attend formal classes. Instead, they relied on the advice of relatives and friends, who told them in detail what the childbirth experience was like and counseled them about how to prepare for it. In the EQ, most women (72 percent) reported they did not attend formal childbirth classes. One woman who attended classes found it unpleasant and reported that she "was not invited back to bring the baby after he was born because of racism."

These incidents and reactions suggest that one reason our study participants did not engage in formal childbirth classes may have been the class and racial bias that underlie some approaches to formal childbirth preparation. Childbirth classes tend to cater to middle-class white visions of what a good childbirth should be (Ginsburg and Rapp, 1991). Women we talked with generally dismissed the practices they heard were taught in the classes (breathing, etc.). Reina, for example, said she did not need "all that" because her mother and aunt had already told her what to do. Many of the women with whom we talked were not concerned about whether their births would be "natural" or would involve some medication or even a cesarean. Ruth, for example, wanted a cesarean and was distraught when she did not have one; she attributed the loss of one of the twins to the fact that she was denied a cesarean (see Nelson, 1986, for differences by class toward birthing).

Even within the medical dimension of care, women practiced a simultaneous process of engagement and distrust. All the women we observed, except Fatima, delivered in a hospital. Noma, as we have seen, did not intend to but ended up having to go to the hospital. In the EQ, most women reported being well treated in hospitals at the time of delivery, using descriptions such as "wonderful" and "they treated me excellent." In the ethnographic work as well, we found that most women reported positive delivery experiences and liked the way they were treated by the staff.

In contrast, women's response to what we can call the "technification" of prenatal care was much more ambivalent. All the women in the study received extensive blood tests and tests for diabetes. Many women had sonograms, and a few were offered amniocentesis. All the women accepted the blood tests and the diabetes tests as a necessary component of their medical care. Low-income women in our study, however, had little sense of the significance of the tests. As we have observed, doctors and medical staff spent little time actually talking to the women in the clinics. Women called the diabetes test the "sugar test" and remembered it well but could not really articulate what risks diabetes posed for them. Only one woman we encountered in fieldwork was actually diabetic during her pregnancy. She worked in a hospital and was well aware of the implications of diabetes and how to monitor herself. Furthermore, few women appeared to understand the purpose of the blood tests.

The sonograms and monitoring of fetal heartbeat also elicited mixed feelings. All were accepted as part of standard medical procedure, but they were generally regarded with indifference. Reina, as described above, was not excited about hearing the fetal heartbeat or seeing the baby in the womb, but Rose was. Aurora regarded the sonogram with indifference. The variation in attitudes and behaviors concerning reproductive technologies is described in the anthropological literature on reproduction (see Ginsburg and Rapp, 1991, 1995; Nelson, 1986; Eakins, 1986). Rapp (1991), moreover, has documented the class and race differences in women's perception and the use of reproductive technologies.

Fraser (1995) describes the ambivalence with which African Americans in a southern town came to view the medicalization and technification of birth practices. She points out that on the one hand, there was considerable regret on the part of African American women about the loss of traditional midwifery practices, which had been strong and prevalent in the South until they were deliberately undermined by the medical system. On the other hand, these women also welcomed modern medical practices because access reflected the inclusion of African Americans into the public sphere after decades of deliberate neglect.

The women we followed, while different from the southerners described by Fraser, nevertheless seemed to have the same ambiguous or contradictory feelings about the medical system. They expected and struggled to achieve the best quality health care. Yet, well aware and sensitive to their treatment in the system, they were careful to maintain their distance from it as well. As we have noted, the perceptions, attitudes, and actions of medical personnel, along with bureaucratic entanglements and humiliation, were among the immediate, experiential sources of this distrust. However, women's positive expressions about the actual hospital delivery of their child seemed to coincide with a compassionate attitude on the part of attending staff.

There was an emerging socioeconomic distinction in women's strategies toward the system. Interestingly, among respondents to the EQ, the number of women who sought advice from doctors or medical personnel dropped significantly with postsecondary education. Fifty-five percent of women with less than a high school diploma went to a doctor for advice, 50 percent of women with a high school diploma went to a doctor for advice, and only 40 percent of women with more than a high school diploma reported going to a doctor for advice. In addition, although 33 to 36 percent of women with a high school diploma or less reported going to a nurse for advice, only 7 percent of those with more than a high school diploma reported doing so.

The ethnographic data, moreover, suggest that although women across educational levels may simultaneously engage with and distance themselves from the medical system, the ways they do so may differ. Among the women we followed, the more educated women seemed to harbor a greater distrust of the standard medical system per se. Noma and Fatima, the two women who chose alternative care, were both highly educated. Diana, who questioned amniocentesis and who went prepared with questions to her prenatal visits, also had a postsecondary education. Perhaps because women with more education often have greater access to alternatives, they may actively strive to disengage (to the degree possible) from the system or to selectively choose how they will engage it. Noma and Fatima had access to a body of knowledge on alternative forms of care available, and both, to different extents, had greater access to economic resources for their care as well. Although Noma was without insurance and had an unstable income because of her profession, she had access to a pool of resources from her family and friends. Fatima was able to prepay in full for her care and then await reimbursement.

Women with less education, having high expectations of the system (see Nelson, 1986), tended to engage with the medical system more fully than those with a higher education. Still, they maintained their distance from the system through attitudes of indifference toward its major practices and through more passive means of avoidance. Thus Reina, for example, remained very matter-of-fact throughout her pregnancy, and Ivory simply sought another clinic for her care. Diana, although having completed high school, was highly limited in her options because of economic constraints. When she felt pressured by the medical staff to have an amniocentesis, she simply avoided it by purposely missing the appointment. In addition, as we have seen, these women's distrust stemmed from the attitudes of medical staff and the nonmedical functions carried out in prenatal care settings more than from the medical services per se.

5.4. EXPLANATIONS FOR PREGNANCY LOSS

5.4.1. Pregnancy Loss and Conceptualizing Bad Outcomes

Although most pregnancies we documented resulted in positive outcomes, involuntary pregnancy loss, here, as in most of the world, was considered a negative experience. Roseanne Cecil suggests that the dearth of ethnographic writing on pregnancy loss may reflect women's painful feelings about pregnancy losses and their reluctance and even inability to talk about them. She cites Leclerc on the difficulty or impossibility of writing about pregnancy and childbirth: "Who could tell me, could I ever express (and what words would I use) ..." (1996:17) and goes on to say "there may not, quite literally, be the words to discuss and describe the event. The feelings concerning simultaneous birth and death, the death of one who never was may be virtually impossible to convey" (1996:2). As we noted when discussing the methodology, although we easily assembled focus groups on a variety of subjects, it was very difficult to convene one on pregnancy loss.

At the focus group that was eventually convened, a 35-year-old participant expressed a sense of powerlessness despite her own efforts to have a healthy baby. Describing the loss of her infant, she stated, "The baby was full-term. I had a good pregnancy. I had pre-natal care. She was like ... she weighed 8 pounds and 10 ounces. And I don't know. It's like still today, I mean, I think about what happened. They said that she died of fetal distress. You know, many hours of labor." A participant in the birth experience focus group said, "It just happened. I didn't plan, but when I found out that I was pregnant, I was happy. This was the first one, and I had just about everything arranged. And then ... it was gone."

A respondent in the birth experience focus group described her hospital experience: "You go to the hospital, and you come home without a baby. That first night you are put in a ward with everyone else, and everybody is bringing their baby. I felt like I was so iso-lated, and I would go out in the hallway or go smoke a cigarette or go talk on the phone, especially at nursing time when they brought in the babies."

Another participant in this focus group described her experience with a miscarriage at 5 months:

> When I found out that I had that miscarriage, I was like OK. I took care of myself and everything, and I was going to the doctor, and they were kind of worried, you know, because they were saying something about my uterus. One night I was just at home, and my girlfriend came over to see me, and we were about to watch a movie, and all of a sud-den I was having pain, and I asked her to get me some juice, and all of a sudden all this blood just burst down my legs, and my girlfriend started screaming, and I just stood there and couldn't move. And then I went to the emergency room, and they told me the baby's head was right there, and they told me to push, so I did, and they said do you want to see the baby, and I glanced, and I was trying to play it off like it didn't bother me, but then I started staying up at night. For two weeks I couldn't sleep. They gave me injections so I would sleep, but I couldn't go to sleep. I sat up in bed.

A preliminary analysis of interviews with 145 mothers who had experienced infant loss in Harlem (Phillips, 1996) confirmed that many believed inadequate explanations of their loss had been offered to them by hospital or medical personnel.

As Scheper-Hughes (1992) notes, a frequent response to infant death everywhere in the world is pregnancy. This observation has implications for understanding the effect of infant loss on subsequent pregnancies. In our longitudinal sample, Sharon had previously lost one baby to fetal distress. Ruth, who, as described in an earlier chapter, lost one of her twins after delayed medical care, soon became pregnant again. Participants in the birth experience and grief-and-loss focus group discussed their need to become pregnant again after the loss of a pregnancy. One said, "I had my son about a year later." Ruth said, "I'm pregnant again, and I think I got pregnant again to try to fill in the void for the baby that I lost." Ruth's response suggests that, perhaps subconsciously, women deal with the power-lessness reflected in pregnancy loss with actions that they can, in fact, control.

Ruth continued:

> I just wanted my baby. 'Cause a lot of people don't understand, "Oh, you pregnant again?"
> I have to fill that void for the baby that I lost, or I'm not going to be no good. I know me.

I know me, you know. So, I'm still going through it. It ain't ... it's far from finished, you know. It's far from finished. Yeah. I gotta fill in the void, people don't understand. Like my mother was like, "How can you just ... how can you go again and get pregnant?" And I try to explain to her that to me, it's an empty void, and I got to fill it. I have to fill in that void. So, I'm having another boy. Can't have no more afterwards, but I'm having another one.

The relationship between loss and replacement was similarly expressed by another participant who described her loss: "It was like something that I felt was missing, and I had to have another baby, and I tried." A participant in the focus group on households headed by women described her perception of the link between life and death:

I have six children of my own and three grandchildren, and with my last two pregnancies, I lost my mother with one, and my father first. My son is going to be 11 in July, and my father died that June before he was born. And with my mother, she died that April, and my youngest son was born that October. A lot of things went through my mind. When there's a birth, there's always a death. This is what they always say. And I also noticed that with my other children, every time one was born, it wasn't in my family, but my husband had lost someone in his family.

Just as the experience of pregnancy itself is structured by a series of social and cultural factors, so too is that of loss. The explanations women in this study gave for the loss of their pregnancies varied and again reflected the interplay of factors over which they could or could not exert control. Leroy (1988:96) suggests that the theme of loss of a child as a punishment for wrongdoing is "a persistent part of human thinking about reproduction." This view was clearly expressed by women who linked their loss to their own behavior. One focus group participant discussed her experience:

I had one son, my first child. But I remarried, and this would have been my husband's first child, so I was really happy all through that pregnancy. But then I took a fall down some stairs. I didn't fall, I just slipped, but I didn't go to the hospital, and a week later I started having pains. The baby had turned around, and it was feet first, and it was very difficult. The doctor had to pull the baby out. And looking at the father I felt really bad, because that would have been his first baby. He was there with me in the delivery room, and somehow or another I felt that he was blaming me, that I didn't do something right, you know, and I never saw my son.

But even now after 10 years he is still talking about it, we get into little arguments about it, so I just tune him out.... He just said that I didn't take care of myself, which I did, I went to prenatal and stuff, and I smoked cigarettes, 'cause he doesn't smoke cigarettes, so he talks about health, so I guess he felt that I could have been a little extra careful. But once you are pregnant you know the infant now, and you go to the maternity leave, you take vitamins, you know, and I did everything else I was supposed to.... You know it really was the fall, and I should have went to the hospital, but I didn't tumble all the way down the steps, you know I just slipped a couple, and I was on my back. But I think they also said it was possible that the baby's kidneys failed. But I didn't go into any further investigation, because I just lost the baby.

What is striking, however, is that many women did not limit their explanations of pregnancy loss to their own behavior. As we saw in a previous chapter, Ruth, while recognizing her own responsibility, also attributed the death of her baby to the action and attitudes of others linked to wider social conditions. Her feelings were supported by others in the focus group. Similarly, when we asked people who lived and worked in Harlem about the reasons for higher rates of infant mortality and preterm delivery among African

American women, although some cited individual behaviors such as nutrition, substance abuse, and lack of prenatal care, most also implicated larger societal issues, such as continued discrimination and cutbacks of government programs. Their explanations of the reasons for infant mortality also give us a sense of how people in Harlem describe the consequences of racial discrimination.

A licensed practical nurse enumerated what she saw as stress-producing situations, including the pressure for African American women to work throughout their life cycle, comparing this situation to white women, who she said may be raised with the idea that a husband will take care of them. She considered relationships in general to be a source of stress during pregnancy: "Men just seem to act funny when you get pregnant." Finally, based on her own experience, she suggested that single motherhood, where one person has to juggle multiple roles, raises the stress level. A registered nurse suggested that the difficult economic situation in which black women find themselves is a major contributor. A certified midwife noted, "Birth weight is an objective measure of lifelong female health status." She went on to say that African American women have more problems with pregnancy because "they live with stress their entire lives, and the pregnancy outcomes reflect its cumulative effect."

Pondering the issue of class, a medical doctor at a large public hospital pointed out that African Americans in every class are less well off than whites in the same class; they are more recent arrivals to middle-class status; they must spend more money than their white counterparts to maintain that status; and the status itself is more precarious for them. Harlem residents who are not in medical occupations may use different terms, but they make similar points. An older community activist said, "It could be stress. Especially if you're having a baby, and you have to work and keep up. Because I know people who work until the last day before they have their baby. And another thing, black people have babies, and they go back to work. White folks have their babies, and they stay home. And you have to wonder who's going to keep the [black] baby."

Another Harlem resident said, "You can't statistically analyze the impact of racism." A secretary put it rather succinctly: "Black women have a hard life and catch hell." Each of these women was cognizant of and responded to the hidden injuries of racism that African Americans must face on a daily basis.

When asked what she would do to change the disproportionately high infant mortality rates among Harlem women, a registered nurse said the community "needs more money." She asserted that the job training program in the welfare system has to change. She recounted her own experience on public assistance before she became a nurse. She said, "Everything is against you." She went for job training and was told she had to wait until the children were school-age to get a job. "And then when you do work, they cut off the assistance." When she was on welfare, she said, she had more money than she does now. She described the inadequacy of child care as another barrier to single working mothers.

At a neighborhood meeting where we presented the research project, one woman questioned its priority. Emphasizing the fact that perhaps there were more pressing problems in the community than infant mortality, she commented, "If you have money to do something, I don't think you should be doing this because there are a lot of little children running around that are hungry." Not only did she consider the need to sustain and nurture surviving children to be just as important, she also insisted on the need to place the problem of infant mortality within a wider context of community problems in general.

In sum, the experiences of women within the health care delivery system must be understood in the context of the wider social conditions and specific circumstances of everyday life. The ethnography points to potential sources of distrust of the system and the subsequent disengagement with it. It is also clear that many people who live and work in Harlem have a sophisticated understanding of the interrelationship between social and economic factors, the delivery of health care, and their own health vulnerability. The implication of this for improving health care delivery is that, in addition to structural changes to facilitate access, improvement in the quality of health care delivery is needed, including the adoption of more holistic views of patient care.

NOTE

[1] As was mentioned previously, stratum or social stratum as used in this report includes variation by level of education, occupation, and income. It is used to indicate a general combination of these criteria but not a confliation of them.

6

RACE, CLASS, GENDER, AND HEALTH

Although this study has focused on reproductive health, African American women and men die younger and have higher rates of morbidity and mortality for most diseases than whites. Mainstream literature in medicine and epidemiology traditionally has attributed these disparities to genetic or cultural differences. Critics of these approaches have pointed to the necessity of studying race, class, and gender as structural constraints on health (Cooper, 1986; Krieger and Bassett, 1986; Krieger, 1999; Mullings, 1984, 1989).

A major problem for theory and policy has been how to conceptualize the effects of multiple forms of discrimination. This difficulty also confronts social scientists, who suggest that race, class, and gender are not additive but interlocking, interactive, and relational categories (see Mullings, 1997). The relationship has been described as "multiplicative" (King, 1988:42) and in terms of "the articulation of multiple oppressions" (Brewer, 1993:13) and of "simultaneity" (Andersen and Collins, 1995:ii). Although highlighting the matrix of interaction is a necessary theoretical intervention, it is not sufficient. The challenge we now encounter is to understand the ways these hierarchies interact to produce consequences such as elevated morbidity and mortality. We must now go beyond an abstract description of the relationship to understand specifically how this interaction, articulation, and simultaneity affect women in their daily lives and may, in fact, be a matter of life and death.

Recent studies have explored the health effects of the way race, class, and gender hierarchies structure the triple day—work outside the home, household work, and community work—for African American women (Mullings, 1984), the health impact of the noneconomic aspects of race, and the gender specificity of racism (Krieger, 1999). This study falls within that tradition in pointing to the multiplicative effects of race, class, and gender on health by framing these in an environmental stress paradigm. It suggests that reproductive experiences can be understood only within the larger context of social, economic, and political conditions within which women live. Such an approach has implications for understanding a range of stress-related health problems.

6.1. IMPLICATIONS FOR REPRODUCTIVE HEALTH

The research found that there were significant stressors and chronic strains associated with environment, housing, and social service delivery. The likely mechanism by which these factors directly affected women's health and well-being was through the day-to-day interactions with these conditions. These included women's daily attempts to cope with these stressors and strains and to modify their quality of life. Women perceived that these sources of stress and strain were modifiable, and, as was demonstrated in the case material, women participated in both individual and collective strategies to address their circumstances. In addition, we found that study participants perceived the negative representation of Harlem in the media, popular culture, and the political arena as attributable to racism and as a direct cause of the negative environmental, housing, and social service stressors. As such, the negative representation was in itself a significant source of chronic strain for study participants across social strata. This was an additional burden that made the day-to-day efforts to cope more difficult. Protective strategies and perceived community assets, however, buffered the women in their daily lives. An important finding was that, in the context of these chronic strains, the occurrence of pregnancy may have served as a catalyst to increase the magnitude of actual and perceived severity of stress. The mechanism appeared to be multiplicative rather than additive. The case material demonstrated how pregnancy became the focal point for the interrelationship between housing, environmental, economic, and other social stressors.

Clearly, the interaction of job-specific stressors and the underlying chronic strain produced by income and employment insecurity resulted in a magnitude of stress that may have had specific implications for reproductive health. The mechanism by which these stressors and strains affected reproductive health is likely to be found in the struggle that women undertook to find or maintain adequate income and benefits both before conception and during pregnancy. The research suggests that, beyond the limitations this mechanism imposes on access to quality health care, it is important to note the further limitations this imposes on access to healthful resources such as adequate housing, nutrition, child care, and a safe environment. Thus it is impossible to separate the effects of economic conditions from the social and political conditions. Public health interventions that target only specific components of job strain are likely to be inadequate unless they include attention to structural issues of gender and race inequality that place large numbers of African American women in severe conditions of income insecurity.

The research found that a consequence of the larger structural forces and changes described in the volume was the decline of marriage and the rise of households headed by women for African American women of all social strata and that the social support networks documented in the case material were an important adaptive coping mechanism. As such, they should be recognized and reinforced, and interventions should incorporate the strengths of these support networks. However, recruitment of social support networks differs by social strata, and this has implications for health and relative exposure to stress during the reproductive years. Middle-stratum women may tend to rely more on friends and may be unable to access the type of instrumental and financial support more likely to be offered by families. Low-income women may continue to rely primarily on families but may find that because of resource scarcity generated by worsening economic conditions, all family members have less to give, and so networks are strained. As such, any intervention should be sensitive to the fragility of these support networks and should incorporate resources that reinforce network ties. Finally, despite value assumptions in popular media and sometimes in the health field concerning African American gender relationships, the research suggested that men, who themselves were strained by economic and social conditions, continued to play more important roles in the lives of women than is frequently recognized. Therefore, interventions to improve reproductive health for women also must include men and must address their conditions.

6.2. THE SOJOURNER SYNDROME

As an aid to conceptualizing the multiplicative effects of race, class, and gender on health, we coin the term "Sojourner Syndrome" (Mullings, 2000). Similar to "John Henryism," the Sojourner Syndrome may represent a behavioral strategy that has important health consequences. John Henry was a legendary "steel-driving man" who was known among late 19th century railroad and tunnel workers for his strength and endurance. In a contest of man against new technology, John Henry and his 9-pound hammer were pitted against a mechanical steam drill. In a close race, John Henry emerged victorious but moments later died from physical and mental exhaustion. For Sherman James (1994), John Henryism describes a strong behavioral predisposition to cope actively with the psychosocial environment stressors, and he hypothesizes that this interacts with low socioeconomic status to influence the health of African Americans, particularly the incidence of hypertension.

We suggest that the Sojourner Syndrome may represent a gendered form of John Henryism. The message of intersecting and overlapping gendered notions of responsibility is found in the symbol of Sojourner Truth, who was born in slavery around 1799 and liberated by the New York State Emancipation Act of 1827. In 1843, she assumed the name Sojourner Truth and began traveling across the country as an abolitionist itinerant preacher. She worked closely with leading abolitionists and became involved in the early women's rights movement. In a speech that underscores the memorable phrase "ain't I a woman," Sojourner Truth dramatically depicts the various responsibilities of African American women carried out in circumstances characterized by racial and gender oppression:

> That man over there says that women need to be helped into carriages, and lifted over ditches, and to have the best place everywhere. Nobody ever helps me into carriages, or over mud-puddles, or gives me any best place, and ain't I a woman? Look at me! Look at my arm. I have ploughed, and planted and gathered into barns, and no man could head me! And ain't I a woman? I could work as hard and eat as much as a man—when I could get it—and bear the lash as well! And ain't I a woman? I have borne thirteen children, and seen them most all sold off to slavery, and when I cried out with my mother's grief, none but Jesus heard me! And ain't I a woman? (cited in Rossi, 1973:428).[1]

The story of Sojourner Truth has become emblematic of the characterization of the lives of African American women. Like John Henry, Sojourner Truth is a larger-than-life legend and assumes extraordinary role responsibilities. Her account embodies the issues we have raised in this volume: the assumption of economic, household, and community responsibilities, which express themselves in family headship, working outside the home (like a man), and the constant need to address community empowerment—often carried out in conditions made difficult by discrimination and scarce resources. In addition, Sojourner Truth speaks to the contradiction between ideal models of gender and the lives of black women: exclusions from the protections of private patriarchy offered to white women by concepts of womanhood, motherhood, and femininity; the experience of being silenced; and, not least, the loss of children. Exploration of the consequences of these intersecting responsibilities that exist for African American women across class may give us insight into the way race, class, and gender structure constraints and choices, and therefore risk, for black women.

The Sojourner Syndrome expresses the combined effects and joint influence of race, class, and gender in structuring risk for African American women. For these women, elevated risk is also observed for those who are college educated, because of the simultaneous exposure to both racism and sexism. This framework may help to clarify the mechanism by which race mediates both gender and class status. First, the consequences of race and gender—of being a black woman—contribute to the instability of class status. Hence we saw this vulnerability in the middle-stratum women in our study. Furthermore, race dilutes the protections of class. For example, middle-stratum black women may have attained the achievements necessary for middle-class status, but they continue to suffer job and occupational discrimination; they are less likely to marry and more likely to become single heads of households because they too are subject to the shortage of "marriageable men" as a consequence of disproportionate unemployment and the prison-industrial complex. The research found that middle-class women may have moved to a black community to avoid racism, but their class advantage may then have been diluted by the discrimination and neglect to which black communities are subject. All these have the potential to become sources of stress.

The Sojourner Syndrome represents a strategy for fostering the reproduction and continuity of the black community. The unusual roles historically assumed by African American women have allowed African Americans to survive through 400 years of slavery, Jim Crow segregation, discrimination, and postindustrial redundancy. During slavery, when the slave family was illegal, African American women's assumption of motherhood and nurturance responsibilities facilitated the rearing of children. After emancipation, when married white women generally did not work outside the home, African American women's work outside the home as domestics and laundresses allowed the family to subsist when wage discrimination against black men and women did not permit a family wage. Throughout, African American women's individual and collective efforts on behalf of their community have facilitated group survival. In other words, the Sojourner Syndrome is a survival strategy. But it has many costs, and among them are health consequences.

In designing public health interventions for this community, the combined effects of various types of social hierarchies on the lives of Central Harlem residents must be taken into account. Public health interventions must, on the one hand, confront the multiple sources of strain women face. These include the ways gender inequity, racial discrimination, and class inequality impose limitations on access to health care and, perhaps more important, on secure jobs, adequate housing, nutrition, child care, a safe and healthy environment, and necessary social service—all of which are necessary for good health. Such interventions must also build on and support the protective mechanisms that women and men have developed, such as individual and collective coping strategies around housing, family, and community.

Central Harlem has a range of community organizations and institutions that overcome tremendous obstacles to render valuable services, some of which we have documented here. Programs developed without reference to the institutions, organizations, and historical and cultural context of Harlem are less likely to be successful and may miss the opportunity to build on the strengths of the community.

Finally, this study suggests that listening carefully to the voices of women, speaking directly through their words and their experiences, gives the scientific and the policy community an opportunity to design interventions that make sense to the people they are supposed to benefit. What women have said here, above all, is that they want to be empowered to take control of resources so they can care for themselves and their children in the best way possible.

NOTE

[1] There are two accounts of Sojourner Truth's address and some controversy about the accuracy of each account.

APPENDIX:
COMMUNITY PROFILE CHARTS

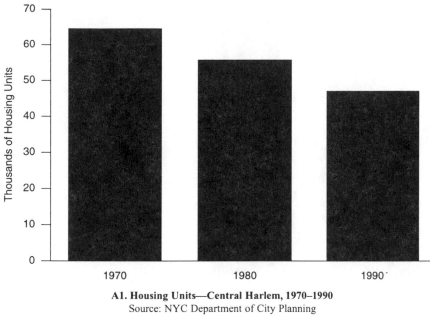
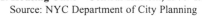

A1. Housing Units—Central Harlem, 1970–1990
Source: NYC Department of City Planning

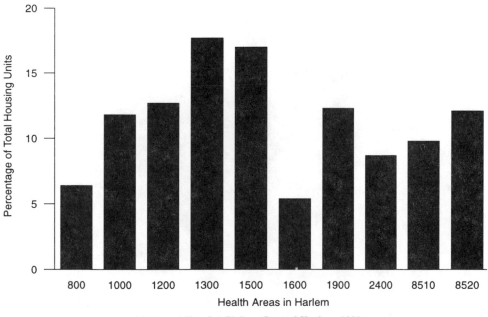

A2. Vacant Housing Units—Central Harlem, 1990
Source: NYC Department of City Planning

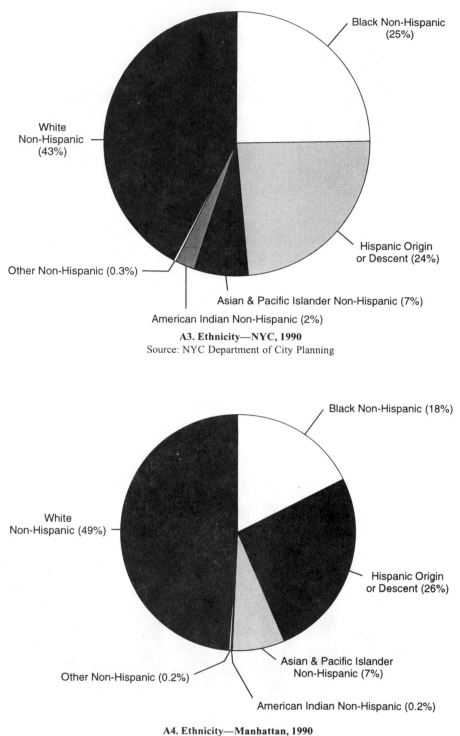

Black Non-Hispanic
(25%)

White
Non-Hispanic
(43%)

Hispanic Origin
or Descent (24%)

Other Non-Hispanic (0.3%)

Asian & Pacific Islander Non-Hispanic (7%)

American Indian Non-Hispanic (2%)

A3. Ethnicity—NYC, 1990
Source: NYC Department of City Planning

Black Non-Hispanic (18%)

White
Non-Hispanic (49%)

Hispanic Origin
or Descent (26%)

Other Non-Hispanic (0.2%)

Asian & Pacific Islander
Non-Hispanic (7%)

American Indian Non-Hispanic (0.2%)

A4. Ethnicity—Manhattan, 1990
Source: NYC Department of City Planning

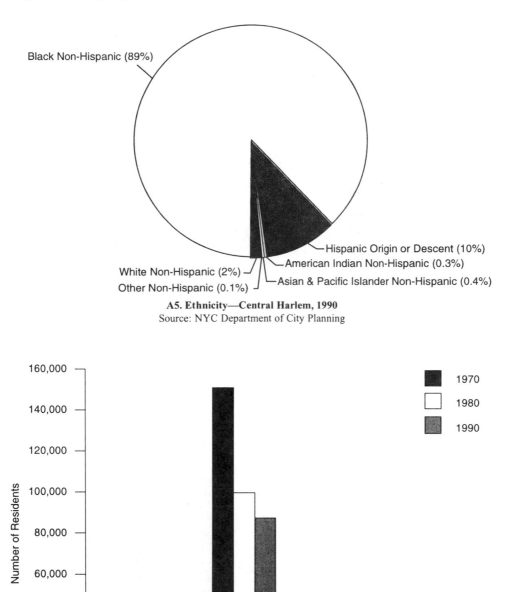

A5. Ethnicity—Central Harlem, 1990
Source: NYC Department of City Planning

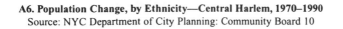

A6. Population Change, by Ethnicity—Central Harlem, 1970–1990
Source: NYC Department of City Planning: Community Board 10

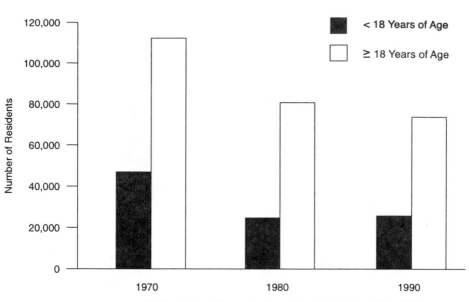

A7. Population Change, by Age—Central Harlem, 1970–1990
Source: NYC Department of City Planning

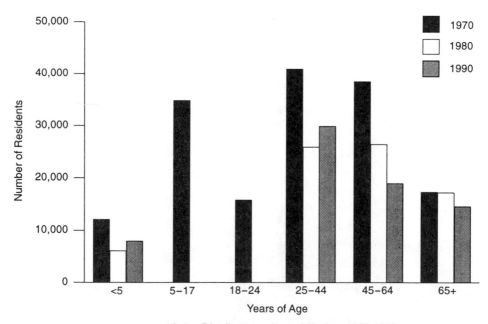

A8. Age Distribution—Central Harlem, 1970–1990
Source: NYC Department of City Planning. Datea unavailable for age groups 5–17 and 18–24 for
1990 and 1990.

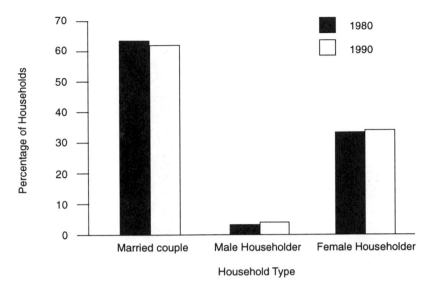

A9. Households with Children (<18 Years of Age)—NYC, 1980 and 1990
Source: NYC Department of City Planning

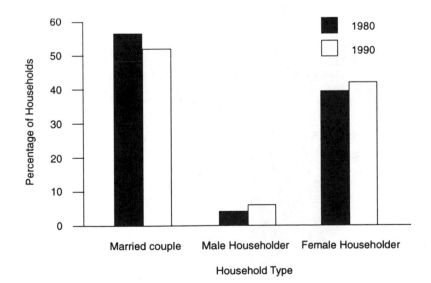

A10. Households with Children (<18 Years of Age)—Manhattan, 1980 and 1990
Source: NYC Department of City Planning

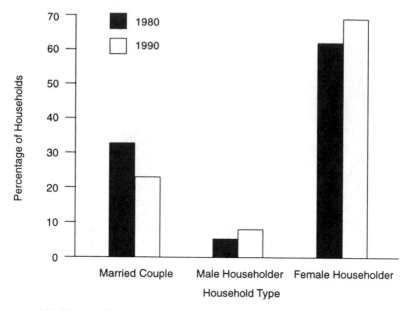

A11. Households with Children (<18 Years of Age)—Central Harlem, 1980 and 1990
Source: NYC Department of City Planning

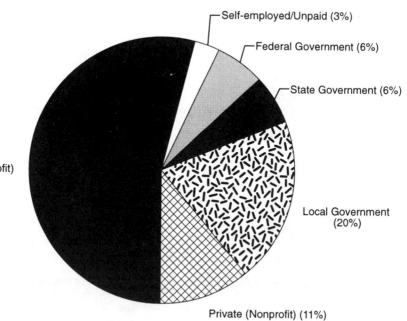

A12. Type of Employers—Central Harlem, 1990
Source: NYC Department of City Planning

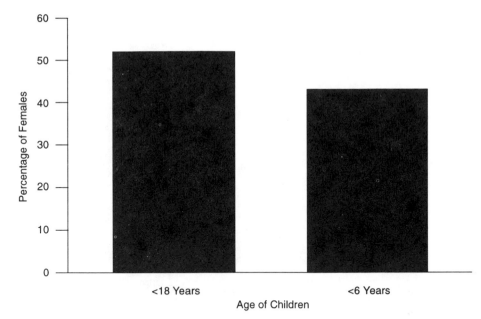

A13. Women in the Labor Force Who Have Children—Central Harlem, 1990
Source: NYC Department of City Planning

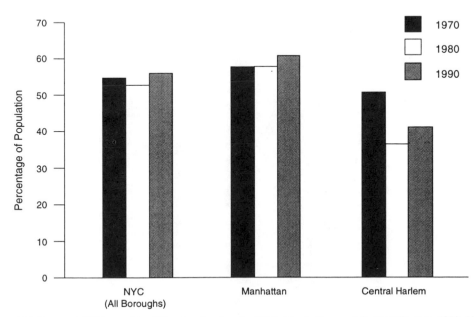

A14. Persons >16 Years of Age Who Are Employed—NYC, Manhattan, and Central Harlem, 1970–1990
Source: NYC Department of City Planning

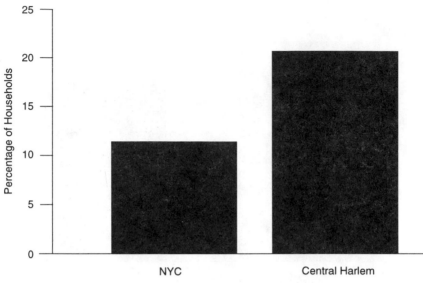

A15. Female-Headed Households—NYC and Central Harlem, 1990
Source: NYC Department of City Planning

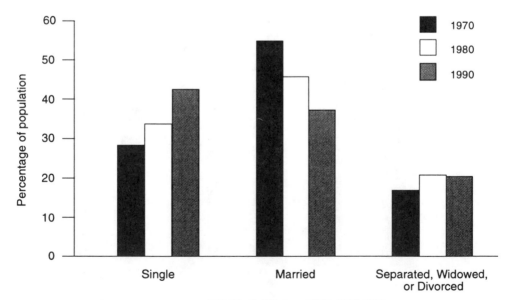

A16. Marital Status—NYC, 1970–1990
Source: NYC Department of City Planning

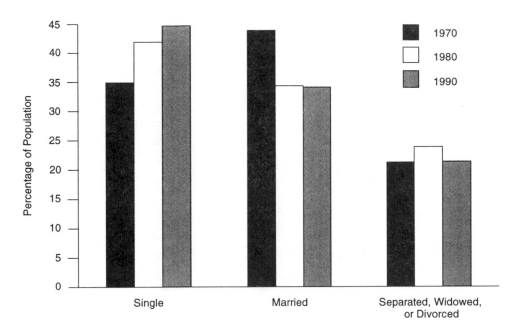

A17. Marital Status—Manhattan, 1970–1990
Source: NYC Department of City Planning

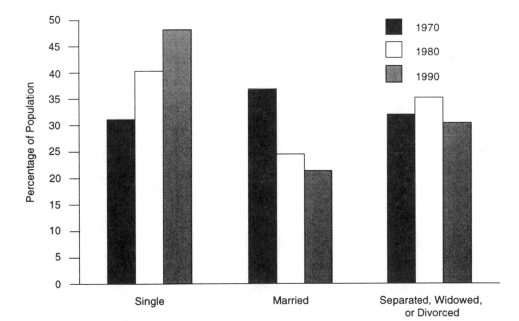

A18. Marital Status—Central Harlem, 1970–1990
Source: NYC Department of City Planning

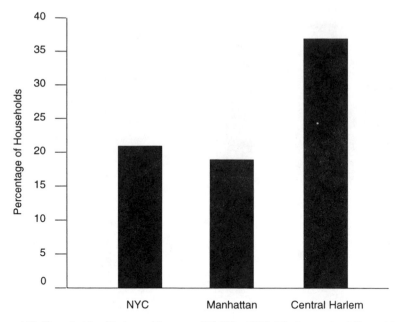

A19. Households with Annual Income <$10,000—NYC, Manhattan, and Central Harlem, 1996
Source: Keeping Track of New York City's Children, A Citizens' Committee for Children Status Report, 1999

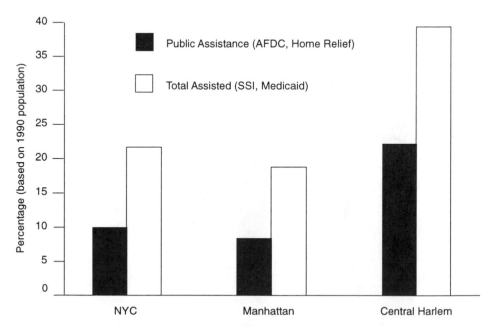

A20. Public Assistance—NYC, Manhattan, and Central Harlem, 1998
Source: NYC Police Department, Office of Management Analysis and Planning, Statistical Report 1998

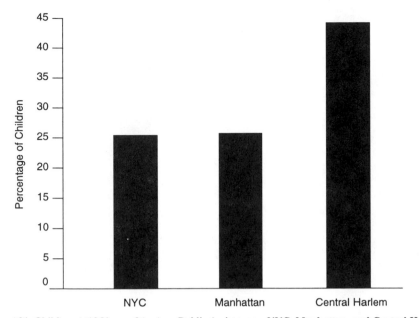

A21. Children (<18 Years of Age) on Public Assistance—NYC, Manhattan, and Central Harlem, 1996
Source: Keeping Track of New York City's Children, A Citizens' Committee for Children Status Report, 1999

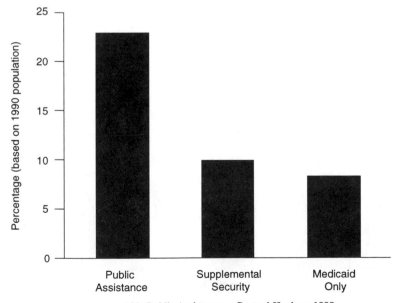

A22. Public Assistance—Central Harlem, 1998
Source: NYC Police Department, Office of Management Analysis and Planning, Statistical Report 1998

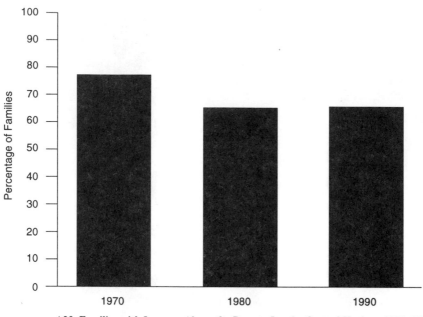

A23. Families with Incomes Above the Poverty Level—Central Harlem, 1970–1990
Source: Department of City Planning, Community Board 10

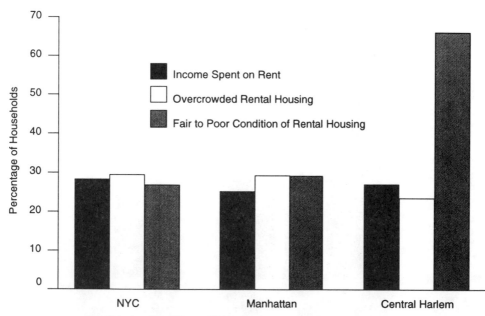

A24. Housing Conditions—NYC, Manhattan, and Central Harlem, 1996
Source: Keeping Track of New York City's Children, A Citizens' Committee for Children Status Report, 1999

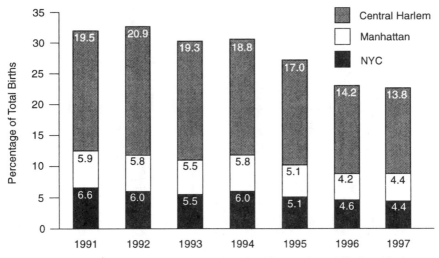

A25. Mother's Cigarette Smoking Reported on Birth Certificate—Central Harlem, Manhattan, and NYC, 1991–1997

Source: NYC Department of Health, Office of Vital Statistics and Epidemiology

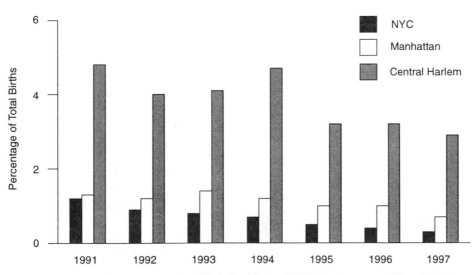

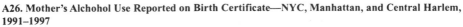

A26. Mother's Alchohol Use Reported on Birth Certificate—NYC, Manhattan, and Central Harlem, 1991–1997

Source: NYC Department of Health, Office of Vital Statistics and Epidemiology

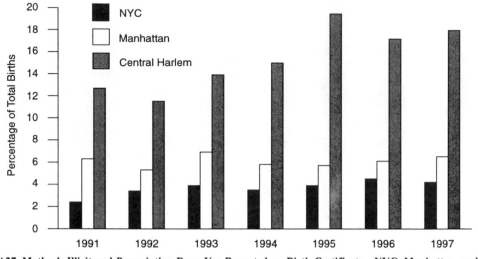

A27. Mother's Illicit and Prescription Drug Use Reported on Birth Certificate—NYC, Manhattan, and Central Harlem, 1991–1997

Source: NYC Department of Health, Office of Vital Statistics and Epidemiology

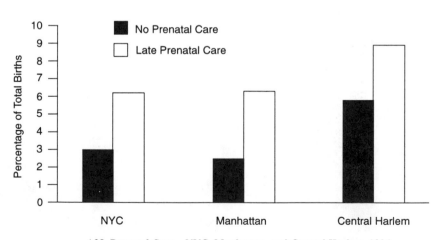

A28. Prenatal Care—NYC, Manhattan, and Central Harlem, 1996

Source: Keeping Track of New York City's Children, A Citizens' Committee for Children Status Report, 1999

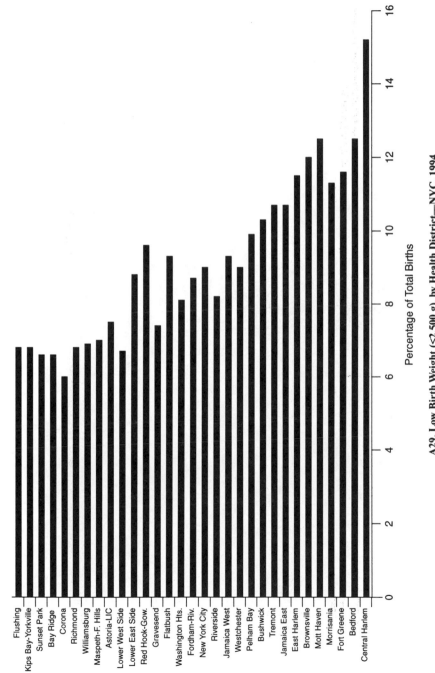

A29. Low Birth Weight (<2,500 g), by Health District—NYC, 1994

Percentage of Total Births

Source: NYC Department of Health, Office of Vital Statistics and Epidemiology

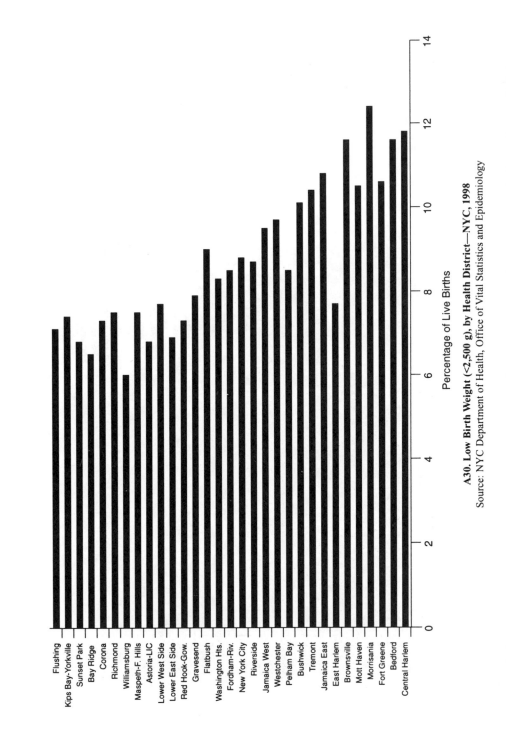

A30. Low Birth Weight (<2,500 g), by Health District—NYC, 1998
Source: NYC Department of Health, Office of Vital Statistics and Epidemiology

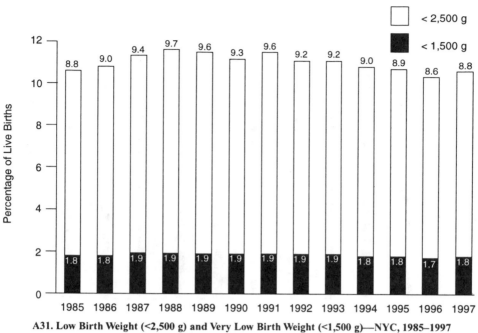

A31. Low Birth Weight (<2,500 g) and Very Low Birth Weight (<1,500 g)—NYC, 1985–1997
Source: NYC Department of Health, Office of Vital Statistics and Epidemiology

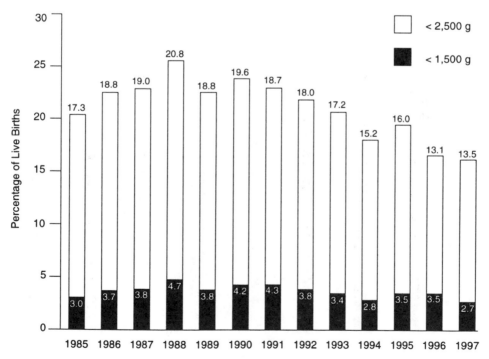

A32. Low Birth Weight (<2,500 g) and Very Low Birth Weight (<1,500 g)—Central Harlem, 1985–1997
Source: NYC Department of Health, Office of Vital Statistics and Epidemiology

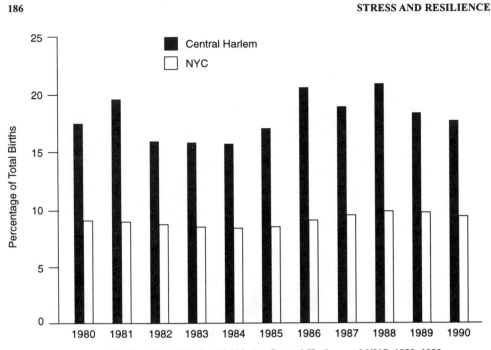

A33. Low Birth Weight (<2,500 g)—Central Harlem and NYC, 1980–1990
Source: NYC Department of Health, Office of Vital Statistics and Epidemiology

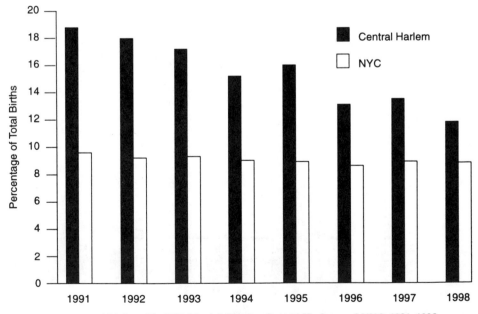

A34. Low Birth Weight (<2,500 g)—Central Harlem and NYC, 1991–1998
Source: NYC Department of Health, Office of Vital Statistics and Epidemiology

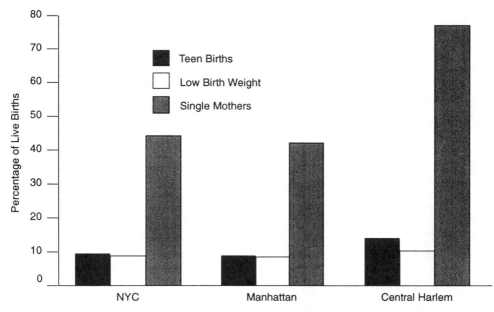

A35. Births by Teens, Deliveries with Low Birth Weight, and Births by Single Mothers—NYC, Manhattan, and Central Harlem, 1996
Source: Keeping Track of New York City's Children, A Citizens' Committee for Children Status Report, 1999

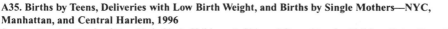

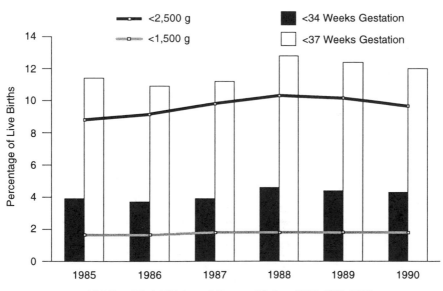

A36. Low Birth Weight and Preterm Births—NYC, 1985–1990
Source: NYC Department of Health, Office of Vital Statistics and Epidemiology

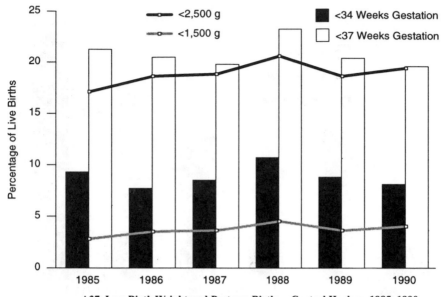

A37. Low Birth Weight and Preterm Births—Central Harlem, 1985–1990
Source: NYC Department of Health, Office of Vital Statistics and Epidemiology

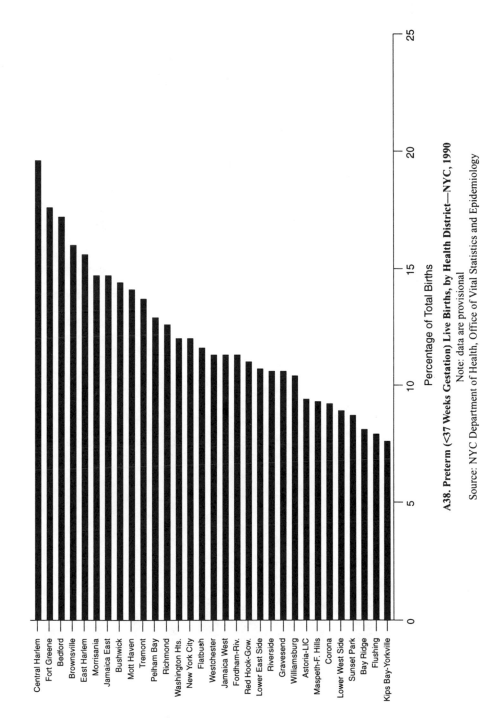

A38. Preterm (<37 Weeks Gestation) Live Births, by Health District—NYC, 1990

Note: data are provisional

Source: NYC Department of Health, Office of Vital Statistics and Epidemiology

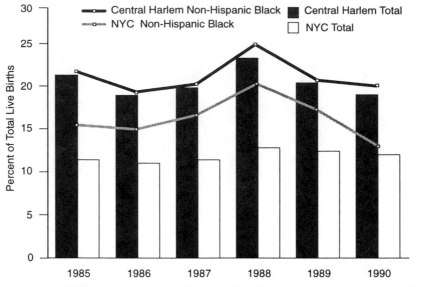

A39. Preterm (<37 Weeks Gestation) Live Births for Non-Hispanic Blacks and All Births—Central Harlem and NYC, 1985–1990
Source: NYC Department of Health, Office of Vital Statistics and Epidemiology

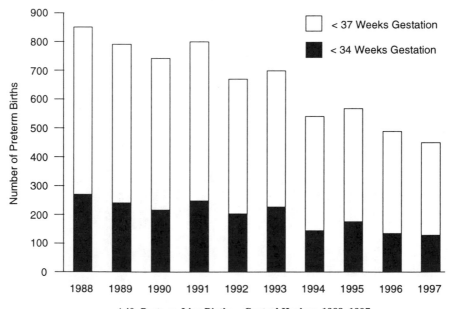

A40. Preterm Live Births—Central Harlem, 1988–1997
Source: NYC Department of Health, Office of Vital Statistics and Epidemiology

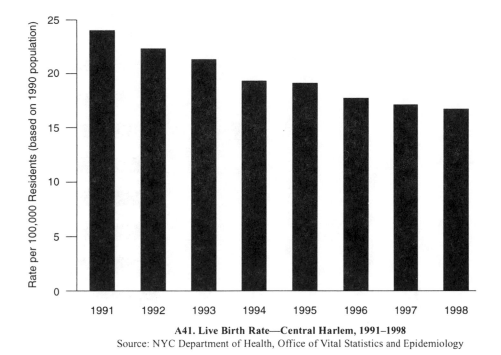

A41. Live Birth Rate—Central Harlem, 1991–1998
Source: NYC Department of Health, Office of Vital Statistics and Epidemiology

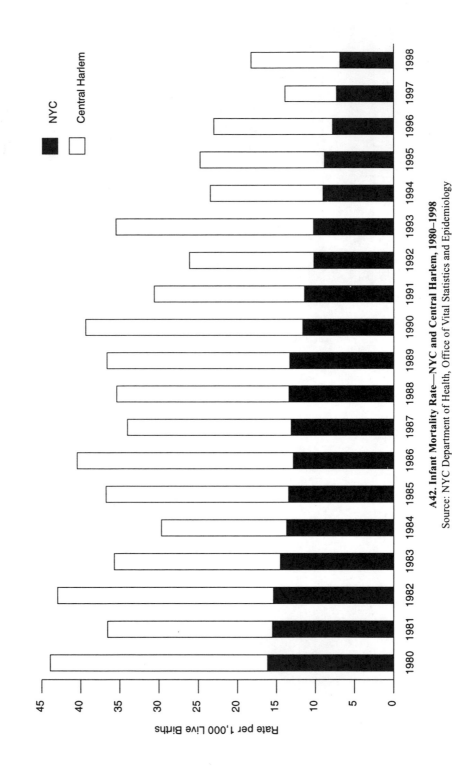

A42. Infant Mortality Rate—NYC and Central Harlem, 1980–1998
Source: NYC Department of Health, Office of Vital Statistics and Epidemiology

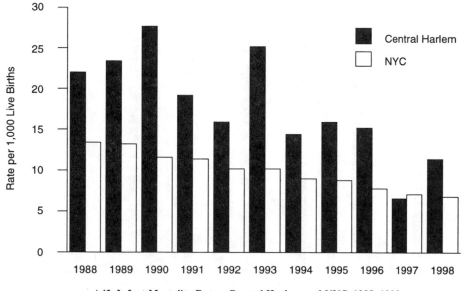

A43. Infant Mortality Rate—Central Harlem and NYC, 1988–1998
Source: NYC Department of Health, Office of Vital Statistics and Epidemiology

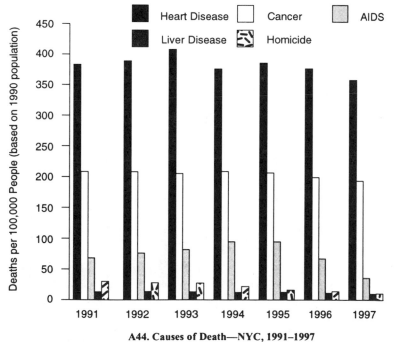

A44. Causes of Death—NYC, 1991–1997
Source: NYC Department of Health, Office of Vital Statistics and Epidemiology

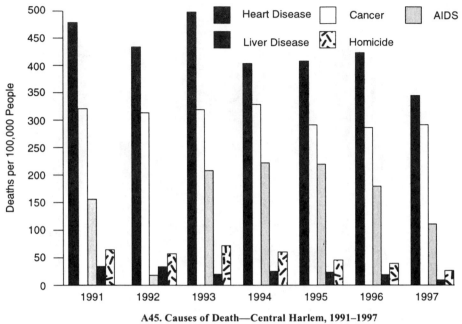

A45. Causes of Death—Central Harlem, 1991–1997
Source: NYC Department of Health, Office of Vital Statistics and Epidemiology

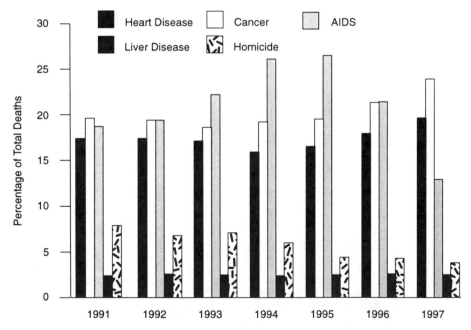

A46. Causes of Death for Persons <65 Years of Age—NYC, 1991–1997
Source: NYC Department of Health, Office of Vital Statistics and Epidemiology

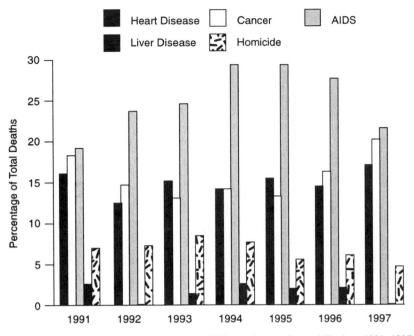

A47. Causes of Death for Persons <65 Years of Age—Central Harlem, 1991–1997
Source: NYC Department of Health, Office of Vital Statistics and Epidemiology

REFERENCES

Andersen, M.L., and Collins, P.H., 1995, Preface, in: *Race, Class and Gender: An Anthology, 2nd ed.*, M.L. Andersen and P.H. Collins, eds., Wadsworth Publishing, Belmont, CA.

Antonovsky, A., 1979, *Health, Stress, and Coping*, Jossey-Bass, San Francisco.

Aronson, R.A., 1999, Coping, coping resources and resiliency, Paper presented at: Expert Consultants Workgroup on Stress and Preterm Delivery, September 23–24, Atlanta, GA.

Bennett, C., 1995, The black population in the United States: March 1993 and 1994, in: *U.S. Bureau of the Census, Current Population Reports*, U.S. Government Printing Office, Washington, D.C., pp. 20–48.

Bernard, H.R., 1995, *Research Methods in Anthropology, 2nd ed.*, Altamira Press, Walnut Creek, CA.

Boone, M., 1989, *Capital Crime: Infant Mortality in America*, Sage, Newbury Park, CA.

Brewer, R.M., 1993, Theorizing race, class, and gender: the new scholarship of black feminist intellectuals and black women's labor, in: *Theorizing Black Feminisms: The Visionary Pragmatism of Black Women*, S.M. James and A.P.A. Busia, eds., Routledge, London.

Brown, G.W., and Harris, T., 1978, *Social Origins of Depression*, The Free Press, New York.

Burawoy, M., et al., 1991, *Ethnography Unbound: Power and Resistance in the Modern Metropolis*, University of California Press, Berkeley.

Burbridge, L.C., 1994, The reliance of African American women on government and third sector employment, *Am Econ Rev* **84**:103–107.

Canada, G., 1995, *Fist, Stick, Knife, Gun: A Personal History of Violence in America*, Beacon Press, Boston.

CBS, 2000, Rich Get Richer, Poor Stagnate, *CBS.com.* 18 January 2000; http://wfrv.cbsnow.com/now/story/1,1597,150545-243,00.shtml.

Cecil, R., 1996, Introduction, in: *The Anthropology of Pregnancy Loss: Comparative Studies in Miscarriage, Stillbirth and Neonatal Death*, R. Cecil, ed., Berg, Washington, D.C.

Chesler, M.A., 1991, Participatory action research with self-help groups: an alternative paradigm for inquiry and action, *Am J Community Psychol* **19**:757–769.

Citizens' Committee for Children, 1999, *Keeping Track of New York City's Children: A Citizens' Committee for Children Status Report*, Citizens' Committee for Children, New York.

Cohen, S., Kessler, R., and Gordon, L., 1995, *Measuring Stress: A Guide for Health and Social Scientists*, Oxford University Press, New York.

Collins, P.H., 1991, *Black Feminist Thought: Knowledge, Consciousness, and the Politics of Empowerment*, Routledge, New York.

Conrad, C., and Lindquist, M., 1998, Prosperity and inequality on the rise. *Focus* **26**:Trendletter.

Cooper, R.S., and David, R., 1986, The biological concept of race and its application to public health and epidemiology, *J Health Pol Policy Law* **11**:97–116.

Dehavenon, A.L., 1987, *Toward a Policy for the Amelioration and Prevention of Family Homelessness and Dissolution: New York City's After Hours Emergency Assistance Unit in 1986–1987*, East Harlem Interfaith Welfare Committee (March 1987).

Devaney, B., 1992, *Very Low Birthweight Among Medicaid Newborns in Five States: The Effects of Prenatal WIC Participation*, U.S. Department of Agriculture, Alexandria, VA.

Devaney, B., and Schirm, A., 1993, *Infant Mortality Among Medicaid Newborns in Five States: The Effects of Prenatal WIC Participation*, U.S. Department of Agriculture, Alexandria, VA.

Devine, T.J., 1994, Characteristics of self-employed women in the United States, *Mon Labor Rev* **March**:20–33.

di Leonardo, M., 1984, *The Varieties of Ethnic Experience: Kinship, Class, and Gender among California Italian-Americans*, Cornell University Press, Ithaca.

Dohrenwend, B.S., et al., 1978, Exemplification of a method for scaling life events: the PERI Life Events Scale, *J Health Soc Behav* **19**:205–229.

Dressler, W.W., 1991, *Stress and Adaptation in the Context of Culture: Depression in a Southern Black Community*, State University of New York Press, New York.

Eakins, P., ed., 1986, *The American Way of Birth*, Temple University Press, Philadelphia.

Edin, K., 1994, *The Myths of Dependency and Self-Sufficiency: Women, Welfare and Low-Wage Work*, Center for Urban Policy Research, Rutgers University, NJ, Working Paper 67.

Edin, K., and Lein, L., 1997, *Making Ends Meet: How Single Mothers Survive Welfare and Low Wage Work*, Russell Sage, New York.

Ellen, R.F., 1984, *Ethnographic Research: A Guide to General Conduct*, Academic Press, New York.

EZ Works: Quarterly News For and About the Upper Manhattan Empowerment Zone, Summer 1998.

Fals-Borda, O., 1984, Participatory action research, *Development* **2**:18–20.

Foster, J.M., et al., eds., 1979, *Long-term Field Research in Social Anthropology*, Academic Press, New York.

Fraser, G., 1995, Modern bodies, modern minds: midwifery and reproductive change in an African American community, in: *Conceiving the New World Order: The Global Politics of Reproduction*, F. Ginsburg and R. Rapp, eds., University of California Press, Berkeley.

Freire, P., 1970, *The Pedagogy of the Oppressed*, Continuum, New York.

Fullilove, M.T., 1996, Psychiatric implications of displacement: contributions from the psychology of place, *Am J Psychiatry* **153**:1516–1522.

Gamble, V.N., 1993, A legacy of distrust: African Americans and medical research, in: *Racial Differences in Preterm Delivery: Developing a New Research Paradigm*, D. Rowley and H. Tosteson, eds., *Am J Prev Med* **9**(6 suppl):35–38.

Ginsburg, F., and Rapp, R., 1991, The politics of reproduction, *Annu Rev Anthropol* **20**:311–343.

Ginsburg, F., and Rapp, R., 1995, *Conceiving the New World Order: The Global Politics of Reproduction*, University of California Press, Berkeley.

Goldsmith, M.F., 1988, Sex tied to drugs = STD spread, *JAMA* **260**:2009.

Greenberg, C.L., 1991, *Or Does It Explode?: Black Harlem in the Great Depression*, Oxford University Press, New York.

Gutman, H., 1976, *The Black Family in Slavery and Freedom, 1750–1925*, Pantheon, New York.

Hack, M., et al., 1995, Long-term developmental outcomes of low birth weight infants, *Future of Children* **5**:176–196.

Hall, J.M., and Stevens, P.E., 1998, Participatory action research for sustaining individual and community change: a model of HIV prevention education, *AIDS Educ Prev* **10**:387–402.

Hamid, A., 1992, Drugs and patterns of opportunity in the inner city: the case of middle-aged, middle income cocaine smokers, in: *Drugs, Crime, and Social Isolation*, A.V. Harrell and G.E. Peterson, eds., Urban Institute Press, Washington, D.C.

Hargraves, M., and Thomas, R.W., 1993, Infant mortality: its history and social construction, *Am J Prev Med* **9**(6 suppl):17–26.

Harlem Urban Development Corporation, 1994, *New York City Empowerment Zone: Harlem, The South Bronx*, Harlem Urban Development Corporation, New York.

Health and Hospitals Corporation, Office of Strategic Planning, 1991, *A Summary Examination of Excess Mortality in Central Harlem and New York City*, New York.

Health Systems Agency of New York City, 1990, *Health Care Forum: Upper Manhattan*, Health Systems Agency of New York City, New York.

Helman, C., 1990, *Culture, Health and Illness: An Introduction for Health Professionals*, Wright, London.

Huggins, N.I., 1995, *Voices from the Harlem Renaissance*, Oxford University Press, New York.

James, S.A., 1994, John Henryism and the health of African Americans, *Cult Med Psychiatry* **18**:163–182.

Johnson, J. W., [1930] 1991, *Black Manhattan*, Da Capo Press, New York.

Jones, B., 1983, The economic status of black women, in: *The State of Black America*, D. Williams, ed., National Urban League, New York.

King, D., 1988, Multiple jeopardy, multiple consciousness: the context of a black feminist ideology, *Signs: Journal of Women, Society and Culture* **14**:42–72.

King, M.C., 1993, Black women's breakthrough into clerical work: an occupational tipping model, *J Econ Issues* **27**:1097–1125.

Kotelchuck, M., et al., 1984, WIC participation and pregnancy outcomes: Massachusetts statewide evaluation project, *Am J Public Health* **74**:1086–1092.

Kramer, M.S., 2000, Association between restricted fetal growth and adult chronic disease: is it causal? is it important? [invited commentary], *Am J Epidemiol* **152**:605–608.

Krieger, N., 1999, Embodying inequality: a review of concepts, measures, and metaphors for studying health consequences of discrimination, *Int J Health Serv* **29**:295–352.

Krieger, N., and Bassett, M., 1986, The health of black folks: disease, class and ideology in science, *Mon Rev* **38**:74–85.

Krieger, N., et al., 1994, Racism, sexism, and social class: implications for studies of health, disease and well-being, in: *Racial Differences in Preterm Delivery: Developing a New Research Paradigm*, D. Rowley and H. Tosteson, eds., *Am J Prev Med* **9**(6 suppl):82–122.

Kretzmann, J.P., and McKnight, J.L., 1993, *Building Communities from the Inside Out: A Path Toward Finding and Mobilizing a Community's Assets*, Center for Urban Affairs and Policy Research, Northwestern University, Evanston, IL.

Ladner, J., 1971, *Tomorrow's Tomorrow: The Black Woman*, Doubleday, Garden City, NY.

Lee, F.R., 1994a, Another America: on a Harlem block, hope is swallowed by decay, *The New York Times*, September 8:A1.

Lee, F.R., 1994b, Another America: Harlem family battles burden of the past, *The New York Times*, September 9:A1.

Lee, F.R., 1994c, Another America: a drug dealer's rapid rise and ugly fall, *The New York Times*, September 10:A1.

Leroy, M., 1988, *Miscarriage*, MacDonald Optima, London.

Lopez, I., 1987, Sterilization among Puerto Rican women in New York City: public policy and social constraints, in: L. Mullings, ed., *Cities of the United States: Studies in Urban Anthropology*, Columbia University Press, New York.

Low, S., 1999, *Theorizing the City: The New Urban Anthropology Reader*, Rutgers University Press, New Brunswick, NJ.

Manderson, L., et al., 1998, The politics of community: negotiation and consultation in research in women's health, *Hum Org* **57**:222–29.

Marable, M., 1996, *Speaking Truth to Power: Essays on Race, Resistance and Radicalism*, Westview Press, Boulder, CO.

Marable, M., 2000, Race-ing justice: the political cultures of incarceration, *Souls: A Critical Journal of Black Politics, Culture, and Society* **2**:6–11.

Martin, E., 1987, *The Woman in the Body*, Beacon Press, Boston.

McCord, C., and Freeman, H.P., 1990, Excess mortality in Harlem, *N Engl J Med* **322**:173–177.

McLean, D., et al., 1993, Psychosocial measurement: implications for the study of preterm delivery in black women, in: *Racial Differences in Preterm Delivery: Developing a New Research Paradigm*, D. Rowley and H. Tosteson, eds., *Am J Prev Med* **9**(6 suppl):39–81.

Mollenkopf, J., and Castells, M., eds., 1991, *Dual City: Restructuring New York*, Russell Sage, New York.

Morgan, D., 1993, *Successful Focus Groups: Advancing the State of the Art*, Sage Publications, Newbury Park, CA.

Mullings, L., 1984, Minority women, work and health, in: *Double Exposure: Women's Health Hazards on the Job and at Home*, W. Chavkin, ed., Monthly Review Press, New York.

Mullings, L., ed., 1987, *Cities of the United States: Studies in Urban Anthropology*, Columbia University Press, New York.

Mullings, L., 1989, Inequality and Afro-American health status: policies and prospects, in: *Race: 20th Century Dilemmas—21st Century Prognoses*, W. Van Horne, ed., University of Wisconsin Institute on Race and Ethnicity, Milwaukee.

Mullings, L., 1997, *On Our Own Terms: Race, Class and Gender in the Lives of African American Women*, Routledge, New York.

Mullings, L., 2000, African American women making themselves: notes on the role of black feminist research, *Souls: A Critical Journal of Black Politics, Culture, and Society* **2**:18–29.

Mullings, L., and Susser, I., 1992, *Harlem Research and Development: An Analysis of Unequal Opportunity in Central Harlem and Recommendations for an Opportunity Zone* [unpublished manuscript].

Mullings, L., Wali, A., McLean, D., et al., 2001, "Qualitative Methodologies and Community Participation in Examining Reproductive Experiences: The Harlem Birth Right Project," *Maternal Child Health J,* **5**[in press].

Naroll, R., 1962, *Data Quality Control: A New Research Technique: Prolegomena to a Cross-Cultural Study of Culture Stress*, Free Press, New York.

National Center for Health Statistics, 2000, *Health, United States, 2000 With Adolescent Health Chartbook*, National Center for Health Statistics, Hyattsville, MD.

Nelson, M., 1986, Birth and social class, in: *The American Way of Birth*, P.S. Eakins, ed., Temple University Press, Philadelphia.

New York City Department of City Planning, 1990, *Persons 16 Years and Over by Labor Force Status and Sex, New York City, Boroughs and Community Districts*, Department of City Planning, New York, DCP 1990 No. 317.

New York Times, August 11, 1997.

New York Times, "A Special-Ed Warning for New York," December 2, 1998. Editorial.

Newman, K., 1986, Symbolic dialectics and generations of women: variations in the meaning of post-divorce downward mobility, *Am Ethnol* **13**:230–253.

Park, P., 1993, What is participatory research? A theoretical and methodological approach, in: *Voices of Change: Participatory Research in the United States and Canada*, P. Park, et al., eds., Bergin and Garvey, Westport, CT.

Phillips, M., 1996, *A Profile of Families who Experience Infant Death During the First Year of Life* [unpublished manuscript], Fordham University Graduate School of Social Services, New York.

Piven, F.F., and Cloward, R.A., 1971, *Regulating the Poor: The Functions of Public Welfare*, Random House, New York.

Putnam, R.D., 2000, *Bowling Alone: The Collapse and Revival of American Community*, Simon and Schuster, New York.

Rapp, R., 1987, Urban kinship in contemporary America, in: *Cities of the United States: Studies in Urban Anthropology*, L. Mullings, ed., Columbia University Press, New York.

Rapp, R., 1991, Constructing amniocentesis: maternal and medical discourses, in: *Uncertain Terms: Negotiating Gender in American Culture*, F. Ginsburg and A. Tsing, eds., Beacon Press, Boston.

Rini, C., Wadhwa, P., and Sandman, C., 1999, Psychological adaptation and birth outcomes: the role of personal resources, stress, and sociocultural context in pregnancy, *Health Psychol* **18**:333–345.

Ross, E., and Rapp, R., 1980, Sex and society: a research note from social history and anthropology, *Comp Stud Soc Hist* **23**:51–72.

Rossi, A., ed., 1973, *The Feminist Press*, Bantam, New York.

Rowley, D., et al., 1993, Preterm delivery among African American women: a research strategy, in: *Racial Differences in Preterm Delivery: Developing a New Research Paradigm*, D. Rowley and H. Tosteson, eds., *Am J Prev Med* **9**(6 suppl):1–6.

Ruiz, V., and DuBois, E.C., 1994, *Unequal Sisters: A Multicultural Reader in U.S. Women's History*, Routledge, New York.

Sanjek, R., and Colen, S., eds., 1990, *At Work in Homes: Household Workers in World Perspective*, American Anthropological Association, Washington, D.C., American Ethnological Society Monograph Series No. 3.

Sassen, S., 1991, *The Global City: New York, London, Tokyo*, Princeton University Press, Princeton, NJ.

Satcher, D., 1999, The initiative to eliminate racial and ethnic health disparities is moving forward, *Public Health Rep* **114**:283–287.

Schensul, S.L., 1974, Skills needed in action anthropology: lessons from el Centro de la Causa, *Hum Org* **33**:203–209.

Schensul, S.L., and Borrero, M.G., 1982, Research based training for organizational change, *Urban Anthropol* **2**:129–153.

Scheper-Hughes, N., 1992, *Death Without Weeping: The Violence of Everyday Life in Brazil*, University of California Press, Berkeley.

Schoendorf, K.C., et al., 1992, Mortality among infants of black as compared to white college-educated parents, *N Engl J Med* **326**:1522-1526.

Schulz, R., and Rau, M.T., 1985, Social support through the life course, in: *Social Support and Health*, S. Cohen and S.L. Syme, eds., Academic Press, Orlando.

Scrimshaw, S.C.M., and Hurtado, E., 1987, *Rapid Assessment Procedures for Nutrition and Primary Health Care*, University of California at Los Angeles, Latin American Center Publications, Los Angeles.

Sharff, J., 1987, The underground economy of a poor neighborhood, in: *Cities of the United States: Studies in Urban Anthropology*, L. Mullings, ed., Columbia University Press, New York.

Smith, N., 1996, After Tomkins Square Park: degentrification and the revanchist city, in: *Re-Representing the City: Ethnicity, Capital and Culture in the 21st Century Metropolis*, A.D. King, ed., New York University Press, New York.

Sowell, T., 1994, *Race and Culture: A World View*, Basic Books, New York.

Stack, C., 1974, *All Our Kin: Strategies for Survival in a Black Community*, Harper and Row, New York.

Stull, D.D., and Schensul, J.J., 1987, *Collaborative Research and Social Change: Applied Anthropology in Action*, Westview, Boulder, CO.

Susser, I., and Kreniske, J., 1987, The welfare trap: a public policy for deprivation, in: *Cities of the United States: Studies in Urban Anthropology*, L. Mullings, ed., Columbia University Press, New York.

Upper Manhattan Empowerment Zone, 1994, *Findings of the Harlem Survey* [unpublished manuscript].

U.S. Census Bureau, 2000, *Historical Income Tables: Households, Table H-5*; http://www.census.gov/hhes/income/histinc/h05.html.

U.S. Department of Health and Human Services, 2000, *Healthy People 2010: Understanding and Improving Health, 2nd ed.*, U.S. Department of Health and Human Services, Washington, D.C.

Wallace, R., and Wallace, D., 1990, Origins of public health collapse in New York City: the dynamics of planned shrinkage, contagious urban decay and social disintegration, *Bull NY Acad Med* **66**:391–434.

Watkins, B., and Fullilove, M., 1999, Crack cocaine and Harlem's health, *Souls: A Critical Journal of Black Politics, Culture, and Society* **1**:36–48.

Wilcox, L.S., and Marks, J.S., 1994, *From Data to Action: CDC's Public Health Surveillance for Women, Infants, and Children*, U.S. Department of Health and Human Services, Washington, D.C.

Williams, B., 1988, *Upscaling Downtown: Stalled Gentrification in Washington, D.C.*, Cornell University Press, Ithaca.

Wilson, W.J., 1987, *The Truly Disadvantaged: The Inner City, the Underclass, and Public Policy*, University of Chicago Press, Chicago.

Wilson, W.J., 1996, *When Work Disappears: The Work of the New Urban Poor*, Knopf, New York.

Wise, P., 1993, Confronting racial disparities in infant mortality: reconciling science and politics, in: *Racial Differences in Preterm Delivery: Developing a New Research Paradigm*, D. Rowley and H. Tosteson, eds., *Am J Prev Med* **9**(6 suppl):7–16.

Zambrana, R., et al., 1999, Mediators of ethnic-associated differences in infant birth weight, *J Urban Health—Bull NY Acad Med* **76**:102–116.

INDEX

Entry numbers preceded by "*A*" refer to charts enumerated in the appendix.